Angela Wales grew up the oldest of five children in Walcha NSW. After the family's move to Sydney she attended the University of Sydney, graduating in English and classics. She was executive director of the Australian Writers Guild for 10 years, after which she moved to the US and became Executive Director of the Writers Guild Foundation (the educational and charitable arm of the Writers Guild of America West) in Los Angeles. Angela returned to Australia in late 2013 to help take care of her elderly mother. *Barefoot in the Bindis* is her first book.

Barefoot
in the Bindis

First published in Australia in 2019 by Affirm Press,
a Simon & Schuster (Australia) Pty Limited company
Bunurong/Boon Wurrung Country
28 Thistlethwaite Street, South Melbourne VIC 3205

Affirm Press is located on the unceded land of the Bunurong/Boon Wurrung peoples of the Kulin Nation. Affirm Press pays respect to their Elders past and present.

New York Amsterdam/Antwerp London Toronto Sydney/Melbourne New Delhi
Visit our website at www.simonandschuster.com.au

AFFIRM PRESS and design are trademarks of Affirm Press Pty Ltd, Inc., used under licence by Simon & Schuster, LLC.

10 9 8 7 6 5 4 3 2 1

© Angela Wales 2019

All rights reserved. No part of this publication may be reproduced, stored in a retrieval system, or transmitted in any form or by any means, electronic, mechanical, photocopying, recording or otherwise, without prior permission of the publisher.

A Cataloguing-in-Publication entry for this book is available from the National Library of Australia

 A catalogue record for this book is available from the National Library of Australia

9781925870213 (paperback)
9781925870749 (ebook)

Cover design by Christabella Designs
Typeset by J&M Typesetting in 12.5/17.5 Garamond
Printed and bound in Australia by the Opus Group

ANGELA WALES

Barefoot *in the* Bindis

memoir of a bush childhood

To my mother, Joan Wales, who brought us through it all with courage, grace and love.

Prologue

I am standing on the hillside, looking down towards the gully. A prolonged drought has leached all colour from the paddocks, withering them to a lifeless brown. In the distance, Trig Hill shimmers blue in the heat.

But the house isn't there. Kicking through a tangle of dry weeds, I find a patch of old concrete where our laundry and dairy must have been. A pile of rubble a few yards downhill might or might not be the remains of the drystone entrance pillars that my father built for us one Christmas. A few blackened stumps are all that are left of the pine trees that had once swayed, so tall and majestic, in all the winds the seasons had brought us.

Where is everything? I look for landmarks, but the once familiar fences separating the paddocks have disappeared. The sheds are gone, both the one near the house and the one we built further up the hill. The cow yards and the chicken coop are gone, too. Some of the hillside boulder clusters, so familiar to us as children, have been bulldozed away. My cousin Anthony is with me, and I want to say to him, 'Here. Here is where your mother, Carmel, taught us to cartwheel,' but I cannot even pinpoint the spot.

The current owner, who has built a cottage down by the boundary beside where our mailbox once stood, had waved us uphill. 'You can see that people once lived up there,' he said, 'and it looks like someone had a sizeable vegetable garden at some point.'

But two blackened and gnarled trunks are all that is left of our apple orchard, and there is no sign of the plum tree.

Much higher up the hill again, someone has tried to clear the dense bush in a haphazard fashion, but despite the drought, a tangled mess of scrub is reclaiming its own. And someone has tried to dam the gully, leaving a pile of clutter and debris across where the road to Cheyenne, now diverted, used to dip. The tall eucalyptus trees that once grew there, home to so many birds, are gone.

A line from Tennyson, one of my mother's favourite poets, comes into my head: 'The woods decay, the woods decay and fall …' And another: 'the tender grace of a day that is dead …'

It's as though we were never there. There are only the memories now.

~

The downhill end of the verandah, before the balustrade starts, is less than two feet from the ground. There I am, perched on the edge, my arms outstretched, ready to fly. Then, screwing up my eyes as hard as I can, waving my arms and wishing hard, I jump. But instead of taking to the air, I land with a thud in the yard below. I head back to the steps, walk down to the end of the verandah and try again, this time wishing harder. Go. Jump. No, this is not flying. My mother has often said, 'If at first you don't succeed, then try, try again.' So I do. I even improvise makeshift wings from two of my mother's aprons. That doesn't work either.

My father has told me that I can do anything I want in life, anything at all, if I want it badly enough and if I try hard enough. Part of the trick, he says, is to see yourself in your mind's eye, doing the thing you want to do. I believe him.

I want to fly more than anything else in the world. I want to be like an eagle, to soar above the earth, to look down on our little homestead with its faded red roof and water tanks and circle of pine trees from above. I want to wheel over our apple orchard and cowshed and then fly so high that the flocks of sheep and my mother toiling in the vegetable garden are just dots below. I want to hear on the wind the distant sounds of Molly and Polly mooing in the cow paddock and my brothers and sisters calling to each other around the house.

But it turns out that flying is not that simple. After several days of trying, I am forced to admit defeat. It seems my father has forgotten to tell me something, and I puzzle over what it is. I suspect that there are some things we are simply not cut out by nature to do, no matter how hard we try.

Or perhaps it's that we can only find out what we're capable of if we attempt the impossible.

~

In 1953 my father, partly for health reasons but perhaps in what seems to me now to have been a fit of romantic delusion, moved the family from the beachside Sydney suburb of Bondi to an underdeveloped sheep property twenty miles east of the small town of Walcha, in the Northern Tablelands of New South Wales. This might have seemed like a surprising step for an inexperienced immigrant from the industrial outskirts of Glasgow to take, but then, Robert Wales could be a surprising man.

This was to be a new beginning, far from the noxious environment of his inner-city textile business and promising, he said, mountain air and wide-open spaces for the children. 'What's wrong with seaside air?' my mother might have asked, but her husband was on a mission. He planned to improve the property and become prosperous, or at least comfortable, from the fat of the land. Did he see it as the serious gamble that it was? Probably not. What he saw was an adventure and a challenge.

At this time, he was twenty-nine and my mother was twenty-seven.

Just over a year earlier, Joan Wales had given premature birth to twin boys. Robert and Joan now had five children under four. To me looking back, this seems like the quintessential Catholic nightmare, but Joan had been taught from birth to accept what God sent her, and she was determined to be a good Catholic wife and mother.

Robert Wales, whom everyone called Bob, was not tall, but he was a good-looking man, bearing a slight resemblance to, say, a young Matt Damon. With his light-brown hair, blue eyes and soft Scottish brogue, he had a twinkle-eyed charm that, along with his warm smile, most people found hard to resist. He made his native town of Greenock, on the mouth of the Clyde, sound mysterious and romantic, but when I visited there many years later it turned out to be a grey and gloomy place, its solid stone buildings soot stained and damp. His father, who originally came from a line of blacksmiths, had established the Greenock Bacon Company, which, apart from curing bacon and hams, made brawn, black pudding, sausages, salamis and other processed meats. The town had grown up around Scotland's shipbuilding industry and it had a solid bourgeois foundation, so our grandfather had prospered. He employed twenty people and was proud of his success. He hoped his only son would take over the family business.

He and our grandmother, strict Presbyterians both, had given all three of their children, two girls and a boy, an excellent education at the fee-paying Greenock Academy. But when their only son, whose first love was painting and drawing, had wanted to go to the Glasgow School of Art, his parents wouldn't hear of it. They insisted that he undertake the daily commute to the University of Glasgow to obtain a science degree. Robert spent a year there before tossing it in to join the Royal Navy. There was a war on, after all.

The navy took him to America for training assignments before sending him to fight, first in the Mediterranean and then in the Pacific, where at some point his ship sailed into Sydney Harbour for repairs. He took a tram from the city to Bondi Beach and instantly fell in love with the place.

When the war was over, he shocked his Scottish family by declaring that he was emigrating to Australia. The Greenock Bacon Company was not for him. He bade farewell to his dismayed parents and sisters and boarded a ship for Sydney.

Robert's maternal grandparents had been weavers and makers of weaving equipment, and he arranged to have their loom shipped out from storage in Dunfermline so that he could begin a small textile business in the rough and tumble dockside area of Woolloomooloo. The gangsters for which it was once famous were giving way to a wave of Italian immigrants, and he enjoyed the colour and bustle of the area's narrow streets and alleyways.

Then one night at Romano's nightclub in Martin Place he saw a girl across a crowded room. To him, as he sometimes remarked to us later, she looked like a young Greta Garbo – slim, with soft brown hair, brown eyes, clear skin and that distinctive mouth and chin. She was with two young men, one of whom Robert knew slightly. Her name was Joan Austin, and the two young men were her brothers. Robert quickly engineered an official meeting and soon the young couple were in love.

Joan Austin came from a staunch and unquestioning Catholic family, and was the eighth of thirteen children, eleven of whom survived to adulthood. Her childhood had been an unsettled one, as the family had moved several times during the Depression, Joan's parents struggling to keep one step ahead of bankruptcy; by the time she was twelve, Joan had already attended four or five different schools. One afternoon she came home from school early to find her mother in the kitchen sitting in front of the open oven with a towel over her head. The kitchen was full of gas. Joan threw open the windows, turned off the gas and telephoned her father. Grandma was rushed to hospital. What neither parent had told the children was that their father had been diagnosed with terminal cancer. He was forty-eight.

Soon after arriving at the hospital, Grandma managed to pick up a large plaster statue of the Virgin Mary from its plinth on the landing and throw it down the stairs, where it smashed to smithereens. 'A nervous breakdown,' they said, and her doctor prescribed a mental institution. Nothing her grandchildren ever knew or saw of her in later years would have pointed to even the faintest possibility of such an incident in her past, and indeed we were all grown-up before we knew of it. As children, we knew her as the matriarch: solid, reliable, pious. She was a major director of her children's and grandchildren's lives.

While their mother languished in the mental hospital, their father struggled to consolidate Australian Cotton, his newly established textile business, while undergoing what little treatment the doctors could offer. Joan and her three younger sisters, Anne, Carmel and the toddler Christine, were sent to live in a convent at Hunters Hill. The school-aged brothers, Larry, Ken and Alan, were sent to St Joseph's College, a Catholic boarding school for boys, also at Hunters Hill. Her brothers were not happy there. The youngest brother, Alan, ran away repeatedly. Their father visited a few times, and then stopped coming. The children felt abandoned.

Then, in early 1942, the girls were sent to another convent in the Blue Mountains, outside Sydney, to keep them safe from the Japanese. No-one came to see them.

Finally, news came from St Vincent's Hospital that their father had died, throwing the family into chaos but jolting their mother onto a path to recovery. Quite soon she was ready to pack her bags, engineer a discharge from the hospital, and take her husband's place at the textile factory.

The shattered family was at last reunited in a large flat in a red-brick building called Rosemont, on Edgecliff Road in Sydney's Eastern Suburbs. This flat was forever after known to the entire family simply as Rosemont, a name that lent it the grand air of a mansion or a vast country estate – the family seat. It was from there that Joan, by now seventeen, was able to finish school and then attend Sydney University. She spent a year or two there before entering the workforce as a teacher. Then came the evening at Romano's nightclub and the fateful meeting with the handsome young Scot.

Grandma was alarmed and distressed when her daughter announced her intention to wed a non-Catholic. There was much saying of rosaries and talking into the night. When the young suitor agreed to take instruction and to allow the children of the union to be raised as Catholics, Grandma finally permitted the wedding to go ahead, although with great misgiving. Of course, any other path short of calling the whole thing off would have meant excommunication for the bride, an unthinkable punishment.

Back in Scotland, our Presbyterian grandparents were no less agitated. Frantic airmail letters came from Greenock, but to no avail. (Airmail was expensive and therefore serious; most mail at the time went by sea.) But the young couple were in love.

Eventually, on the day of the wedding, a telegram arrived from our Scottish grandmother, which said, 'Kindly never communicate with me again.' Our resigned grandfather took a more charitable view; unknown to his wife, he sent a bank draft for one hundred pounds, a good deal of money then.

So, in spite of all opposition, and as if to underline the gravity of the groom's commitment, they were married in St Mary's Cathedral, Sydney's grandest Catholic church, in August 1947.

Over the next few years they lived in various flats and had three daughters in quick succession: Angela, Katrina and Philomena. As Robert's business prospered, they bought and renovated a picturesque Victorian cottage in their dream suburb of Bondi, with a large backyard and a granny flat out the back for live-in help. Then twin boys came along: Aidan and Robert.

The arrival of the boys was the young family's first serious challenge. The twins were born very premature, only ten months after Philomena, the youngest daughter. They each weighed less than two pounds at birth, and for many weeks they struggled for life. Grandma offered up rosaries and paid for masses to be said, until finally, months later, the tiny bundles were brought home. But only a few months after that, they developed eczema from head to toe. The women in the family tried oatmeal baths, calamine lotions, lanolin creams, potions and everything else anyone and everyone they knew could think of. Nothing worked. Doctors advised that the poor little boys be returned to the hospital, where they remained for many more months, wearing tiny white mittens and sometimes with their hands tied, so that they could not scratch themselves.

The family suffered another unexpected setback soon after: my father came down with a flu from which he could not quite recover. Then he began to experience alarming respiratory problems, including wheezing and uncontrollable coughing.

'It's the cotton fibres in that factory,' said the Macquarie Street specialist. 'You could be developing a form of white lung. You might need to think of some other career. You need fresh air and a change of environment.'

So here was a dilemma. The shadow of our grandfather's premature death still hung over the family. There were long discussions. Then, in deliberations between Grandma and my father, a possible solution emerged.

The oldest and youngest of my mother's brothers, Jack and Alan, had bought a largely uncleared six-thousand-acre sheep property in the New England district of Walcha as a business venture. Grandma had probably hoped that the project would make men of her two most difficult sons: Jack had been in and out of trouble since his schooldays, and Alan's education had been hindered by his frequent truancies from school. But they were mainly city boys and spectacularly unsuited to life in the bush. It was becoming clear that they were failing to make any headway, and then Jack, as was his wont, lost interest altogether. Alan, who was having difficulty managing alone with a young wife and baby to look after, applied to Grandma for a way out of his predicament. Grandma suggested to my father that he might be interested. He was.

He went up to visit and came home full of enthusiasm. 'The place certainly needs more clearing,' he said, 'but I think I can manage that, no trouble. Wool prices are high – it'll be a good living eventually.'

Grandma, anxious to help her daughter, and possibly even more anxious to have something good come out of Jack and Alan's failing venture, offered to buy my father's textile company to fold into her own so that our parents could purchase the Walcha property for themselves.

The infant twin boys were to be left behind in the hospital in Sydney, and it was agreed that Grandma and our Aunt Phil would bring them to us when their treatment was successful. That would be soon, we were told.

So it was that we, city people with Bondi sand between our toes, entrusted our belongings to a removal company, loaded our little Austin Seven with suitcases, boxes and packages, and said goodbye to the house and its garden with the mulberry tree. We took one last look at the nearby gleaming sands of the beach, and set off north, up the Pacific Highway and beyond.

What nobody mentioned was that our uncle Jack had skipped town leaving both unpaid bills and bad feeling all over the district.

~

I was only five years old, but I remember the journey well. We stopped for the night at a hotel in Scone and I recall rising in the dark, the hotel's rooster crowing out the back, and eating boiled eggs and toast at a table laid with a white tablecloth and hotel silver.

We strapped our bags onto the luggage rack of the little Austin Seven as the sun came up and Katrina, Philomena and I tumbled into the back, with our dog Dizzy on the floor. The road passed the straggling towns of Murrurundi, Willow Tree, Quirindi and Wallabadah and finally there was Tamworth, sun-sleepy on its flat plain. I remember the car struggling up the Moonbi Hills, and Dad's curt 'Stop asking that,' when we ventured to enquire if we were there yet.

At the hamlet of Bendemeer we turned onto the much narrower Oxley Highway, and continued to climb. But here in a dip was Walcha Road – a railway station, general store, war memorial and a pub.

'Oh, we're here,' said Mum.

But no, we were not.

'Still another eleven miles to go,' said Dad. 'They couldn't get the railway up the steep hills, so they had to put the station here.'

Walcha, when we reached it, was just another drowsy country town – two wide main streets that intersected in the town centre, with dust-covered cars and trucks parked at an angle to the pavement. A colonnade of shops on either side of the street included a couple of milk bars, banks, stock and station agents, and the library. Four pubs, two picture theatres, a post office and court house stood alone.

After filling up on petrol, we drove up the Derby Street hill, turned right at the showground and out of town. We were soon churning dust from the dirt track. Fences, mailboxes, the occasional homestead set back from the road, a shearing shed here and there, sheep and cattle dotting the paddocks. On a distant hillside was a man on a horse with his dog, rounding up his flock.

Past the Emu Creek, Bark Hut and Table Top turnoffs, through Winterbourne, up a hill, through a couple of gates and then …

'There it is,' said Dad.

A circle of tall pine trees, a sagging wire fence, a roof that had once been painted red. We were looking at a weather-beaten bungalow surrounded by a verandah, a cylindrical water tank at one end. Weeds everywhere, a corrugated iron shed across the yard, more ramshackle buildings, one of which turned out to be the outhouse, door swinging off its hinges.

Our mother said nothing.

Uncle Alan and Aunt Beverley appeared to help us inside, picking their way around some rotting verandah floorboards. The front door opened straight into the living room, and from there we walked down a hallway past the main bedroom and a small bathroom to an enclosed back verandah and the kitchen with its large blackened fireplace. Everything, walls and floor, tilted a little downhill. All the doorways leading to the outside had flyscreen doors in addition to the wooden ones. The sound of the flyscreens squeaking and banging as we came and went was to become part of the background music of our lives, along with the sighing of the wind in the pine trees, the drawn-out lament of crows circling overhead, and the screeching of a passing flock of black cockatoos. We girls found chickens and a calf. There were trees to investigate, rusty machinery to climb, an old buggy up the hill. There were horses, too, one a dappled grey. 'The Old Grey Mare,' said Dad. The name stuck.

The shock to our mother must have been incalculable. Rotten floorboards. No running water. No telephone, no electricity. How, she must have thought, are we going to live here?

Chapter 1

It's Pronounced 'Wolka'

The town of Walcha lies on the eastern edge of Northern Tablelands of New South Wales, approximately halfway between the small cities of Tamworth and Armidale. It's not on the New England Highway, which runs between them, but some twenty miles to the east of it as the crow flies. The only time you would drive *through* Walcha would be if you were heading for the coast and Port Macquarie from the New England Highway. In the 1950s it was a small town of perhaps a thousand people, but the population of town and district together brought it to almost three times that.

The region is one of rolling hills, fertile valleys, green pastures and granite outcrops bordered by stretches of almost impenetrable bush with wild rivers and deep gorges, most spectacularly to its east. Summers are mild and winters harsh. It has traditionally been sheep country, and has historically produced some of Australia's finest wool.

Tendrils of road stretched in all directions from the main town, miles and miles of unpaved dusty tracks, winding through hills and valleys and over rivers and creek beds leading to farms and properties, five, ten, twenty, thirty miles away. Our trip had brought us almost to the end of one such road - the wooded end with the shale and the granite outcrops.

So here we were. Our new, somewhat rickety, old home. Apart from the glimpse of the Winterbourne homestead among the trees in the valley below, the view from the kitchen windows was just the pines, and beyond them hills and more hills, brown and hazy blue and rolling on forever. From the front verandah, we looked down towards a gully. Beyond the gully was a rise and some pasture and beyond that there were more and higher hills, including Trig Hill, the highest in the area. If you stood on our front verandah and cooeed loudly enough, Trig Hill would echo your call back to you, a trick Dad showed us once that we loved to attempt from time to time. The far hills were virgin bush, full of mysterious wildlife, but from a distance blue and beautiful, frequently with a plume of tightly wadded white clouds behind them, promising a rain that never seemed to come. Until it did.

Uphill from there was an apple orchard, with six large apple trees and one orphan pear tree. The apples were all one variety, small green Granny Smiths, and each tree produced hundreds of apples every summer. They were not particularly sweet eating, although good for cooking.

Our six thousand acres were originally two lots: when we bought it the front part was called Glenoak and the back part was Dingerolla, but we renamed the entire place Arran, after the island in the Firth of Clyde, on the banks of which my father had grown up. The original block of 5813 acres had been awarded in a land ballot in 1911, possibly devolved from the original Winterbourne run. The Glenoak homestead – our new home – had been built in about 1912, but the dense bush, rocky soil and unreliable climate must have defeated the poor settler, and he was long gone. The back lot of Dingerolla had been neither settled nor cleared. There had very likely been Dunghutti people there before the settler, particularly up by the spring and down around Winterbourne Creek, but if so, they had trod lightly upon the earth and had left no trace behind them, not that our European eyes could see, anyway.

Uncle Alan and Aunt Beverley and our young cousin Michael were to stay for some months after our arrival to show us the ropes – to the extent that they themselves had mastered them. My mother's initiation came within a day or two of our arrival on wash day, in the little lean-to out the back of the house.

'Since I'm pregnant,' said Aunt Beverley, 'do you mind carrying the water?' So Katrina and I trailed along as our mother carried buckets and buckets of water from the tank to fill up the copper and rinse tubs.

Aunt Beverley lit a fire under the copper. The lean-to filled with thick white smoke, which billowed out into the yard, making everyone cough.

'Oh, it always does this to begin with,' said Aunt Beverley as my mother arrived with two more buckets, 'but it'll be all right when it gets going.'

Struggling through the smoke, they added the dirty sheets and Rinso soap powder into the steaming cauldron, along with a bag of Reckitt's Blue whitener. They took turns stirring with a large wooden stick for about half an hour before using the stick to lift the wet, heavy items into one of two large concrete tubs. Then they passed the sheets and towels and clothes through the wringer, turning the handle all the while, into the adjoining tub of cold water for the rinse. Back through the wringer again to tub one, then the washing was ready to hang on the line, or rather, several lines, strung on poles between the plum tree and the apple orchard uphill from the house. There were more poles to hoist the lines up high once the washing had been hung. The next load was nappies, this time in the same water, and there was another load after that, which meant starting all over again with clean water.

Earlier Katrina and I had followed with curiosity as they surveyed the vegetable garden, between the house and the apple orchard, close to the clothes lines. Aunt Beverley, chatting all the while, pointed out the scanty collection of bug-eaten carrots, tomatoes, beans, squash and the Queensland Blue pumpkins. My mother frowned.

While the women washed and swept and discussed the spring planting, the men were out on horseback surveying the land and taking stock of things. Now that he had read a book or two about sheep farming, this inspection must have come as a sobering reality check to my father, as the laundry and vegetable garden had for my mother. It must have dawned on them quite quickly that they weren't taking over anything like a going concern; they would have to start almost from scratch. But they were committed now, and there was no going back.

It must have been impossible to know where to start. There was so much to do – fixing the house, clearing the bush, mending fences and making new ones, keeping the rabbits at bay, building up the infrastructure needed to be successful at the business of sheep – but if my father was overwhelmed at the magnitude of the task he had undertaken, we children were not aware of it.

Images of those first weeks and months flicker in and out of my memory like a grainy old movie now: Dad and Uncle Alan going out in the cold mornings to milk the cows, and setting off after breakfast to chop down trees, set the traps, tighten slack fence wires, dig ditches and tend to the very few sheep that Alan had managed to hold onto. There they are, sawing and hammering to fix up the back of the house. There is Mum, standing on the front verandah, arms crossed, insisting that the men fix the rotten floorboards as soon as they could order the timber from town. What if a child were to fall through the gaps? There are the two women in the kitchen, cooking, washing, cleaning and chasing children with a broom. In the evenings the firelight flickers across the men sitting by the fire and smoking, Aunt Beverley reading *Woman's Day*, my mother frowning over the accounts at the kitchen table.

Our black and white Cocker Spaniel, Dizzy, took to her new home with gusto. She followed my father everywhere, except when he went out on the Old Grey Mare, whom she did not like. She was part of our family and we loved her, although Dad often said, 'She's silly as a two-bob watch, that dog. She'll meet a sticky end, one of these days.'

Dizzy liked to chase rabbits, and there were plenty to chase. We girls had thought that rabbits were cuddly, furry creatures, but now we had to learn to think of them as the enemy. Not only did they gobble up pastures, but their habits caused serious soil erosion and threatened native species. Bundles of rabbit traps with their fierce jaws hung from hooks in the shed, and no day ended without a haul of dead rabbits. They were good food for the dogs.

The weeks went by. Aunt Beverley went to town and came back with a new baby. Every day we looked down the track for the removals truck carrying our goods and chattels, but there was no sign of either the truck or our things. Finally, messages were sent to Sydney and Grandma was put on the case. Perhaps a month after that a dilapidated truck showed up with about half our furniture, and half of that was damaged. The man eventually made another run, but there were still pieces and boxes missing, including our dining suite, which we never recovered.

Then a letter came for Uncle Alan with an offer of a new job up north, and he and Aunt Beverley and toddler Michael and baby Colin packed up their car, said their goodbyes, and rattled off down the track. It was just us now.

Chapter 2

This Little Hillside House, Our Home

The house didn't seem emptier for long. In early 1954, the doctors finally discharged Aidan and Robert from the hospital. The twins had been there for more than a year and were nearly two years old. Our aunts Phil and Carmel brought them to us on the train, and my father drove out to Walcha Road to pick them up. This was Phil and Carmel's first visit to Walcha, and they were shocked by what they encountered.

We girls had been excited for their arrival, and we rushed down to the gate to greet the car as it pulled up. But when we went to help lift the little boys from the car, they wailed and sobbed and held out their arms to their more familiar aunts. They clung to Phil and Carmel for days and cried when they left the room. We tried to cheer them up with lots of attention and little rhymes, but they just glared at us before breaking into more sobs.

Aunt Phil, short for Philomena, was much older than my mother, probably in her late thirties at the time. She had never married. Every day of her stay with us, she appeared at breakfast perfectly coiffed and dressed in twinset, tweed skirt, stockings, sensible heels and red lipstick. She had standards to maintain. Nevertheless, after breakfast she fastened her apron strings and pitched in. She made beds, stirred the washing in the copper, ironed, stoked the fire in the stove, carted water, cleaned the kitchen and washed dishes. She busied about the house organising and tidying, dispensing instructions, advice, comments, maxims and not a few tuts of disapproval. When we went to town she added pearls, a little starched collar and a hat and gloves. Carmel, on the other hand, a petite brunette with sparkling eyes and a broad, winning smile, was happy to lark about with us in her trousers, still having something of the tomboy in her. She would have been about nineteen.

The handing over of the boys was one of the very few times our aunt Phil ever visited, but I suspect we had her to thank for some later improvements. She must have had words with her brother-in-law about priorities, and may well have made a financial contribution from her own funds.

With the twins home, the household chores tripled overnight and Katrina and I were pressed into childcare service. Gradually, and with a lot of help from Dizzy, whom they loved, the boys began to adapt to their new home. My mother tried to toilet train them as quickly as she could. We girls unwittingly assisted in this endeavour by encouraging them in peeing competitions against the fence posts.

By now my father, with much sawing, banging and hammering, had completed the work of turning the back of the house into a small, three-sided courtyard. On one side was the boys' bedroom (the old store room) in which he had installed wooden bunk beds. The room was too small for anything else. This room adjoined the girls' bedroom which opened onto the front verandah. On the other side of the courtyard he had built another small wing, which included the new laundry – housing the copper, double tubs and wringer – a dairy, and a new storeroom. The lean-to wash house had gone.

The kitchen, as in most country homesteads, was the hub of the house. At the downhill end was the work area: an alcove with a wood stove at a right angle to the sink, which was set under the window, between two benches. Another large workbench stood opposite. We spent most of our indoor lives at the pine kitchen table in front of the great fireplace. The worn linoleum floor, the kerosene refrigerator, the old pie-safe cupboard with its wire mesh doors, the Singer pedal sewing machine and a big armchair by the fireplace took up the rest of the space.

Our daily lives now began to settle into a rhythm, sunrise to sunset. At dawn my father went out to milk the cows and my mother got up to light the stove, coaxing it into a blaze before going out to fetch buckets of water from the corrugated iron rainwater tanks at the back of the house. The tanks were our only source of water. They collected rainwater from the gutters and we depended on regular rain to fill them. Rain or no rain, we learned that water was always precious – it was something you never, ever, wasted. You never knew when the next rains would come.

After Mum had brought in the water and put on the porridge to cook, there began an endless round of child management, meal preparation, washing, cleaning, tending the vegetable garden and sewing.

My father brought the steaming milk buckets down from the cow yard, slapping them onto the kitchen counter to be strained into a large bowl through a muslin cloth. He would scarf down his hot porridge, and then it was time to saddle up the Old Grey Mare and set out into the paddocks.

His first task was to ringbark trees to clear more land for pasture. It was back-breaking work, and slow. If we were to survive here, he needed to clear at least another two thousand acres this way, but it was a constant battle against the regrowth. The clearing was in addition to work on the house and to the daily toil of taking care of the sheep.

Uncle Alan had left us a few sheep, but there were not as many as we eventually hoped to have when more clearing was done. As the flock thinned the grass in one paddock they were moved to another with the dogs and the Old Grey Mare, who in fact was not all that old and decidedly frisky. She was a one-man horse; my mother could not ride her, nor visitors who prided themselves on their horsemanship. She would only accept my father, and it had taken him some time to tame her. Behind the house, beyond the courtyard and the backyard, stood a majestic cherry plum tree, under which sat an anvil on a large wooden block. Every six weeks or so my father would shoe the Old Grey Mare there, clanging the red-hot horseshoes into the right shape and size with a big hammer. I don't know where he learned to do this. Perhaps his blacksmith grandfather had taught him, back in Scotland.

None of us were old enough for school yet, but we were expected to pitch in with the daily tasks right from the beginning. In the mornings Katrina and I helped to clear the table after breakfast and wash up. Standing on wooden stools, we helped with the laundry and to hang clothes on the line. In the afternoon, we helped sort and fold it. Mum taught us how to weed the vegetable garden, and which greens to pick for dinner. Katrina was charged with bringing the cows Molly and Polly in from their paddock to the cow yard, uphill from the orchard. She locked the calves in a small covered pen so that they could not suckle overnight, leaving us the best of the milk for the morning.

It was my job to sweep the kitchen floor. This was a task that needed to be performed several times a day, as was the carting of water from the tanks. We took it in turns to feed the chooks.

Most afternoons the boys played in the dirt in the yard, making roads for their Matchbox and Dinky cars, throwing sticks for Dizzy, or racing each other back and forth to the gate. By late afternoon, it was time to peel potatoes and help prepare for dinner. We girls helped bathe the boys and get them into their pyjamas before dinner. This involved filling the tin tub that we put in front of the fireplace with more water from the tanks. My mother added some hot water from the large black kettle that hung over the fire and then we sluiced the boys down with a flannel. We girls could wash ourselves, and we took it in turns with the same water.

As the sun began to go down, we waited for the Old Grey Mare to appear over the top of the northern hillside, prancing her way sideways down to the flat and up the rise towards the house in her excitement, the sheep dogs nipping round her hooves. Dad would hang up her bridle, park the saddle on an old saw horse in the shed, rub the mare down and put her out to graze. When we heard his boots crunching on the gravel path near the back door, we rushed out to greet him, clinging to his trousers, which smelled of sweat and horse and soil.

In the evenings, the kerosene lamps lit up the kitchen with a warm, flickering glow. After the washing up, my father might read us a story by the fire while my mother sewed. But quite soon Dad would say, 'It's Wee Willie Winkie time,' and we were sent to brush our teeth and then to get into bed, the boys and Philomena first, and then Katrina and I.

Mum would come in to supervise some prayers – 'Now I lay me down to sleep' and 'Matthew, Mark, Luke and John' – before removing the lamp.

Chapter 3

Five Little Australians

So who were we, these new little farmers?

First, me: blonde, earnest, curious, a little anxious, eager to please, eager to fly.

Next up, Katrina: a year younger than me, and the only brunette among us. She took after our mother's side of the family, the Austin side, and our father used to call her his 'nut brown maiden'.

Her brown hair and olive skin were not the only differences. She had little interest in schoolwork and books, whereas I enjoyed them. Katrina wanted to be out in the paddocks, mustering sheep, building yards, putting in posts for new fences. She became very capable, very young. For a long time, she didn't like to wear dresses or skirts, preferring pants, and insisted on having her hair cut short, like a boy. 'She's a tomboy,' people said. She must have realised, way sooner than I did, that girls were often regarded as the inferior sex, and she simply wasn't having it. Anything a boy could do, Katrina could do better.

My father used to say of her, 'Though she be but little, she is fierce.' Even when very small, if exasperated, she would pronounce to Mum with the lisp she had in the early days, 'I'm thick of you!' One lunchtime, after a fierce difference of opinion, she packed a small suitcase and announced that she was leaving us. We watched her as she marched down the road to the mailbox, and then turned right along the boundary fence, her eight-year-old form and small Globite suitcase disappearing into the bush. She had already gone further than I had imagined she would.

'Aren't you going to stop her?' I begged my mother. 'What is she going to eat? Where will she sleep?'

Mum's reply was brisk. 'Don't worry, she'll be back when she gets hungry. I'll give her till five o'clock.'

This struck me as rather calm – and even callous – but indeed, in the afternoon when I went into our bedroom, there was Katrina, sitting on her bed.

'I jutht wanted to teach Mum a lethon,' she said.

Katrina and I were best friends. Our two beds were side by side, separated only by a small chest of drawers, and we would talk for hours at night, about our dogs and cats, stories we had heard, or the mysterious Brennans, a wild family that was said to live deep in the gorge. We were fascinated by the Brennans. Did they have a hut down there or did they sleep under the stars? How many of them were there? We had heard that there were several brothers. Where was their mother? How did they get their supplies?

Next down the line was Philomena, named after our Aunt Phil. She was three years younger than I was and two years younger than Katrina. She was only two years old when we moved to Walcha, and would not have remembered much about life in Sydney. As a small child she had fine white hair that stood straight up, like a mohawk cut. There was nothing Mum could do to dampen it down. For our first year at Arran, Philomena was the baby. To begin with, she was excused chores, a situation that she must have hoped would be lasting, because she was rather shocked when they started coming her way. One of her first was to feed the chooks, and she would head out, a tiny scrap of a thing hardly bigger than the chooks themselves, in dirty overalls a bit too big and falling from one shoulder, her hair standing straight up, with a large pocket full of chook food.

Philomena liked to colour, draw and paint. She was fussy about her clothes, and objected vociferously to the hand-me-downs she had no choice but to wear. She also spent a good deal of time arranging all our dolls artistically around the bedroom. She was a sweet-natured little girl, but she was the one who wanted the princess outfit, or perhaps a tulle ballerina skirt, something that would have been unthinkable to our mother, and a major sign of an impossibly spoiled child.

It must have been hard for Philomena when the twin boys arrived; now she had not one rival, but two. And they were less than a year younger than she was.

Aidan and Robert were very late to start talking. Instead of English, they had developed a language all their own and talked to each other in a rapid, incoherent babble that they seemed to understand perfectly. Our parents were worried and wrote to Grandma, describing the symptoms. Grandma consulted a paediatrician friend after Mass one Sunday. 'Oh, it sounds like cryptophasia,' he said, 'although some people call it idioglossia. It's not uncommon with twins. Don't worry, they'll grow out of it.' Reassured, we all began to learn some of their language. *Gaga, pintoob, mikmak.* As time went by, of course, the boys did grow out of it, but they were well past their fourth birthday before they became fluent in English.

With their white-blond hair and cheeky grins, Aidan and Robert were a handful. They climbed every piece of furniture in the house and every tree within reach, and sometimes needed to be helped down. They loved to play in the shed with our father's tools, which would infuriate him; the tool he needed at any given moment always seemed to be missing. On one occasion, the boys got in the car, released the handbrake, put the gears in neutral and drove it down the hill to the flat above the gully. The miracle was that they stopped short of the gully itself.

Because they were identical twins it was difficult to tell them apart. Robert had a small birthmark on his right thigh, so often we had to ask them to bare the relevant leg, so that we could tell. Dad got around the problem by simply calling them both 'Boy'.

An early chore for the boys was finding eggs for me and Katrina to collect. Our chooks were locked up in the evenings to shelter them from the foxes and feral cats, but during the day they wandered about the place, pecking in the yard unfettered, free to drop their offerings in unlikely places: the shed rafters, perhaps, or the front seat of the car, or behind the laundry copper. The boys, being closer to the ground, often found what Katrina and I had overlooked in our searches. Every egg was precious.

Our mother was for the most part a loving, gentle woman, whose soft voice, as we well knew, belied stern stuff underneath. She was far more patient than our father, although even she had her limits, which she reached on some days more quickly than on others. Life was hard for our mother, her days a constant round of backbreaking work and her nights a turmoil of anxiety about money. She loved poetry and music. She also loved us, and we felt secure in her love, although she was a strict disciplinarian, and we often gave her cause to grab for the wooden spoon. We were used to the whack of the spoon on the back of our legs – that was just part of life. Though we laughed when she sometimes missed and broke the spoon on the back of a chair.

We all adored our father, and I especially. A relatively reserved man with a short store of patience where children were concerned, he was sparing with both his praise and his affections. It was rare to get his undivided attention, and he was certainly not demonstrative – we did not get kisses or hugs from him. But he was generous with information. 'See this plant?' he would say. 'It's wild hops. That's the plant that people use to make beer. Oh, and that one over there – it's wild tobacco.' Or, out of nowhere, 'The city of Budapest is actually two cities, on different sides of the Danube. One is called Buda, and the other is called Pest.'

When he was working near the house, fixing tackle in the shed, say, or fixing pipes to the bathroom, I would hang about at his side. I seized upon the precious bits of information he would offer as though they were rubies or pearls. 'You know, Columbus didn't really discover America,' he would grunt, mixing cement in the wheelbarrow in the back courtyard. 'A Viking called Leif Erikson did.'

If we went too far with Dad's patience, talked back or left a gate open, off came the belt, and very occasionally the beating would be severe. Still, we were anxious for his attention and approval, and tried hard to extract from him some word of praise. He became easier with us after a beer or two, or perhaps a whisky, when he became gregarious and outgoing. It was very much a drinking culture then, and in town on a Saturday the men would drink heavily, but my father, like most men, worked hard all week without it. Drinking was reserved for weekends.

Chapter 4

In Which We Make Some Improvements

From the very beginning my mother had been chafing about there being no electricity at the homestead. Each room in the house sported a single light bulb hanging from its ceiling. The living room, used only for special occasions and company, had two, one at either end. But they were for decoration only, since they shed no light. There was a generator in a small lean-to out the back, but when we first arrived it didn't work, and Uncle Alan and my father together had not been able to fix it. One cold Monday afternoon, a box of parts arrived on the back of the mailman Mr Grieve's truck. My father carried the box to a new shed he had built, also out the back, where he had installed the uncooperative generator.

An hour or two later we heard a sputtering noise and, following that, the unmistakable sound of an engine throbbing. Dad came rushing into the kitchen and flicked the switch by the door, the one that had never worked. And lo and behold, the single bulb lit up, bathing the kitchen in a kind of anaemic pall. We had electric light now, 32 volts of it, however dim.

But only for some of the time. And we children were never allowed to turn on the lights in our rooms. We still had to go to bed in the dark, or perhaps, on a moonless winter night, with a torch or a lamp.

And then, the most miraculous thing of all: we could have a radio, a major lifeline to the outside world. Grandma sent up a plug-in radio for the kitchen, which had a battery back-up for those times when the generator would sputter and die until attended to. This meant I could now listen to the ABC Children's Hour at five o'clock, which included the Argonauts Club. I joined up as soon as I could write, and quickly became addicted. I could not hear the show's opening tune 'Come, Old Mother Hubbard and Jack and Jill and Tom the piper's son …' without a quiver of excitement. I listened eagerly to the banter between Mac, Jimmy and various other collaborators before Ruth Park's famous long-running serial *The Muddle-Headed Wombat* came on; then would come a weekly discussion about writing, music, painting, or science and nature – all led by extremely distinguished Australians, I was later to discover – then an adventure serial for older children before the end.

Of course, there was work to do while listening to the Children's Hour: peeling potatoes, topping and tailing beans, shelling peas or, as I got older, ironing or mending. Because, as Mum was fond of pointing out, 'The devil finds work for idle hands to do.'

On 2AD, the Armidale station, which we tuned into sometimes to get local weather reports, we could hear Doris Day ('Once I had a secret love …') and Tony Bennett ('Take my hand, I'm a stranger in paradise …') and Rosemary Clooney ('Hey there, you with the stars in your eyes …').

At a deceased estate auction, my father had picked up a brand-new record player along with the farm machinery he had gone there for, and once we had electricity, it was our chief diversion for a brief period. Our parents had a few new-fangled LP records stored up from their Sydney days, so sometimes after dinner when the weather was warm, we retired to the living room where they played Frank Sinatra or Bing Crosby, or a musical, maybe *South*

Pacific or *Carousel*. My mother had some classical favourites: Chopin, Rimsky-Korsakov's *Scheherazade,* and Beethoven's Violin Concerto. In our bedroom, Katrina and I strained to listen through the adjoining wall.

One year our neighbours, Mr and Mrs Bloo, gave my mother a recording of *Oklahoma* for her birthday. That evening we girls were allowed to sit up and listen to it. We already knew some of the songs from the radio. What excitement, what pleasure! 'Oh, what a beautiful mornin',' we bellowed from the front verandah into the bright blue sky the next day. 'Oh, what a beautiful day!' we shouted at a startled flock of passing rosellas.

The pleasure was brief because when the bills for the diesel fuel for the generator began to arrive, reality set in. We could not afford the extra electricity. Record playing was limited to when we had company. We became sparing with our electricity, and the generator only ran when we needed it; but even on those nights we often heard the generator begin to sputter, fade and die. And out would come the hurricane lamps.

Around this time my father discovered a small spring up the hill from the house. With the help of Mick Brien, our neighbour from Winterbourne, he installed a small pump and some copper piping down to the house. He connected them to the formerly non-functioning taps and now we had cold running spring water in the kitchen, laundry and bathroom. We still had to heat water in the large kettle over the fire or on the stove, but this one small thing made an even bigger difference to our lives than the generator had. No more carting water on washdays, only drinking and cooking water to be lugged to the kitchen. We began to use the bathroom for bathing, instead of the tub in the kitchen. This felt like progress to us.

Indeed, each one of these improvements, electric lights, the radio, the record player, the running water, seemed to us a minor miracle. Collectively they made an enormous difference to our lives. But they didn't solve everything. There was still plenty of work to do.

Once the cold weather started, for example, the kitchen fire in its great fireplace was lit first thing in the morning and stoked and coaxed into a warming blaze. The stove had to be lit, too, because it always went out overnight. Other people, perhaps richer people, had Aga stoves that stayed alight, but we were not so wealthy and had to make do with what was already there: a bulky, iron-topped, enamel-fronted substitute, which used a lot of wood and, like almost everything else about the place, required constant feeding and attention. Each winter my father would amass a huge woodpile behind the shed, but the trips back and forth with the wheelbarrow to fetch wood for the kitchen seemed endless. And every afternoon Katrina or I were sent off to collect kindling for the next day's fire. We would return with armfuls of eucalyptus bark, pine cones and twigs, which we dumped in a basket beside the stove. As the winter wore on, however, the pickings close to the house became slim, and we needed to wander further and further afield. On really cold days, and these were many between May and September, no-one really wanted to leave the house. My father was out, of course, rounding up sheep or clearing scrub or killing rabbits or building fences in the biting cold, but we were in no hurry to join him.

Chapter 5

In Which We Learn The Sheep Business

Our first new mob of sheep, mostly ewes, arrived dusty and hungry, in the charge of a drover on horseback and his dogs. They had walked all the way from the other side of town and now they straggled up the hill from Winterbourne and jammed through our boundary gate. They spread out, bleating, into our front paddock, slightly bewildered to be now free of the dogs who had been snapping at their heels for days.

Sheep were our business. They were going to be our livelihood. When the time came, we would shear them and send the wool to market, and breed them. The lambs they produced would give us more sheep, and thus more wool to send to market each year.

This turned out to be both more complicated and more arduous than it had seemed.

We could not run many sheep to the acre because most of our six thousand acres were useless for sheep until we could clear them. And while my father was constantly trying to clear as much land for pasture as he could, occasionally hiring a bulldozer from town to help, progress was slow and the going tough. Still, the clearing resulted in an abundant supply of tall young trees suitable for using as posts for yards, sheds and fences, so after a year or two on Arran, not only could my father fell a tree within a matter of seconds, but we had a respectable pile of logs for building projects; we did not yet have our own yards, dips or shearing shed, all essential trappings in the raising of sheep, so we were going to have to build them.

Rearing sheep is an exceptionally labour-intensive business. Our lives became a long round of shearing, lambing, marking, dipping, drenching, crutching, feeding, watering and general sweat and toil. Whenever it was time to move sheep from place to place for food or water, my father, the Old Grey Mare, and several dogs were often joined by a child or two, on foot. Our job was to open and close gates, as well as to help the dogs. The dogs usually kept the sheep corralled in a tight bunch, running furiously back and forth and around the flock in circles. If you needed the sheep to move in a certain direction, you would call the dogs back. This involved a number of ear-splitting whistles and basic bellowed instructions: 'Come behind there, Annie! Come behind, you stupid drongo! Come behind, Baxter! No, not that way, you bloody galah! Come behind here!' The dogs worked hard to please, despite the heavy verbal abuse. Four-letter words were absolutely forbidden across the threshold of our house and in social contexts of any kind then. But with the dogs, my father, as did all the farmers, let loose his frustrations with language that would have lifted the lid off a witch's cauldron.

Also used to control and call back the dogs was a piercing whistle, made by putting two fingers in one's mouth and, well, blowing. Every man in the district was adept at this whistle, and Katrina and our boys learned it early.

The fences required constant maintenance, the boundary fence most of all. The tall boundary fence, with wire mesh set a foot or two into the ground beneath to discourage burrowing, was supposed to be dingo proof, but it wasn't always, because sometimes dingoes would manage to tunnel under the wire mesh. This not only meant dingoes in the paddocks, but the possibility of sheep getting through and rambling off onto Winterbourne or perhaps into the gorge, where they might be caught and cooked by the fabled Brennans. Just one or two dingoes could wreak tremendous havoc, killing dozens of sheep in a night. They seemed to maul sheep rather than eat them, eating part and leaving them to die, or even just killing them without eating them. Every now and then we would find ragged, bloody sheep carcasses scattered around the paddock. Everyone set dingo traps around their boundaries, and neighbours put together drive days to try to catch or shoot them.

Every few months, my father took off on the Old Grey Mare with a swag, a billy can, and enough food to last a few days, to ride the boundary, check and reset dingo traps, and fix any problems with the fence. Our boundary was maybe twelve or thirteen miles around, and much of it was in rough and hilly bushland. If there were no problems he could be back in two days, but if there were holes to fix, it might take him three. On the afternoon of the second day we began an anxious watch for his return over the crest of the hill above the gully and we were always happy to see the Old Grey Mare rearing and prancing down the hill and across the flat in her pleasure to be home.

Our busiest time was the spring. We knew it was coming when the wattle bloomed. The abundant clumps of golden yellow flowers, which generally appeared in late August and early September, were full of summer's promise. They smelled to me of sunshine and honey. In our early years, I longed to pick some to put in a vase, but Mum said no, it was unlucky to have wattle in the house.

After the wattle, our plum tree would burst into blossom,

followed by the apple trees in the orchard. Spring meant the shearing, and close upon it the lambing, then the dipping, then the marking. For our first few years at Walcha, we did not have our own shearing shed, so we drove our sheep to the Winterbourne shed to be shorn there, following their own shearing, somewhere between late August and early October. Our neighbour Mr Brien kept two or three of his five or six itinerant shearers on for us and the whole family worked around the clock to assist.

The commotion and excitement of shearing was the culmination of twelve months of care and sweat, and a high point in our year. The woolshed pulsed with the whine of the electric shears, the rattle of sheep's hooves on the wooden floor and the shouts of the crew as they yelled for tar or had a fleece ready to throw. A good shearer could shear a hundred sheep in a day and they competed to see who could clip the most sheep, keeping their tallies on a blackboard. Those with the highest earned bonuses.

We all loved to hang about in the shed, but perhaps Katrina loved it the most, watching carefully as the fleeces were thrown on the sorting table and the expert wool classer sorted the wool. The wool was tossed into cubicles according to its grade – A, AA, AAA, sometimes even AAAA – ready to be pressed into bales. The smaller children threw themselves into the half-full bales and bounced around in the wool, which helped pack it down; 'Just watch out that you're not squashed flat by the press and sent to market,' warned the classer.

Shearers, even if there are only a few of them, eat a lot. Mr and Mrs Brien hired a cook for their own shearing, but we couldn't afford to. So we were up before daybreak to prepare breakfast for the shearers: sausages, bacon, eggs, fried tomato, mushrooms, even steak. After cleaning up their breakfast we made scones, pikelets, biscuits and cakes for their morning and afternoon smoko breaks, and stews and shepherd's pies for their dinners. We all loved the extra scones and biscuits we could nick from the kitchen during shearing.

For me, it was fascinating to hear the shearers talk. They had a language all their own and when I came in at smoko with a basket of scones and cake, they might say, 'Bewdy. Bonza scones, luv. Yer blood's worth bottling.'

'Give us another cuppa, luv. I'm parched as a Pommie's bathmat.'

'How's yer mum today, luv? Good lookin' sheila. S'pose with all you kids she's flat out like a lizard drinking, eh?'

'Stone the crows, Bluey! Yer took the last piece, yer big galah! Well, may all yer chooks turn into emus and knock yer dunny down.'

When one of them, a tall, stringy man who never spoke, left the room for a moment, one of the others remarked, 'Just sits there like a shag on a rock, that bloke. Got a few kangaroos loose in the top paddock, I reckon.'

And then, when they had finished, one might say, 'Well, it's back to the hard yakka. Roarin' to go, now. Fit as a Mallee bull.'

Most of these expressions were familiar to me, some weren't, but I knew I was not to call a woman a 'sheila', describe work as 'yakka' or something good as 'bonza' at home. My mother regarded this kind of talk as common, although my father enjoyed it. When I asked what 'parched as a Pommie's bathmat' meant he explained that 'Pommie' was Australian slang for an Englishman, and it was widely believed in Australia that Englishmen didn't bathe, so therefore didn't dampen their bathmats.

The bales of wool went off on trucks, the origin and grade stencilled on the side of each bale, and then our parents waited to hear what it had fetched at market. Our first cheque was not very big, but my father was optimistic. 'Never mind, it'll be more next year,' he said. Every year, waiting for the cheque was an anxious time and the cheque, when it came, never seemed to be enough, but to begin with we children did not concern ourselves with that.

About a month after shearing, and before they had grown too much fleece, the sheep needed to be dipped – shunted through a bath of chemicals designed to protect them from lice, ticks and flystrike. That, too, required driving our flock to Winterbourne, so that we could use their yards and dipping trenches.

Around the same time came the lambing. Then we patrolled the front paddock constantly for two or three weeks, watching, waiting, and giving a helping hand to any ewe having trouble. Again we began our days before dawn, because the crows, hawks and eagles circled from sunup to sundown, seeking a chance to attack. Only once did we see a large eagle flying towards her eyrie with a newborn lamb in her talons; a more common problem was the ewe in difficulty who might have her eyes plucked out by an opportunistic crow. If my father managed to shoot a circling eagle, which he sometimes did, he would spread its wings out along a fence and secure it there with wire and string, leaving it to rot as a warning to others

Every spring, when the plum and apple blossoms bloomed, we found ourselves with a few 'poddy' lambs in the kitchen. These were the lambs that had lost their mothers to the crows, the cold or simply a difficult birth. They slept near the fire in cardboard boxes lined with hessian bags. My father said that the important thing with a brand-new lamb was to make sure that we milked the dead mother to obtain her colostrum, which the lambs needed to drink to protect them from various diseases. After that we bottle fed them with a special formula and teats. For us children, being allowed to feed the lambs was a privilege earned by being good and doing one's chores, and the little creatures were gratifyingly appreciative, nuzzling the teats and wagging their tails. We gave them names. Two of the first that we had were Barbie and Betty, named after Barbie Laurie and Betty Borthwick, glamorous young brides who had married into the district recently.

One cold winter's day during lambing season, we went over to visit Dick and Tony Blomfield at Karori. Although it was afternoon, there was still frost in the fence-post shadows and under the trees. We walked into Mrs Blomfield's kitchen with its blazing open fire to find the floor carpeted with lambs, curled up in their little cardboard cartons, some bleating pitifully for their mothers. She must have had more than twenty lambs, and she kept her two boys, Peter and Rob, busy feeding them all.

After a few days in the kitchen the lambs could be turned out into a pen in the yard and then the yard itself until they were big enough to join the main mob. We could always tell a sheep that had once been a poddy lamb: they were the ones that would come running to greet and headbutt you when you walked through a grazing paddock, or when you began a muster, hoping for a caress or a treat. When my father was selecting a sheep to kill for our food, he had to be careful to avoid a sheep that we had raised as a poddy lamb, because that would send us into a tailspin of anguish.

When the lambs were about six weeks old, it was marking time. This meant docking their tails and castrating the males, an activity that took several days. Up in the yards, we sat on the top fence rail at the end of the race, and swung the gates back and forth to separate the lambs from their mothers. My father docked their tails and earmarked them as ours, then castrated the males. We used the same method for both docking and castrating: applying a tight ring around the tail or testicles to cut off circulation. The part or parts would drop off in a few weeks. The tails had to go because the discomfort and misery of flystrike later would have been far greater than the temporary discomfort of losing a tail. We might leave one or two promising male specimens from mothers who had produced fine wool to grow into stud rams, but the rest of the males would become wethers.

These practices were standard in the industry, and we completely took them for granted. If one of us children began to worry about the lambs being in pain, my father would explain that the pain was short lived, would not be remembered, and was for the sake of the animal's future wellbeing. Like most farmers, we loved our animals and cared for them deeply. We would not have subjected them to any process that would cause them unnecessary pain, and neither would any farmers we knew.

Chapter 6

A Woman's Work

When I think of my mother back in those days, I see her in an old dress and scuffed lace-up shoes, her hair pulled back, an apron tied around her waist and wearing either a pair of rubber gloves or gardening gloves. Rubber gloves were something of a luxury then, but on her first visit Aunt Phil had seen what the washing and the gardening were doing to her sister's hands. 'You may be stuck out here in the middle of nowhere, but you're not going to ruin your hands, Joan,' she warned. So Aunt Phil left her own rubber gloves behind, sending more from Sydney from time to time, until eventually they became available in McRae's in town.

The first meal of the day was not a complicated one, because it was always porridge. We children ate ours with milk and brown sugar, but my father made a point of eating his with salt, the Scottish way. Scooped out of a ten pound bag that sat beside the stove, the oats were set to soak in water in a big pot the night before, making them quicker to cook in the morning, especially since the stove took a while to heat up.

Lunch was sandwiches, so long as the bread lasted. In the early days, before the boys had arrived from Sydney, my mother had made our bread, but it was a tricky business, because our oven was unreliable. Somebody had to stand by the stove and feed it with wood to keep the heat constant. In the end she gave up, and our bread came from town on Mr Grieve's mail truck, wrapped in butcher's paper and fastened with a rubber band.

Monday lunchtime was a big event in the week, because that was when Mr Grieve came to the house, bringing our week's supply of bread: two large high-top loaves that came apart in the middle, the blackened, rounded tops promising a delicious crust. There was nothing better than a Vegemite sandwich with garden lettuce and homemade butter on fresh, crusty Walcha bread. Often we ate our sandwiches standing around in the kitchen, on the run in a break between chores, lessons and play.

As the week wore on, however, the bread would get staler and less delicious and the slices thinner. Sometimes we ran out, and we fell back on tinned baked beans or tinned spaghetti, or even potato pancakes or soda bread.

That we killed and ate our own meat was a given; we had paddocks full of sheep out there. When we were running low on meat, my father would select a sheep from the mob to slaughter, careful to choose one that would not fetch too much at sale – a bit too old, perhaps, or with inferior wool quality. Often the victim would be penned up in our yard for a day or two to fast before meeting its fate, and sometimes, depending on the season and how much of a fleece it had, my father would shear it first. But when the time came, the end would be swift. I was often his appointed assistant in this task, especially as I grew older, but I didn't mind – I loved the extra time I could spend with him.

The slaughter happened in the laundry. My father took his sharp knife, slit the victim's throat and broke its neck in an almost simultaneous movement, swiftly and surely. The sheep would struggle for a moment, hooves scrabbling on the concrete floor, and then its body would relax as its blood gushed out into the dish held below the neck.

'You see,' said Dad, as he set aside the dish for the blood to set, 'it dies straight away. It's not cruel, it hardly feels a thing. Besides, sheep don't feel pain the way people do.' Later he would give the blood to the working dogs, along with the heart, lungs and other offal.

He strung the sheep up by its back heels on a large hook screwed into one of the back verandah posts and quickly removed the hide, making slits along the length of the sheep's front, around the anus and up the legs and then peeling the hide away from the carcass. He had been tutored by his brother-in-law, our Uncle Alan, and butchered swiftly and expertly, naming the parts for me as he went: heart, lungs, kidneys, liver, stomach. The carcass needed to hang and 'set' before being eaten.

The butchered meat was kept in a Coolgardie safe, a large cabinet with double walls lined with tin. The tin was punched full of holes. Between the outer and inner walls was a layer of charcoal and on top was a drip system that kept the charcoal wet and the meat cool.

Sometimes Dad saved the hides to tan and then make into a sheepskin rug for the house, but usually he would just wash them, accumulate a few and drop them off in town; they didn't fetch much but it was something, and every little bit helped.

We always ate lambs' fry – liver – on the same day we killed a sheep; it was best eaten fresh, whereas the rest of the sheep would not be ready to eat for a few days. The meat was thinly sliced, coated in seasoned flour, and quickly fried in the large cast-iron frying pan until crisp on the outside but still a little pink in the middle, and we loved it. The next day Dad ate crumbed brains, and we would have braised kidneys in gravy with vegetables.

For dinner, there was no other choice than lamb, or more precisely, mutton. Younger sheep were too valuable, and besides, an older sheep went further. It was most frequently chops, with a large serve of mashed potatoes, and a green vegetable from the garden. The only parts of this meal that ever varied were the cut of mutton and the vegetables, since we could eat only what was in season. In summer there were beans, peas, cucumbers, lettuce, tomatoes, squash and corn; in winter, cauliflower, parsnips, spinach, cabbage, Brussels sprouts, carrots and broccoli, all home grown. Often boiled or mashed pumpkin was added to the mix, although my father refused to eat it, because he said that in Scotland, pumpkin was fed to the pigs. But it had been an Australian staple since convict times and we children liked it. We picked our pumpkins in the autumn and stacked them on the floor of the pantry, where they lasted for most of the winter.

No dinner was complete without dessert, or 'sweets' as Mum called it. Usually it was stewed apple (the younger ones pronounced it 'chewed apple') and custard, but sometimes there might be blancmange, rice pudding or junket, an old standby. The custard was made with custard powder, which should have had powdered eggs in it, but didn't. Sometimes Mum made sago or tapioca puddings, cheap and supposedly nutritious, but we all hated them, and they eventually disappeared from her repertoire.

Dinner was the time when the family talked. Our father talked about what he had done that day, or about things he had seen – quolls, enormously long snakes, goannas – while riding the boundary. He would tell us about our grandparents and his sisters in Scotland, and about his uncle Charlie, who was a 'wag'. He told us about his grandfather Alexander McKenzie, a man of so few words that the family stories about him became legendary. Once, without explanation, he wore his hat to dinner for a week, but no-one was allowed ask why. It turned out that he had been injured by a falling piece of masonry, but was not willing to discuss it. Alexander was fond of occasional visits to the pub, of which our great-grandmother disapproved. He would return to her with a box of chocolates, handed over with his finger to his lips. Mum did not seem to think that this story was so funny.

Dad told us about Sunday trips down the coast to Largs, where the men, as 'bona fide travellers', could get a whisky at the pub (pubs were closed to locals on Sunday, but open to those who had travelled a certain distance). There would be squabbles between his mother's brothers over who was to drive the family car, but once there, while the men were at the pub, the women and children could enjoy delicious ice creams at Nardini's, near the seafront. 'I still sometimes dream about Nardini's chocolate ice cream,' he said. He told us about places he had visited while in the navy: New York, Gibraltar, San Diego. He told us that some people in New York said 'toity-toid' instead of 'thirty-third'.

But better still, he would answer questions, at least until he tired of our constant babbling, or blethering, as he called it. How does the radio work? Why aren't there bears in Australia? What's the hottest place in the world? Had he been there? What makes the rain? How many people live in London? What's the biggest city in the world? He seemed to know the answers to many of our questions, and it became a kind of game to think of questions he could not answer. How many stars are in the sky?

On Sundays, the fragrant smell of roasting lamb wafted through the house all morning, an aroma of comfort and anticipation. Sunday lunch, with its traditional roast dinner, was both a more formal and a more leisurely affair. Mum usually put some effort into a special Sunday pudding, perhaps apple cake, or baked apple, or apple crumble, or apple brown betty or a steamed apple pudding. Once in a glorious blue moon, if we were having company, there might be enough butter to make pastry for an apple pie.

It was then that Dad would tell us stories of films he had seen, or maybe of how Christopher Columbus had proved the world was round, or of Bonnie Prince Charlie's escape to Skye. Sometimes Mum would recite us one of her poems. 'Tiger, tiger, burning bright …' she would begin. We didn't know what 'fearful symmetry' was, but it sounded both scary and very grown-up.

Our parents paid a great deal of attention to table manners. No matter how hungry we were, we had to wait until Mum sat down and picked up her knife and fork before we could begin. We were not permitted to leave the table during the meal without asking, 'Please may I leave the table?' We were taught how to set the table (a job for the boys, from very early on) with napkins (cloth, of course, and washed once a week) on the left, and how to hold our knives and forks properly, using both implements to eat. Never hold your knife like a pencil. Never, ever, ever put a knife in your mouth. We ate with our mouths closed, and there was to be no smacking of lips or loud chewing. We did not speak with food in our mouths. No arguing or fighting at the table. No elbows on the table. When we were finished our meal we lined up our knives and forks together neatly, the knife's cutting edge facing inwards, on the plate in the half-past-six position.

Our mother was not going to run the risk of our being thought 'badly brought up', or worse, 'common', and so excluded forever from social acceptance in the highest possible circles. After all, her great-grandmother had been a maid in a grand house in Ireland and had come to Australia on an assisted passage. She had passed on to her children and grandchildren the manners she had learned there. Of course, at that time those same table manners were almost universally taught in English-speaking homes around Australia. (Several of my mother's more distant forebears had also been transported to Australia at the pleasure of Their Majesties George

III and IV, but they were never mentioned. No doubt this fact had been conveniently forgotten by the family as soon as possible.) Besides, what if one day one of us were to be invited to Buckingham Palace for tea? One never knew where this life might take us. She did not imagine that one of us might end up in Hollywood, where such niceties counted for naught.

Manners were not the only issue. We had to finish every single piece of food on the plate, but for the gristle and bones, which went to the dogs or the chooks. If someone was reluctant to finish their pumpkin or mashed potatoes Mum would say, 'You need to be grateful. A child in Africa would love to have that,' and of course we would grumble that we couldn't send our mashed potatoes to Africa so what difference did it make? Only years later were we to understand what she meant.

Putting food on the table meant hours of labour each week in the vegetable garden, our mother doubled over as she hoed and dug and planted. Tending was crucial: nets over the beans and tomatoes and celery to protect them from the birds, potions to ward off insects and constant, constant weeding. We helped with weeding, as well as with picking.

As winter approached, we spent two or three hard days in the orchard picking the apples and carting them in buckets and baskets down to the house. Then we spent more days peeling, coring, stewing and bottling. The large Fowler's Vacola jars, sterilised in bubbling vats on the stove, were filled with stewed apple, capped with rubber rings, lids and clamps and set back in the vats to seal. To ensure a good seal, the clamps stayed on until the next day.

By late April the walk-in pantry outside the kitchen was crammed with jars and bottles, its shelves buckling under the weight. Apart from the dozens of jars of stewed apple, there were jars of tomatoes, corn, green beans, a few precious jars of pears for a special occasion, and stewed plums. These were our winter stores.

The growing and preparation of food was only part of my mother's burden. Sewing, sweeping, carting water, washing, ironing, all were part of her day. And although she tried to keep ironing to a minimum, sometimes it had to be done. We had a set of very heavy cast-iron flatirons with a detachable handle. You sat three irons on the stovetop and waited five or ten minutes before they were hot enough to begin. When the iron you were using began to cool you would put it back on the stove and transfer the handle to a hotter one. It was a strenuous task, and one soon handed to me, as soon as I was old enough.

Chapter 7

Oskar Kokoschka

We had bought a small mob of cows and heifers as a sideline to the sheep. The cattle, too, had come straggling through our boundary fence after a two-day walk from town. If wool was not keeping us in shoes, perhaps the sale of some calves would help. And cattle were far less labour intensive than sheep, although they did require drenching and more dramatically, branding. After they arrived, Dad took about sixty of the cattle down to graze in Kitty's Gully, halfway to Cheyenne, where there was a good, grassy meadow. But when he went to collect them a few weeks later, some forty-five head of our new mob of cattle had simply disappeared. Where had they gone? Did they get through the boundary fence and wander into the gorge? It turned out that Mick Brien was missing some cattle too. Many thought they had been stolen, and some thought the Brennans were to blame. Whether the police ever caught any thieves I don't know, but the loss was a blow, which we could hardly afford.

We branded the rest of the herd as soon as possible. My father had designed, registered and made his own brand, and he and Clennell Fenwicke spent a couple of days penning our cattle up in the Winterbourne yards and throwing them to the ground before searing the brand into their poor rumps.

But if we wanted calves to sell, we would need a bull.

We could see the line of dust moving across the opposite side of the valley. This was the delivery we'd been expecting all afternoon. Mum put on the kettle.

As the massive dirty truck crossed the boundary ramp and began to rattle towards the house, Dad directed it to head up the hill to the cow yards, where there was an old wooden cattle ramp. The driver managed to manoeuvre the truck so that it backed onto the ramp, and then they opened the doors. Out clattered a gigantic dun-coloured monster, backwards down the ramp and into the yard, roaring and snorting. Katrina and I had been perched on the top rail of the yards inspecting this operation, but when the bull got us in his sights and started pawing at the ground with menace, we leapt down.

Here was a giant of a beast, much bigger than our milk cows or placid grazing cattle – even his hooves seemed enormous. He had a glossy coat, sharp, curved horns, and huge balls that hung halfway to the ground.

'Well,' said Dad, 'he's an impressive gentleman, isn't he? I think we'll call him Oskar. Oskar Kokoschka.'

Oskar Kokoschka? This was the most exciting, exotic and tongue-twisting name we had ever heard. We rolled it around our tongues: *Oskar Kokoschka, Oskar Kokoschka*. We danced around in circles, singing, 'Oskar Kokoschka, Oskar Kokoschka,' in convulsions of joy.

Dad decided to leave Oskar to settle down in the yards before letting him out into the paddock, and so he and the driver headed back down to the house for scones and tea. We were in the kitchen enjoying the pleasure of a visitor when one of the boys came rushing into the kitchen, waving his arms and shouting something unintelligible in his twin language. We hurried out and there was Oskar, racing around the cow paddock as though he hoped to win the Melbourne Cup. He had managed to break down the wooden gate in the cow yards and leap into the paddock. The two milk cows, Molly and Polly, were cowering together in the paddock's top corner.

We left him there for the time being, but later in the day it was Katrina's job to bring in the cows for the night, and due to the presence of Oskar, Mum decided to accompany her. Dad had already fixed the cow yard's broken gate so that the cows would not get out overnight, and had gone back to some fencing away from the homestead. As Mum and Katrina entered the paddock, Oskar came at them. The very ground shook as he thundered towards them, nostrils snorting. They quickly scrambled back over the fence.

I had heard somewhere that bulls liked red rags, so Philomena and I rushed to the house and grabbed an old red shirt from the rag bag. We took the shirt up to the gate that led into the back paddock, opened the gate and waved the shirt, shouting to get Oskar's attention. Then we tumbled over the fence. Oskar came charging across the cow paddock and through the gate into the back paddock, the one that bordered Millbank, the Blakes' place. When he had raced far enough in, we leapt over the fence, shut the gate behind him, and leapt back again so that Katrina could get the cows into the yard on the opposite side unhindered. This was all quite an operation, and not something we looked forward to repeating every day.

The next morning, when my father went to see what Oskar had been up to overnight, there the bull was, charging at the boundary fence into Millbank, which he had almost, but not quite, destroyed. He was within inches of getting at Eric Blake's heifers. Apart from being unfriendly, Old Eric was known to have a bad temper. Oskar needed to be banished from the back paddock, quickly.

My father was obliged to fix Eric Blake's fence, not for the last time. For wherever there was a cow, wherever there was a heifer, there was Oskar, trying to make her acquaintance. No gate was too much for him, no fence too high. Morning after morning, he would be found to have rearranged his accommodations. Day after day, my father would be mending gates and fences.

Eventually my father began to wonder whether the bull was more trouble than he was worth. Too much of his time was being wasted fixing gates and fences, and worse, he was not in control of the reproductive arrangements of his cows and heifers – Oskar was. It wouldn't do.

It was when the bull broke down the gate of the vegetable garden and trampled over our newly sprouted spring lettuce that Oskar's fate may have been finally sealed. My mother was distraught at all her wasted work, although there was an upside. She had been pressing for a new vegetable garden, with a strong high fence and a stile rather than a gate, and now she had a perfect and urgent excuse. Since Oskar had been his idea, my father was forced to do as she asked.

Six months or so after the vegetable garden incident, the truck came back and took Oskar away. He had lost a little of his belligerence by then, but he never lost his enthusiasm for the opposite sex. We were to have other bulls, although never one as impressive or as determined as Oskar.

Years later, in an art history class at school, I learned a little more about the real Oskar Kokoschka. He was an artist, my father had said, but he was the kind of artist who would have been known mostly to intellectuals and critics. The mystery was, how did my father know of him? Digging a little deeper, I found that Kokoschka, banished by Hitler as a degenerate artist, along with Max Ernst, Paul Klee and others, had lived and painted in Scotland for a period during the war. The Scots would have known about him. In any case, over the years, in a museum or gallery in New York or London or Vienna or Berlin, when I have happened upon a display of Oskar Kokoschka paintings, I have been reminded again of Oskar, the iconoclastic and amorous bull.

Chapter 8

Cheyenne And Winterbourne

The Winterbourne Road was some twenty-six miles long. It snaked east from town and finished at Cheyenne, the homestead five miles further on from us. On the way out from town there were other, subsidiary roads, mostly rough gravel and sometimes just rutted tracks – Moona Plains Road, Table Top Road, Florida Road (which diverged from Table Top Road), the Blue Mountain Road, and more. Along these roads, miles apart from one another, lived some of our friends and neighbours.

Cheyenne, at the end of our own road, was the home of the Blomfield family. Pat and Buddy Blomfield would become our close friends, mentors, protectors and second family. We could not have survived on Arran for as long as we did without their help and generosity. We called them Mr and Mrs Bloo, partly to distinguish them from the other nearby Blomfields, their cousins, at Karori over the hill. Mr and Mrs Bloo had three children: Vaun, Burgh and Bunky. Vaun and Burgh were at boarding school in Armidale; only Bunky, aged six or seven when we first met her, was still at home.

Not long after our arrival in Walcha, Mrs Blomfield had come over and shown my mother how to preserve the apples, bringing her preserving equipment and a supply of spare bottles and jars with her. She made it her habit to call in on her way to and from town, sometimes to deliver surplus items from their garden or extra milk, or something she had picked up for my mother in town. The Blomfields always had spare milk because they made and used large quantities of butter.

We loved Mrs Bloo. A member of the prominent Joyce family from The Overflow in Beaudesert, Queensland, she was short, energetic and a rapid talker – a cheerful and kind soul who loved children. She was older than my mother; already she had grey hair streaking the brown. As soon as we saw her coming in the distance we lined up along the verandah, waiting to run and greet her. 'Hello, my little chickadees,' she would cry, her arms outstretched as she alighted from her dusty old Land Rover.

Buddy Blomfield, in his blue overalls and tough work boots, was as tall and laconic as his wife was petite and lively. He had a slight stammer, and his American accent only added to his intrigue. Buddy had been a flying instructor in the Air Force during the war, so he could fly a plane, which was another source of awe and fascination. Buddy's father Alfred (who, Walcha people would always say in reverent tones, was the seventh son of a seventh son) had been born in nearby Uralla. Being more than usually clever, he had attended university and become a mining engineer, and in his youth had befriended another young mining engineer, visiting from America, by the name of Herbert Hoover. Encouraged by his friend, Alfred had sailed to California and spent several years working in mines in America and Canada, remaining friends with Mr Hoover, who, despite a long sojourn in London, eventually went into US politics.

Alfred, deciding that he wanted to give his sons an Australian education, had brought back his American wife, two young sons and many American ideas with him. It was Grandma Blomfield who had supervised the building of the homestead at Cheyenne, which was in every respect an American house. She stayed long enough to see their two boys through The Armidale School in Armidale, but eventually the isolation proved too much for her. She and Alfred retired back to Canada to live in Vancouver, leaving their sons to run their two Australian properties, Colorado at Quirindi in the Hunter Valley and Cheyenne at Walcha.

The Cheyenne homestead was to us an enchanted and exotic place. The Virginia creeper that almost covered the homestead's stucco walls had the effect of blending the house into the surroundings of native and American trees that peppered the spacious and well-manicured grounds. The front verandah of the house was perched right at the edge of the Hole Creek Gorge, which formed part of the larger Blue Mountain Gorge. The gorge was a deep, wild chasm of untouched bush that stretched almost to the coast, eighty or ninety smoky-blue miles away as the crow flew. The view was magnificent. The immense, steep and seemingly bottomless canyon was both wide and wild. Kangaroos, wallabies, dingoes, possums, goannas, koalas (which we anxiously looked out for but never saw) snakes and dozens of bird species abounded there. The gorge led into what is now part of the Oxley Wild Rivers National Park, which is an area of sheer inclines, virgin rainforests, abundant waterfalls and spectacular beauty. Parts of it at the bottom were leased by the Crown for stock grazing. We children were endlessly intrigued by the idea of the wild Brennans who supposedly lived there. Bunky Blomfield said that they survived on kangaroos, rabbits and livestock that had strayed from the properties surrounding the gorge's rim, and whether this was true or not, we seized on new information about the Brennans hungrily. Sometimes the gorge filled with a thick fog, and if you stood on the front verandah, it felt as though the house were floating on the clouds. It was the closest thing we knew to pure enchantment.

At the back of the house, near the kitchen door (which was the customary entrance) was a small separate building, also covered in

Virginia creeper. This building housed the generator, the laundry and the dairy, which had a milk separator and a large butter churn. This seemed a most sophisticated arrangement to us – the last word in dairies. The family had several dairy cows and always had plenty of milk and butter. Mrs Bloo loved butter. To our enormous satisfaction, she used it lavishly on just about everything she served us.

The large walk-in pantry off the kitchen was a riot of colour. Grandma Blomfield had amused herself on winter nights by decorating tins and canisters with green and red and black waves of paint, everything artistically labelled – SUGAR, FLOUR, HONEY, SALT, BISCUITS, BROWN SUGAR – all neatly lined up along the shelves. We thought it very artistic and civilized.

The house had a most unusual feature for Australia: a cellar, with a large coke burner that in winter dispensed heat through large ducts to all the rooms in the house. The outside door to the cellar was a kind of double trapdoor, and you had to lift the two sides of it up before descending the steps. On one of our first visits to Cheyenne, Bunky led us down the steps into the cellar to show us the jewel in the household crown: the pet carpet snake. It did not have an interesting name like many of our own animals; it was just called Snakie. It was huge, maybe eight or nine feet long, ranged over a thick beam in the ceiling, its olive and cream diamond pattern catching the sunlight streaming through the open trapdoor. Its thick body might have been more than twenty inches in circumference.

'He's a diamond python. He eats all the mice and rats,' said Bunky. 'It's his job. Sometimes he eats possums. Once,' she went on, 'he ate one of our cats.'

We stared at her, horrified, as she described the process in detail. 'But he's not poisonous,' she reassured us. 'He's harmless.'

But all the times we stayed at Cheyenne – and there were many – we were never tempted to play in the cellar. Sometimes, however,

Snakie would emerge from the cellar and wind himself into a neat coil beside the kitchen steps, where he might bask in the sun for days. We kept a wide berth, shooting up the steps and leaping into the kitchen as quickly as possible.

There was a gravel path leading uphill to the 'kids' house'. This was originally intended as a guest house in the American fashion, but now it was where the Blomfield children lived. It was designed rather like an American east coast beach house. There were two bedrooms, a bathroom with a flushing toilet, and a large verandah running the length of the house, closed in with glass shutters and containing a table and chairs and a row of beds. These beds were where Katrina, Philomena and I slept when we stayed at Cheyenne. In the mornings, when the light streamed through the glass shutters, the chorus of birds from the gorge was riotous, carolling, chirping or screeching us awake: the musical magpies first, then the currawongs, koels, lorikeets, cockatoos, finches, kookaburras and rosellas.

Each day at Cheyenne there was something different to delight us. There were ponies that Bunky taught us to ride, Misty and Billy Boy, and all kinds of board games, which we played frequently. There were Bugs Bunny records to listen to, and a full set of *Dr Dolittle* books by Hugh Lofting, who had also been a friend of Alfred Blomfield. Mrs Bloo made us pancakes for breakfast, which she served with butter and maple syrup. This dish was a great novelty in Australia at the time. These intriguing items – records, games, maple syrup, books – all came in regular boxes on the back of Mr Grieve's mail truck, sent from distant Canada.

~

Although they were to become our closest friends in Walcha, the Blomfields were not, in fact, our nearest neighbours. That honour fell to Mick and Budge Brien at Winterbourne, down the hill from us. Their house, with its brightly painted green roof, was in the valley on a small rise above the creek. This was the creek whose rocky bottom we had to ford to get to and from town, and it was passable when the weather was relatively dry, and hazardous when it was not.

When we first arrived in Walcha, and for quite a long time thereafter, our house had no phone; we were on a long waiting list for a phone line. People wanting to get in touch with us would contact Budge Brien (Mrs Brien to us children) at Winterbourne and she would hang a red towel from the top of their garage. If we saw the red towel it meant there was a message for us, and if Mum was busy, Katrina or I would be sent to get it, half a mile down the hill and back up again. It seemed a long way downhill when we were young and even longer back uphill, but Mrs Brien always gave the small messenger a biscuit, even if it was only a Sao biscuit with Vegemite, to send them on their way.

The Winterbourne homestead was a little older, larger and much more elegant than ours. It was surrounded by various buildings. Close by were the remains of six long-abandoned split-slab huts, three on either side of a little alley, plus corrugated iron sheds, outhouses, yards and barns. The original Winterbourne Run, one of the oldest properties in the district, had been settled with convict labour in 1837. The huts would have housed convict workers, and been used for laundry, dairy and blacksmith purposes. One might have been a bakehouse. Essentially, it had been a small village. The original homestead had been built on top of the hill on the opposite side of the creek, and most of its stone walls still stood, but it had long been abandoned, perhaps because of a deep crack running down one wall. We called it the Old Stone House. Winterbourne was a good place to play.

In one of the newer sheds were a couple of ancient tractors and an imposing old car – was it a Bentley? – which deteriorated as the years went by, and was used mostly by spiders and the Winterbourne chooks (the car was a convenient spot in which to lay their eggs). The Briens had lots of chooks. They often let us keep some of the eggs that we found tucked in nooks and crannies about the place, as they frequently had more than the two of them could use. There were ducks and even geese.

As children we thought that married people were at least supposed to be friends, but Mr and Mrs Brien didn't seem to be. They spent a lot of time apart. When together, they fought ferociously and often. Once we saw her push him into the fish pond.

Budge Brien, a petite and slightly stocky bottle blonde, had a sharp tongue and plenty to say about most subjects and most people, but she was capable of occasional benevolences. She was some sixteen years older than her husband. She had three grown-up children from her first marriage (her first husband had died young) and they sometimes came to visit: Doug, Mary and Andrew Laurie. Andrew was a famous rugby player. Budge did not grow much in the way of vegetables, but she kept a magnificent flower garden, with roses, peonies, hydrangeas and zinnias, and a lush lawn kept green by water piped up from the creek. At some point my father built them a fish pond and a sundial as a thank-you gift, and that added to the garden's charm. But best of all to us, there was a swing seat on the verandah.

Mr Brien was a tall, good-looking man with pronounced black eyebrows, who bore just a passing resemblance to Gregory Peck. He had been in the Middle East and later New Guinea during the war, and perhaps it was these experiences – or perhaps merely a misalliance with Mrs Brien – that had developed in him a taste for beer and whisky. He took to showing up on our front verandah with several large bottles of Tooth's KB or a bottle of Scotch and insist that my father take a drink with him. And then another. And another.

Mick Brien liked company when he drank. He was known far and wide as a dangerous man to encounter in one of the Walcha pubs, or even in the street anywhere close to a pub. His habit was to collar a victim, often a young person or a visitor to the district, and ply him with beer after beer, followed by whisky chasers. Mick would not take no for an answer. Travelling salesmen and other unwitting callers at Winterbourne could be delayed for hours, and sometimes even days.

On the other hand, when there was serious work to be done, fencing or shearing or crutching, he could remain sober for days and weeks at a time.

Mr Brien liked nothing better than to sit at our kitchen table and fill our parents in on all the ancient gossip of the district, talking of this character and that old mate. Sometimes he would talk about his mates in the war. Then he would shake his head sadly and say, 'It was the grog that got him in the end, you know. Yeah, the grog'll get a bloke.'

We would sometimes watch from our bedroom window as he staggered to his car, shouting and muttering, and then churned off down the hill. We children thought this was terribly funny, although it usually meant that my father would have a headache the next day. One evening after the family had gone to bed, Katrina and I were awoken by the sound of a car pulling up outside the house, and the bang of its loudly slamming door. We went to the window to see Mr Brien staggering up the steps onto our verandah. 'Bob!' he called. 'Bob, I know you're there!' Waving a bottle of whisky in one hand, he staggered through the living room into the hall outside our parents' bedroom.

'Bob!' he yelled, as he yanked open their door and flung himself across our parents in their bed. 'Your shout!'

Katrina and I were astonished. Our parents' bedroom was sacrosanct; none of us dared to enter it after bedtime. How did Mr Brien get away with it? In the end, we could only giggle.

~

Like Mr Brien, a good many of the adult men in Walcha whom we knew growing up had served in the war, often in the Middle East, North Africa or New Guinea, or sometimes all three. Our father had been in the Royal Navy, both in the Atlantic and the Pacific. Buddy Blomfield had been in the RAAF, although as a flying instructor he didn't get to see overseas service. Some of the men had been in Changi and some even on the Burma Railway. Few of them, however, except occasionally Mick Brien, ever talked about it, and Mr Brien talked about his mates, not about battles. On Anzac Day there was a march through town with a local band, and many of the veterans from both wars would gather together afterwards in the Apsley Arms Hotel or the Memorial Club to drink and play two-up. Some, however, never went, preferring to leave their emotional wounds buried deep in their breasts.

One of those most damaged by the war, however, had in fact been a civilian, known to us all as Old Bill. He too, lived on Winterbourne, a grace-and-favour tenant of Mr and Mrs Brien. Old Bill couldn't have been more than sixty when we met him, but with his white hair and stooped shoulders, he seemed much older. He lived in one of the old slab dwellings that had once been a labourer's hut, part of the original Winterbourne settlement. His full name was William Murray Borthwick Laycock, and many years since, he and his brother Blakey had been two of the district's most eligible bachelors. At the prestigious King's School in Sydney, Bill had been both an excellent scholar and an exceptional athlete. In 1925 and 1926 he played rugby for Australia as a Wallaby, which would have given him hero status not just in the district but throughout the country. The brothers had owned Millbank, where the Blakes now lived, and whose boundary adjoined both ours and Winterbourne's. The brothers were well liked. Sometime in the late thirties, when the Depression had taken its toll and a new drought had hit the area, they had sold their stock, left their place untended and bought a mine in the Philippines.

When the Japanese had invaded in 1941 and 1942 Bill and Blakey, too old for war service, had been captured and thrown into Changi Prison. From there they were sent to another prison camp, where, along with other British and Australian captives, they were starved and tortured. Blakey tried to escape, and Bill had been forced to watch while their Japanese captors tortured Blakey and then forced Bill, at gunpoint, to bury his brother alive.

After the war, Bill had returned to Australia a broken man. He spent some time in Sydney, but eventually he had washed up back in Walcha, to all intents and purposes a homeless swagman. Mick and Budge Brien, who had known him for years, allowed him to set up house in one of the old slab huts. Bill basically lived in one room behind a little enclosed verandah piled high with rubbish. The hut was flanked by two small water tanks, and an ancient dunny without a door. For furniture, Bill had a rusted iron bed with a sagging wire mesh base. Yellowing newspapers served as a mattress. He had two straight-backed chairs with saggy cane bottoms, and a small table on which stood a couple of enamel mugs, a tarnished knife and fork, and a chipped enamel bowl and plate. On the hearth was a blackened kettle and an equally blackened cast-iron frying pan. The makeshift shelves beside the fireplace held piles upon piles of books, newspapers and magazines, which overflowed onto the floor. There may have been an old pie cupboard hidden somewhere under the magazines. Mr Brien had had electricity put on to the hut, so that Bill could listen to the radio.

It turned out that Bill was an intellectual, a lover of literature, art and music. Here was someone for our parents to talk to on subjects they thought they had left behind in the city. Bill had *The Listener* magazine sent all the way from England, while *The Bulletin* and other magazines came from Sydney, and *Meanjin* and *Overland* from Melbourne, and he would share these with my father. The magazines, it turned out, were partly because Bill wrote poetry, and he lived in hope that one of these publications would eventually accept one of his efforts. He had no typewriter and wrote in longhand, although he had a clear and elegant hand. Sometimes *The Bulletin* published his letters and comments, which kept hope alive.

Every so often Old Bill mentioned a wife, a teacher in Sydney, to whom he wrote long letters two or three times a week, but we never knew her to visit. Nor were we aware that he ever visited her. 'We just can't live together,' he said.

Occasionally Bill walked up the hill to have dinner with us. He might stay to listen to a radio play with our parents, but often when the chairs were pushed back, and the plates were being cleared, he would make his excuses and leave. Perhaps there were too many children, and too much noise. Afterwards we would watch his lonely, bent form fading down the hill into the summer dusk.

In summer, Bill might frequently disappear for weeks at a time. He had built a mineshaft deep in the Winterbourne State Forest, not far from our boundary, and was hoping to strike gold. He found just enough to keep his hopes up, but never enough to be rich. Once or twice he was away for such a long time that my father took a detour from his boundary riding to go into the forest to look for him. He always found Bill safe and sound, whistling over a boiling billy, and sometimes he was persuaded to stay a while to help Bill follow a promising lead. It always came to nothing.

Chapter 9

A New Dunny – And The Table Top And Florida Roads

My father was out the back with his shovel, digging a large hole. Each rasp of the shovel was followed by a thud as another load of dirt hit the growing pile of earth beside the hole.

It seemed that Dad was always building something, and there was much building to be done. Apart from the new shed for the generator, quite early on he had built a new chook house, because the foxes, and perhaps the tiger quolls, were getting into the old one and stealing our chooks far too often. The new one was much more comfortable for the chooks and much more secure, but the war with the foxes was one of continuing attrition. We had bought a rooster, Andre, so that we could breed some chickens, but the numbers barely kept pace with the losses.

This time, in the spring of 1954, Dad was at work on a new dunny, a pit latrine, labouring for hours and days over the six-foot hole. It was a huge source of entertainment for us, watching him shovel the earth over the edge of the pit. Some of this soil would be used to cover up the old pit, which was now almost full. Eventually the new pit was so deep that he had to get a ladder to climb out of it, and the earth needed to be hauled up in a bucket tied to a rope. He didn't want to have to undertake this again for a long time. It was my job to keep the boys at bay so they didn't fall into the hole, but we were happy to spend hours watching our father work, sitting on our haunches around the pit's edge, providing a running commentary.

'Are you nearly finished, Daddy?' Philomena asked about, oh, every half-hour.

'Go and help your mother in the kitchen,' Dad panted, the sweat glistening on his neck and shoulders.

When it was finally finished, the new outhouse seemed like the height of luxury to us – the memory of flushing porcelain was fading fast. It was bigger than its predecessor and smarter, too, with its straight corner posts, fresh yellow timber floor slabs and walls of corrugated iron that didn't flap in the wind. It even had a wooden door that closed and bolted properly. There was a new can with a wooden seat and lid. A spike in the corner was where our toilet paper – that is, cut-up used newspapers and pages of the *Reader's Digest* – would hang.

But no-one wanted to trek out in the dark, through the back gate and along the track through the pine trees to eventually reach the dunny, so at night we continued to use our potties, enamel and plastic chamber pots. We kept them under our beds in case we needed to go at night, and in the morning we emptied them out into the dunny.

One day Mrs Bloo called in on her way from town. She had with her a little black kitten, wrapped in a baby blanket. We gathered around it in a frenzy of excitement. It was the sweetest thing we had ever seen. Dad said it would keep the mice out of the shed, so, miraculously, it seemed we would be allowed to keep it.

We made a little bed for the kitten in a shoebox in front of the fireplace. There was fierce discussion about a name. My father suggested we call her Miranda ('O brave new world,' he said), so Miranda she was. We competed to have her sleep on – and in

– our beds. To my father's surprise, she and Dizzy became friends, frequently snuggling together by the fire.

Then one afternoon Katrina ran into the kitchen sobbing and waving her arms. 'Mum, Mum, come quickly, come quickly! Philomena dropped the kitten down the toilet!'

We hurried out, through the back gate and along the path, our mother carrying the kitchen broom.

The pit was deep and the little black kitten was frightened and couldn't seem to get a grip on the broom. We children were all wailing and crying. 'Just stop it. You're no help at all,' said Mum, exasperated. It seemed to me we spent an eternity there, trying to coax the poor kitten onto the broom, the afternoon shadows closing around us, and in the end, it was my father who achieved the rescue. He just lowered a thick piece of knotted rope into the pit, Miranda found a grip and, cautiously, we pulled her up.

Our parents speculated that Philomena must have been still chafing from the unwelcome appearance of her twin rivals and had decided to make a dramatic bid for attention.

Almost as soon as she was old enough, Miranda became pregnant. This was amazing. How could this happen, with no recognised father to hand? We were mystified. Her tummy was as tight as a drum, and her little teats began to swell. The culprit was probably a feral cat, or maybe a stray from the Winterbourne sheds, wandering the half-mile up the hillside on a cold night in search of some fun.

When the time came, we all crouched around the little nest my mother had made for her using a cut-down cardboard carton lined with hessian sacks and watched as Miranda gave birth to one, two, three, four, five, six kittens. We were entranced by these little bundles, who blindly crawled to nuzzle at Miranda's teats. We each picked one out for ourselves to have as our own special pet and

Miranda licked her blind little brood all over, quite pleased with herself, it seemed. From now on, she would mostly be known in the family as Mummy Puss. Miranda was no more.

Only a day or two later, however, we were to learn one of life's painful lessons – new kittens were not things to be welcomed and cherished. Dad asked us to select the two kittens we most wanted to keep. What? Only two? He was taking four of the kittens to drown in the dam. We were distraught, but he was adamant.

'I've enough bloody mouths to feed as it is,' he said, pushing past us as we clung to his trouser legs, crying and pleading for mercy. 'Do you have any idea how fast cats can breed? You're lucky you're getting to keep two. If I had any sense you would be keeping just one.'

We stood on the front verandah and watched him trudge down the hill to the waterhole in the gully below the house with his squirming hessian sack as the evening gathered around him.

Little Aidan, still a toddler, was the most upset. He mourned the lost kittens for days and appointed himself guardian of the two remaining kittens, watching over them as though he was their mother. One of the kittens we chose to keep was jet black all over. My father called him Othello and in due course he and his sister Portia were taken to the vet in town to be spayed. In her next litter, Mummy Puss produced a pure white kitten, which we also kept. She was named Desdemona. Dad explained to us who Othello and Desdemona were, but did not tell us their sad story.

Eventually my father learned how to spay male kittens himself, which he did on the kitchen table, but somehow Mummy Puss escaped the knife. Perhaps it was too late for her. In any case, we still ended up, after several years, with quite a lot of cats. They kept the house and its surrounds relatively free of the mice, rats and possums that might otherwise have plagued us, although the occasional possum would risk death by venturing across the roof at night. The cats did occasionally kill a willie wagtail, although at the time we thought nothing of it.

~

Table Top Road branched off from the Winterbourne Road, a half mile or so back from the Winterbourne boundary towards town. Florida Road branched off Table Top, and each rutted and dusty road led to several outlying properties, spread miles apart from one another. Early on, my father made the acquaintance of Clennell Fenwicke, who lived on Earsdon, off the Florida Road, about five miles from us. Not long after the twin boys arrived from Sydney, Pas Fenwicke, his wife, invited us to afternoon tea.

So, dressed in our second-best clothes, we presented ourselves at their little homestead. Mrs Fenwicke served up brownie (which to us was a kind of fruit loaf), pikelets, both spread with butter, and a passionfruit sponge cake. A robust woman, Pas was lively, wryly funny, capable and, we were to learn, long-suffering. In a short time, she and my mother were close friends and allies. Pas was a trained nurse, and friends and neighbours for miles around relied on her experience for first-aid and general health advice, both of which she dispensed with generosity and good cheer. 'Well, you have to laugh, don't you?' she would say, and sometimes there was a touch of determination in her smile.

Her husband Clennell, dark haired and fine featured, with long, thick eyelashes, had a kind of boyish good looks. But he was not an easy man. He had a mistrustful nature and was quick to take offence. It was easy to 'set him off', as my mother used to put it. We children learned to stay out of his way.

Millbank, which bordered both us and Winterbourne, was

owned by Eric and Eva Blake. Their house was over the far side of our hill, on the Table Top Road. They had bought Millbank from Bill Laycock after the war, probably for a song. The Blakes were a relentlessly hard-working family who kept to themselves. Old Eric, as he was known, had no patience with leisure or frivolity, so the family did not participate in the Walcha social scene. Although they had two young sons – Keith, a little older than we were, and Neville, about our age – invitations to tea were never exchanged. Offers of help were neither received nor given. If Mr Blake needed a hand he would call on his brother Ronnie for it, no-one else. It would be fair to say that we were not friends with them. Not many people were.

Dick and Tony Blomfield lived on Karori, further along the Table Top Road. Their back boundary was quite close to ours, although their homestead was a twenty-minute drive away. Their sons, Peter and Rob, were around the same age as Katrina and I. An older daughter, Gillian, was away at boarding school. Tony Blomfield was so called because her father had wanted a boy, for whom he had picked out the name Tony. So Tony she was, and nobody ever called her by any other name. She was another kind and generous person – blonde, slightly built, cheerful and brisk, a positive soul with not a mean bone in her body. She also loved children and we loved her. We were always happy to visit Karori. Dick Blomfield, her husband, a wiry man with a lived-in face and a deep tan, was much older than Tony. A compulsive worker, he seemed to be the strong, silent type, not much given to small talk. He, too, had seen heavy war service, both in the Middle East and New Guinea, but he never talked about it.

One day when my father was fencing, Clennell Fenwicke came to help, bringing his brother John and John's daughter, Anne, who was the same age as Katrina. John and his wife, Barbara, managed and lived on a property called Waterloo, closer to town, a little to the south of Walcha. John and my father were to become good friends, and so were Anne and Katrina.

A fast-talking man with an ever-changing moustache, John Fenwicke was a man of boundless energy and endless curiosity. He collected things. He built weathervanes and elaborate mailboxes in his shed. He had been an eager boxer and field athlete in his youth and was even now a keen horseman. He had been a little young for war service, but had raised his age and gone anyway. He loved a party and took pleasure in singing and dancing. He threw himself into each new interest with everything he had. And he always had a scheme going.

Barbie Fenwicke, his wife, was a lively soul with a distinctive, rather low-pitched, raspy voice, with which she dispensed frequent good-natured advice and instruction to us children. In another life, she might have had a career in the creative or decorative arts, but as a bush housewife, she threw her energies into baking, knitting, spinning, weaving, flower arranging and dressmaking, frequently winning prizes at the local show. It was Barbie who taught Katrina and me the rudiments of knitting and flower arranging on our visits to their house at Waterloo.

The two Fenwicke brothers had grown up on Europambela, off Moona Plains Road to the west of us. It was one of Walcha's oldest and most prestigious properties, and they were part of an extended clan of Fenwickes in Walcha. The family had been there for several generations. Some were prosperous, but John and Clennell came from a less affluent branch of the family, and in any case, had not yet come into their own modest inheritances. Did this fact contribute to Clennell's anger? Was it the fact of being the younger brother? Or did he simply inherit the bad temper from his father? Who knows? Who can explain the vagaries of human temperament?

Bumping along the gravel roads from remote mailbox to remote mailbox three times a week, connecting us with all our neighbours, was our mailman, Mr Grieve. Though we children called him Mr Grieve, to the rest of the world he was simply Old Tom. Other people might come and go to no particular timetable, but Mr Grieve arrived at our house every Monday lunchtime, to deliver our mail, packages and supplies from town.

The dust from his old white truck raised a streak of small clouds across the hillside opposite, disappearing into the dip in the valley when he stopped at Winterbourne. We waited for the nose of the truck to appear over the hill and begin its rattling climb to our boundary ramp and from there traverse the rutted track up to the house, to come to a stop at our front gate in a flurry of dust. We were always there, waiting to greet him. My mother, hair pulled back, apron damp, took a break from her wash-day labours to come down to the gate.

Mr Grieve never stepped down from his dusty truck without first looking around for Dizzy, who had to be kept in the kitchen, or at least behind the gate. Mr Grieve seemed not to care for dogs. Then he would scramble onto the back of the truck and toss down our deliveries, as well as our bag of mail. *The Women's Weekly* for my mother and perhaps the *Ladies' Home Journal* or a catalogue from David Jones, Sydney's big department store; bills, circulars and letters; and the Sunday papers from Sydney. Then, as he climbed down, Mr Grieve and my mother began to exchange vital pieces of news and information. Who had had some rain, who hadn't. Who had had a tiger snake on their place. Who was in the hospital. Who was engaged, or having a baby. Who was having trouble with dingoes. All this gossip was in a mumble that my mother understood better than we did, because Mr Grieve had no teeth, only bare gums. Mr Grieve confided to us that he had lost his teeth eating too many lollies when he was young, but it was all right, he reassured us, he was saving up for a new set.

With the Sunday papers came the comics – *Dagwood, Ginger Meggs, Brenda Starr, Prince Valiant.* Oh, how I loved *Prince Valiant*. I longed to have a dress like Queen Aleta's. A good haul of mail would bring letters from family and friends in Sydney, and sometimes a big excitement in the form of a blue envelope with red-striped edges from Grandpa in Scotland or from my father's sister, Aunt Nessie. Because my grandmother was still angry at her son for marrying a Catholic, it was only Grandpa who wrote. And because Granny had also forbidden Grandpa to write, his letters were written in the name of the family dog, Fergus. 'Summer came on a Tuesday this year,' Fergus would write. But quite often there was a postcard addressed to us children from our Scots Granny, as she called herself, from Blackpool, or Robin Hood's Bay in Yorkshire, where they liked to holiday.

We had never met Grandpa and Granny, and they remained remote and romantic to us, left behind in the grey mists of Scotland by our father after the war. But they always remembered our birthdays, and books came from them in the mail, wrapped in brown paper and tied up with string. These distant grandparents were something exotic we could claim when other children required us to pull something out of the hat in the boasting department.

Mr Grieve brought other bounty. He delivered not just the mail, but fresh bread from the Walcha bakery, a sack of potatoes, a roll of barbed wire, medicine from the chemist – anything we might have ordered from town. Often he came inside for a cuppa, once Dizzy was banished, and the gossip could continue in the kitchen. But if he was running late, he might set out on the bumpy three mile run for the Cheyenne boundary without the tea. That was the end of the road for him, and he always aimed to get to the Cheyenne mailbox by 2pm. One of the Blomfield family drove from the homestead to meet him and their Land Rover waited under the shelter of the massive old gum tree beside their boundary ramp. They also had ready a thermos of tea and some biscuits. The homestead was several hilly miles further on from the boundary itself, and Mr Grieve did not care to venture so far on such a rough road, nor, it seems, did his job description demand it of him.

Although Mr Grieve delivered mail to our part of the world on Mondays, Wednesdays and Fridays, it was only on Mondays that he came to the house. The other days he left our mail in our box at the Blue Mountain turnoff, about three miles back along the Winterbourne Road, on the opposite hill. Our family had two mailboxes – old petrol drums set on posts – one next to the boundary ramp at the bottom of the track that passed the house about a hundred yards down the hill, and another at the Blue Mountain turnoff. On the very occasional Monday, if it was raining or bitterly cold, Mr Grieve left the mail at the bottom of the road and we had to walk down and get it. When you got back to the house with the bundle of mail and papers on a frosty winter's day, there was excruciating pain as you attempted to warm your frozen fingers into some kind of life by the kitchen fire. Sometimes on his way back from Cheyenne, Mr Grieve would leave in our box an offering from the Blomfields: some spare milk in a large gallon bottle, perhaps, or some surplus from the Cheyenne vegetable garden.

Monday in and Monday out we waited to see the dust of the mail truck along the opposite hill, the signal to put the kettle on the stove and to get ready to go down to the gate to meet him. Then, one December, there was an interesting surprise.

Mr Grieve arrived sporting a full set of new teeth, which utterly transformed his appearance. He flashed his new white smile at us proudly. 'What do you think? I've been saving up,' he said. 'My wife's friend in Armidale works for a dentist and they gave me a deal. Not bad, eh? Just in time for Christmas. Best Christmas present a bloke ever had.'

We admired the new teeth from all angles.

One Monday a month or so later, prompted by Bunky Blomfield, Katrina and I begged to be allowed to ride with Mr Grieve to the Cheyenne boundary and back. To our surprise, Mum said yes. After we passed through our house paddock, the road became quite rough, although we enjoyed bouncing on the springs of Mr Grieve's passenger seat. Until we hit a large pothole. The jolt was so violent that it sent Mr Grieve's new false teeth flying onto the dashboard. We were amazed, and not quite sure how to react. Did this mean that Mr Grieve had lost his new teeth and would have to save up to get more? Was this a catastrophe? Was it all right to laugh, as we so badly wanted to do?

Then Mr Grieve turned to us and gave us his familiar old gummy grin. 'Well, fancy that. Would you like me to do it again?'

'Yes, yes!' we cried.

And he put his teeth back in and went over another bump, and out flew the teeth again. We began to roll around the cabin, laughing. We laughed so hard we were crying. When we got to the Cheyenne boundary we were still laughing. We asked him to take his teeth out to show Bunky, who was there with her mother to meet him. Mrs Bloo admired the teeth and deftly managed to change the subject.

When we finally arrived home, we persuaded our mother to let us all go with Mr Grieve the following week so that the others could see it too. 'Go over a bump, Mr Grieve, go over another bump!' we cried, and he did, just to please us. Since there wasn't room in the cabin for all of us, two of us had to take turns sitting in the back of the truck with the mailbags and packages, getting covered in dust, sliding down to the back as Mr Grieve took his run at the Steep Pinch, a short, sharp and very steep hill that had defeated many a would-be visitor to Cheyenne, but we didn't mind. What could be more fun than this?

Chapter 10

A Tale Of Two Dogs

The wind howled and raged around the house. The pine trees, tall and strong as they were, bent with the force of the gale. Curled under several layers of scratchy army blankets, I waited for one to fall on the roof. Behind the roar was the sound of rattling corrugated iron, of branches falling and tumbling, of the cows in distress up in the cow yard. We had had severe storms before, but not like this. This one was ferocious. Philomena and I crept into Katrina's bed and we huddled together, whispering. Then, after a particularly frightening crash, we made a dash along the verandah and through the living room, ending up outside our parent's bedroom, shivering together even though we were wrapped a blanket. We trembled there for a few minutes, summoning up the courage to knock and enter. When we did, we found the boys were already there, snuggling between our parents under their pink satin eiderdown. In the end, we all huddled the night out while the gale screamed around us and unknown objects bounced off the roof, no-one but the boys and possibly Dizzy, under the bed, getting any sleep.

As the sun rose, we went outside to find the entire corrugated roof of the shed sitting in one piece near the flat above the gully, a hundred yards away. The paddocks were littered with broken branches, and indeed, some trees had been uprooted altogether. We might have imagined sheets of iron blowing off, but not the whole roof. The shed was home to the workshop and tool room, the garage for the car, a stall for the Old Grey Mare and a small tack room.

We lost one or two sheep that night, but most of our remaining livestock seemed, miraculously, to survive, though the cows and the Old Grey Mare were a little skittish for a few days. We all were.

It took days to get the roof back on. Clennell Fenwicke and Buddy Blomfield came over to help with the frame, and then of course the sheets of corrugated iron had to be disassembled before they could be replaced. We took it in turns to hand up nails and eventually it was finished. My father could ill afford the lost time, but afterwards he needed to help our good neighbours fix the fences that had been broken by falling trees, and that was more time lost for them all.

It had also become clear that progress demanded a bigger and more functional workshed. My father chose a site just above the cow yards. Once again, there was a round of tree chopping, bark stripping, log hauling, post digging, sawing and hammering. The old shed remained in its overall capacity as stable, tackle room and garage, but in the hayloft in the new shed my father could cure and tan sheepskins and the occasional cowhide, as well as store hay and grain. Underneath, in his new workshop and tractor garage, he installed a bench saw so he could cut the wood for the shearing shed he planned to build next and pile up logs for the winter.

~

Our beloved Dizzy was a small black and white tornado of frenzied activity. She was named because of her habit of chasing her own tail. She followed my father wherever he went – to the shed, to the old truck and to the cow yards in the morning when he went to milk the cows. She chased rabbits and even kangaroos with boundless zeal, although she never caught one, or even came close. She disappeared down rabbit holes, but usually had to back right up again. She fetched sticks for hours on end if you could be bothered throwing them, dropping them at your feet and then raising her eyes to yours in soulful appeal. *Just one more,* she seemed to plead. She greeted visitors with an almost unseemly excitement, circling them as her tail wagged with its own frenzied rhythm. She went wild when we sang a song Dad had taught us that we adapted for her.

> *Dizzy, Dizzy, give us your answer do,*
> *I'm half crazy, all for the love of you,*
> *It won't be a stylish marriage,*
> *I can't afford a carriage,*
> *But you'd look sweet upon the seat,*
> *Of a bicycle built for two.*

Dizzy was a house dog – she was not to be mistaken for a working dog. The three working dogs we kept, a black and white Border Collie sheepdog named Annie, a brown Kelpie named Baxter and a blue heeler named Bluey, lived out the back of the house. They were bred to herd sheep and cattle and we were not permitted to play with them, lest they be spoiled. They were never allowed in the house. The working dogs accompanied my father on his horse or in the truck and were out most of the day. At night, they ate rabbits, kangaroo or meat scraps and were chained to kennels made from old water tanks or oil drums. Sometimes when it was windy or cold or they sensed a dingo nearby, they would howl and keen at the night sky, making us pull the bedclothes tighter around our shoulders. Not Dizzy. Dizzy got to sit by the kitchen fire, lie under the table during mealtimes, and take it in turns to sleep on the end of Katrina's bed or my bed. On a cold winter's night, we squabbled about who got Dizzy, or perhaps a cat, to sleep with.

About a mile to the north of the house, over a little rise in the direction of Trig Hill, was a small gully with a creek that gushed with water when it rained, but only retained a trickle and some small ponds when it didn't. The gully had a tea-tree thicket, which was fun to play in, and also a profusion of wild blackberry bushes. Every year in late summer, when it was time to pick the blackberries, we set out in our oldest clothes, bringing whatever gloves we could find and every bucket, saucepan and bowl in the house. Our mother drove us there in the car along a little track that led to the gully. If we became bored, we would take a quick break and have some fun with the not-very-deep quicksand that was part of the creek. After a few hours, the bowls and buckets were full. We competed to see who could pick the most, and bickered over the end result. But after a bit of sampling our hands clothes and mouths were all stained dark purple.

One blackberry day, our mother said that she would load up the car with the berries and that I could lead the party back to the house on foot while she got dinner ready.

So off we set. At that time I was learning to sing sea shanties from the school broadcasts on the radio, so I led a chorus as we walked. 'Blow the man down, bullies, blow the man down, with a way, hey, blow the man down ...' we yodelled, our song echoing back to us from the hills. We were well into 'In South Australia I was born, heave, away, haul away' and were indeed in sight of the house when Robert tugged at my sweater and said, 'Gaga, gaga.' That was still their name for each other. At the same moment Philomena said, 'Where's Aidan?'

We looked around. Where, indeed, was he? Then I asked,

'Where's Dizzy?' For she was not with us either.

'I think she went back with Mum,' said Katrina. We couldn't remember. She had been with us, but where was she now?

Robert began to wail. He turned back, wanting to return to the creek.

'Shouldn't we go and tell Mum?' Katrina asked. We were torn. Finally, we agreed that Katrina should go ahead to the house with Philomena while Robert and I would go back.

We set off to retrace our steps, by this time weary and dispirited. It was getting late. We were almost at the little gully when Dizzy came bounding up to us, running back and forth between us and an old log. She was trying to tell us something. Then we spotted him. Aidan was curled up in the grass, fast asleep beside the log. Robert and I ran to shake him awake, but he would not wake up. Dizzy licked his face and he stirred and moaned a little but went back to sleep. Robert shouted at him in the language that only the two of them understood.

I was panic stricken. This was all my fault. I should have been watching more carefully. How could this have happened? How much trouble was I going to get into? Would I get the belt?

This was a real concern. If the offence was bad enough or my father angry enough, I might get a belting. The sound of the buckle coming undone was enough to strike fear into our hearts. But it seemed to be accepted practice then – just the way things were. 'Spare the rod and spoil the child,' was a saying we heard often.

But then along came my mother and the others in the car, bumping over the track, over sticks and stones and potholes. She gathered Aidan into her arms, bundled him into the front seat, and we headed back to the house in silence. We got the blackberry-stained little boy onto his bunk bed, and discovered a large red welt on his leg. Something had clearly bitten him – not a snake, but what?

Aidan, now awake but dopey, was rushed down to Winterbourne in the car for a telephone consultation with Dr Morgan in Walcha, who said that it was probably a centipede bite. His advice was to wash the wound, administer aspirin crushed in some honey and keep a watchful eye.

For the next day or two the bite was painful, but Aidan didn't really seem to mind, since he was now the centre of attention, the hero of the hour. Dizzy did not leave his side for days, and she too, was hailed as a heroine. Strangely enough, and to my great relief, I did not get into trouble.

~

Right after Christmas we took a train trip to Sydney to visit our grandmother and assorted relatives. Dad was only staying in Sydney a week; the rest of us would stay another two. He took all the dogs, Dizzy included, out to Cheyenne, where Mr and Mrs Bloo were going to take care of them in our absence.

The train to Sydney was a steam train then. The giant black engine puffed through a distant gap in the trees and huffed around the bend towards the station, belching steam and smoke. We shuddered with anticipation as it rolled majestically along the platform and its great wheels ground and squealed to a stop. The guard opened the doors and we clambered up the high step, struggling with our luggage and packages. Then the doors banged shut, the whistle blew, and the train lurched forward just as we were trying to position everything, including our lunch packets of baked bean sandwiches. The journey took almost ten hours, stopping at Woolbrook, Bendemeer, Kootingal, Tamworth, Werris Creek, Quirindi, Willow Tree, Murrurundi, Scone, Aberdeen,

Muswellbrook, Singleton, Maitland, Broadmeadow, Wyong, Gosford, Hornsby, Strathfield and finally Central, where it was evening and Grandma and various aunts and uncles were waiting for us.

With all the excitement of train journeys, trips on the Manly Ferry and to the beach, and then being back at home with some new improvements to the house that had taken place while we were gone, it was not until the day after out return, during unpacking, that I thought to ask, 'Where's Dizzy? When are we getting her back?'

My mother must have been steeling herself for this question. She made me sit down. 'Well,' she said, 'you know the snake in the Bloos' cellar?'

Oh no. Oh no, no. For a moment, I couldn't breathe. My head spun. Just like that, I could see it all. Dear sweet Dizzy had been sniffing and wagging her innocent friendly tail at Snakie, who, like the snake he was, had taken advantage and attacked. He had squeezed her in his grip, tightening it every time she tried to take a breath, till she couldn't breathe any more and then he swallowed her whole, her little body making a huge lump in his long sinuous shape.

It was too much to bear. All these years later, and even though I didn't see it and wasn't there, this image has often haunted my dreams. Poor Dizzy. The only person for whom this cloud had a silver lining was Mr Grieve.

A few weeks after Dizzy's gruesome end, I officially started school. I had been in kindergarten at a Catholic school in Sydney, so my parents had wanted me to start the year before, but since I had not turned six by the official state school start date, I had had to wait another year. There were two schools in Walcha, of course, but since we had no school bus, and town was too far away, the only option for us was correspondence school.

Now I had my own mail: a large manila envelope with an important OHMS in the corner. OHMS, my mother had explained, stood for On Her Majesty's Service. The OHMS was above a line that said Blackfriars Correspondence School. This school was first established by the New South Wales Government during World War One for the education of isolated, itinerant or sick children and had since grown into quite a large enterprise. I was in first class and under my mother's supervision was learning to read, write and spell, starting with an annoying and boring book called *Fay and Don*. In my packet, along with the new lessons for the week, were the workbooks from two weeks earlier, corrected and graded by my teacher in Sydney.

Not long afterwards was my seventh birthday. A brown paper parcel from Scotland had yielded a book called *Pedro the Portuguese Cat* by EJ Foote. Then, on a trip to the Blue Mountain turnoff to collect the Wednesday mail, we found another package in the mailbox, this time holding a red-covered book called *Winnie-the-Pooh*, sent from Grandma in Sydney. Grandma had eleven living children and by then a great number of grandchildren, but she remembered all their birthdays.

These books looked much more promising than *Fay and Don*. I read *Pedro the Portuguese Cat* to myself about ten times, slowly and haltingly at first, and then with increasing fluency, until, there it was, I could read. Furthermore, I went with Pedro on his voyage around Africa and across to India, meeting monkeys, elephants and tigers on the way. It was then no trouble to launch into AA Milne's *Winnie-the-Pooh*, which was a different kind of discovery. I loved Pooh getting his head stuck in the honey jar, Piglet sitting under his sign saying Trespassers Will, Rabbit and all his relations, Kanga and baby Roo and poor old sad-sack Eeyore.

Another cat book, *Orlando the Marmalade Cat* by Kathleen Hale, came from Scotland for Katrina's birthday in May. By now I was hooked. I would creep behind the sofa in the living room (which was off limits) with a precious book, and was, for a short while at least, transported to other worlds. Eventually, though, my mother's calls would become more insistent, and it was back to the kitchen.

Once my reading was fluent, however, I could be left to do my weekly lessons more or less unsupervised, as I was an eager student, hungry for knowledge.

~

Later that year, on one cold night in early spring, my father returned home from town carrying a bundle under his arm. It turned out to be a skinny young dog, still a pup, all legs and angles, with a long narrow face, shaggy grey coat and big soulful eyes. We gathered round to stroke him. We hadn't seen this kind of dog before.

'He's a Scottish Deerhound,' said my father, 'and he's going to be called Cassius, because "Yond Cassius hath a lean and hungry look".' My father had bought Cassius because he reminded him of Scotland. Here in this dog was a piece of home.

We children soon learned that Cassius was nothing like Dizzy. He was placid. He seemed a lot smarter. And he took up a lot more room by the kitchen fire. He grew to be tall, so tall that sometimes one of the boys would sit on his back and ride him, although when my father discovered this, he put an irate stop to it. The gentle Cassius himself didn't seem to mind. He was a noble dog. Like Dizzy, he loved to follow my father, and accompanied him fencing or clearing or building or chopping and dragging logs.

One day we were sitting at our lessons when Cassius began to growl. I had been trying to teach Aidan and Robert to read, but they were getting bored with it. The growling became louder, and there was an edge to it that made us look down. There, squeezing itself through a hole in the floorboards, was a red-bellied black snake. We all started to scream, overturning chairs and backing away in fright.

My father was away riding the boundary, but my mother came running and before we knew it she had grabbed a shotgun from the locked cupboard in the pantry where my father kept his guns. As we cowered behind Mum, she loaded the shotgun and took pot shots at the snake. She really hadn't had that much to do with guns, and at each shot she staggered backwards, causing us even more panic. But miraculously, she managed to hit the snake and it retreated down its hole. Now there was the problem of a venomous snake under the house. Not just a snake – an angry snake. We went outside and, peering under the verandah, Mum took a few more pot shots under the house, but we could not tell whether she had hit it or what state it might have been in.

'Crikey,' said Dad when he came home and saw the shot holes in the walls and floor. 'It's straight out of "The Drover's Wife". We'll be getting "The Loaded Dog" next.' He had been doing his due diligence as a new Australian and reading Henry Lawson. He shone a torch around under the house, but there was nothing to be seen and not much to be done. We waited nervously for several days, but we never saw the snake again.

Snakes may have been interesting to Cassius, but what really excited him was a kangaroo. We had plenty of kangaroos on Arran, although as a rule they didn't come too close to the house. Every now and then, however, a few kangaroos or wallabies would bounce shyly into our house paddock and hop by our front fence, perhaps hoping we wouldn't notice. But Cassius could smell them coming. Kangaroos can be dangerous to a dog if threatened, so he wasn't allowed to chase them, and we were not supposed to let him. But he could easily slip through our small fingers and go wild, springing after them and circling and growling, hoping for a chance to attack. We would all chase after him, shouting and struggling to grab him by the collar, even though by now he was bigger than we were, and much, much faster. He could run like the wind.

One day my father took Cassius in the car down to Kitty's Gully, which was reached by a rough track leading off the road to Cheyenne. There was a beautiful clearing there, a grassy meadow where we kept a mob of cattle. When he returned in the afternoon, he was carrying Cassius in his arms. Both were covered in blood. Cassius had bailed up one kangaroo too many. An old man kangaroo, balancing on his tail and one hind leg and lashing out with the sharp claws of the other leg, had inflicted a huge bloody gash that ran from Cassius's throat to his gut. My father lay the half-dead dog down on the kitchen table and called for cloths and hot water. The dog was whimpering softly. Dad carefully washed his wounds, doused them in Dettol and then sewed them up with a sacking needle and strong thread.

Cassius recovered remarkably well. In a few weeks, he was the same dog, and life went on pretty much as before. He was no longer allowed on expeditions if there was a chance of encountering kangaroos, so he was at home much more. He often sat at our feet while Katrina and I did our lessons. He was more precious to us now that we had nearly lost him.

One day, two or three years later, when I was about nine or ten, my father was again setting out for Kitty's Gully. 'Don't let Cassius chase the car,' he warned as he started the engine. Cassius and I were on the verandah, and I took him by the collar, struggling to restrain him, as the car bumped over the ramp and started down the track. It was hot, and the car windows were open. It only took a couple of seconds, but Cassius gave a great tug and broke free of me, leaping over the ramp and bounding after the car. My father sped up, but the little Austin was no match for Cassius. I ran down the road after them, shouting to them both to stop. But in a bound, Cassius leapt through the car's back window. My father did not stop, and off they bumped down the track, making the right turn towards Cheyenne.

Later that evening when I heard the car coming up the track, I ran out to greet my father as he pulled into the shed. Cassius wasn't with him. A sudden fear clutched at my heart. 'Where's Cassius?' I asked.

My father didn't look at me. 'I couldn't do a thing,' he muttered. 'Not a thing. It might even have been the same kangaroo, it just slit him from the knave to the chops. Poor dog didn't have a chance.'

It was a minute before I could take this in. 'But why didn't you bring him home? What about burying him?' By then I was choking through my sobs. This was all my fault.

'I couldn't bear to bring him back. He was just too mangled up. I buried him down there in the gully.'

Cassius simply disappeared from our lives. It would be nice to think he died doing what he loved to do, but he was still a relatively young dog, and he should have lived for many more years. I was racked with guilt and remorse, although my father gently told me it wasn't my fault. 'I could have stopped and brought him back to the house,' he said, 'but I didn't. It's more my fault than yours.' This was unusual for a man who was not slow to punish when punishment was due, and I was thankful to him for not blaming me, and grateful, too, for his consoling arm across my shoulders, another unusual gesture for him. It was a rare moment of intimacy.

We were united in our sorrow. But there was to be no cheer that day, nor for many days afterwards.

We were all of us grief stricken. There is a part of me that grieves still for gentle, brave, beautiful Cassius. We never acquired another house dog. From then on it was the working dogs and the cats.

Chapter 11

No Man Is An Island

In Erratt's General Store, our mother, dressed in her hat and high heels, was at the counter trying to open an account. It was one of our early trips to town. The man behind the counter listened, frowned, then turned and went into the office at the back. 'Sorry, madam,' he said on his return, 'but the boss says I absolutely can't allow it. No account. Cash only for you. At least until the debts are paid, anyway.' For a moment our mother looked perplexed. What debts? Then she reddened.

'Come on, children,' she said, her head held high, 'we're not shopping here again.' We trailed out after her, confused and anxious.

It was Uncle Jack. He had run up a big bill at Erratt's and had never paid it. There were other establishments, too: the vet supplies, one of the garages, the fencing and hardware stores. The slowly dawning comprehension of the scale of Jack's havoc was humiliating and embarrassing for our family. It was one more obstacle to overcome, as though there weren't enough already.

We were already regarded with the wary suspicion that met all newcomers to the community. But there were some people who did not stop for a chat in the street or turned the other way when they saw us coming. That was because of Jack, and was made worse by the fact that he and his family were Catholics.

The question 'Catholic or public?' hung in the background of almost everything we did, everywhere we went. In the 1950s about a quarter of the Australian population was Catholic, mostly of Irish descent, but Catholics had historically been shunned in polite society. For the most part, Protestants and Catholics did not move in the same circles, and until immigrants began to arrive from southern and eastern Europe, and later from Asia and the Middle East, thus providing new generations of people to look down on, the Irish were at the bottom of the white Australian pecking order.

And that wasn't all. Much of Walcha's squattocracy was long established, and its members regarded themselves as a cut above. They sent their children to the state's most expensive and exclusive private schools, took beachside holidays at the coast, and every now and then journeyed by ocean liner to Europe, leaving their properties in the hands of a relative or manager. Anti-Catholicism was an essential component of their sense of superiority.

So here we were, children of a 'mixed marriage' who were being raised as Catholics, my father, despite his atheism, being true to his marriage pledge. It was rather shocking to have been an atheist then; most people paid at least lip service to some Christian denomination or other. From our time in Sydney, Katrina and I were familiar with much of the Catholic ethos: holy water, genuflection, the sign of the Cross, the Rosary, fish on Fridays, Sunday Mass, the Hail Mary, Heaven, Hell and Purgatory. Although we did not question our Catholic status, I was relieved to have left behind me the tyranny of Sister Matthew at Holy Cross Convent on Edgecliff Road, with her cane and her frequent order to 'Go and wash your mouth out with soap' if you talked back. Sister Matthew was a fervent believer in the crackling, roaring fires of Hell, and she threatened the kindergarteners daily with them. I suffered from recurring nightmares in which both my parents were falling from a bridge into the flames of Hell and I could not save them. For some reason in this nightmare they were wearing their pyjamas and dressing gowns, which only made the vision worse.

In Walcha, however, life was different. Sunday Mass was out of reach – twenty miles away on a rough road. There was no fish and our chooks did not lay enough eggs for Friday dinners. In the beginning my mother did make the occasional attempt to take us to Sunday Mass (which was held at the early hour of 7.30am) from time to time, but after the boys arrived it became impossible. So she visited Father McKeon, the parish priest at St Patrick's, the church set on an unpaved street up the town's steepest hill, and asked for a dispensation from weekly Mass and Friday fish. Poor benighted Father McKeon had a vastly spread-out parish to attend to. On Sundays, he would say three masses, one in Walcha and two others in towns chosen from a rotating array of several outlying hamlets, some of them thirty or forty miles away: Nowendoc, Bendemeer, Walcha Road, Brackendale, Yarrowitch, Glen Morrison, Niangala or Weabonga.

The dispensation was granted and for us children, our Catholicism receded into the background a bit (and I cannot say we missed it). My nightmares of Hell disappeared. Although our mother made up for the losses with efforts to see that we said our nightly prayers, our Sydney grandmother was not one to allow her mixed-marriage grandchildren to lapse into heathen ways. She visited often enough to see to it that we were getting at least some Catholic guidance. We all knew, when a visit from Grandma was imminent, that it was pull-up-our-socks time.

Grandma had been born during the reign of Queen Victoria and she was every inch a Victorian. With her stays and corsets and sensible dresses and suits with matching hats, all in shades of grey, brown and mauve, she seemed, like the old Queen, to be in a lifelong state of dignified mourning for her departed husband.

She was not the kind of grandmother who hugged and spoiled her grandchildren. From our point of view, she was stern and forbidding, and we were in awe of her. Her arrival in the house meant that grace was said before every meal, not just dinner. There were morning prayers. She insisted on being taken to Sunday Mass and on the whole family saying the Rosary together after dinner. That was going too far for my father, who would leave his fireside post with some pointed harrumphs and see to things in the shed until we had finished.

Grandma brought us a set of Rosary beads each. 'They're very, very special,' she told us. 'They're blessed by Our Holy Father, the Pope. Father Damien at St Joseph's brought them back from his trip to Rome.'

On one visit, she brought a special gift for the family: a small porcelain statue of the Holy Infant of Prague. The Infant was very pretty. He wore a white robe under a red fur cloak with a ruffled white lace collar. He had a large crown on His head and held a golden orb in His left hand. He had *Made in Japan* stamped on the bottom. Grandma sat Him on the mantelpiece over the kitchen fireplace with great solemnity.

'You pray to him if you have money problems, and if you need better weather,' said Grandma.

'Will he make us rich?' asked Philomena, who possibly wanted one, just one, dress that wasn't a hand-me-down.

'Let us hope so,' Grandma said.

After she had gone back to Sydney, whenever we needed rain, my father would shake his finger at the inscrutable little red-robed figure on the mantelpiece and say, 'Come on, old moneybags, do your stuff!'

Grandma brought with her other things, of course: hand-me-down clothes from older cousins and family friends; books with titles like *Stories from the Bible* and *The Illustrated Gospels*; and dress lengths and patterns for our mother, which she would help her make up during her visit. Best of all, she would also bring a large tin of Sao biscuits, enough to last us for months, if eked out carefully. Grandma was a big fan of Saos and so, fortunately, were we. Afterwards we used the large square tins, with their picture of the rosella eating his biscuit with his foot, for storage: toys, dressmaking items, shoe cleaning equipment or knitting wool.

On one occasion, she brought me a coat, proudly handing it to me to try on.

'But it's a boy's coat,' I protested, feeling its scratchy grey tweed. I wanted a pretty red coat with a black velvet collar.

'It's a very good quality coat – the best that money can buy,' she said. 'Look at the label, Harris Tweed. It belonged to Basil.' Basil was the young son of Peggy, a well-off family friend in Sydney, but he was very much a *boy*.

After Grandma's first long visit, Katrina, who was a favourite with Grandma, began to take religion seriously. One day, when she was out in the paddocks with my father, she asked him whether he believed in God.

'No. Well, I don't know,' he said. 'And anyway, if there was a God, why should he care about us?'

'But he does, he does! He watches everything you do. You have to believe in him or you will go to Hell!' Katrina cried. For months afterwards, she anxiously prayed at night that Dad would be moved to believe.

So being Catholic was a liability in Walcha then, and we and our mother were Catholics. But our father was not Catholic, and he was a handsome and charismatic man; he made friends easily, he was a good sport, an entertaining raconteur, and was well informed on most subjects. He was the one who could play the piano at parties, most of which would end up in sing-alongs. People liked him.

Though it was Pat and Buddy Blomfield who saved us. They were well liked and respected in the community and not only were they in our corner, they offered useful advice and guidance. So, gradually, the district began to accept us, but there were some of the old landed squattocracy families who never really did, despite my expensive Harris Tweed coat.

We did not know many other Catholic families, since most of them lived in town, but eventually we got to know the Hallorans and their daughters Wisty and Wainie, the Cummins family and Leo and Kerry; and Justin and Betty King, who ran one of the two pharmacies in town.

Every now and then at the homestead we would receive a visit from someone, a new stock and station agent, say, or the bank manager, who would bring their children with them. While our parents discussed business, we would be left to entertain the children. 'Are you Catholic or public?' they would ask. These seemed to be the only two choices available. Catholics versus everyone else. As time went by we began to realise that admitting to being Catholic was not necessarily a popular move, so we would say we were half and half.

~

Saturday. Clean faces, clean hands, hair brushed, faces washed, shoes polished, good clothes: riding jodhpurs and our good jumpers, plus lace-up shoes for the girls, and wool short pants for the boys. If it was a special occasion, we girls might wear our pleated tartan skirts, of which we had one each, to be handed down to the next girl after we had grown out of it; mine were usually inherited from an older Sydney cousin. Mum wore a dress, stockings and high heels, and Dad a shirt and tie, moleskin or corduroy trousers, a sports jacket and a hat. Everyone got dressed to go to town.

As we children grew a little older and as our parents began to feel their way into their new community, we began to go into town a little more regularly. Our father's health had improved considerably, and although he still wheezed occasionally, his hacking cough had all but disappeared. We did not expect to be rich yet, but there was hope for the future.

We all squeezed into the Austin Seven for the twenty-mile trip. There were no seatbelts, and no bucket seats in the front, just a bench that seated three. We took this trip every two or three weeks, and it was a highlight. We knew every inch of the road. First we rattled down the hill past Winterbourne, then over the rocky ford through the creek, then up the steep hill past the Old Stone House; on past the Blue Mountain turnoff with its collection of mailboxes sitting on their posts, through the Winterbourne boundary gate, past the Table Top Mountain turnoff, past Annandale and a goodly stretch of Emu Creek, the Aboriginal reserve, then the Ohio Boys' Home and over the hill past the sawmill, and finally the showground, a left turn and up and then down into Derby Street. In years gone by, the journey to town would have meant opening and closing more than a dozen gates along the road, but people were installing ramps now.

We rarely encountered anyone else on the road, but when we did we always exchanged waves. Anyone who didn't return the greeting was immediately a subject of speculation and suspicion. The journey was also fraught with potential hazards: potholes, broken windscreens, a boiling radiator, flat tires, the possibility of getting bogged after rain, and general mechanical failure. All these things happened to us at various times, and most of them more than once.

If he was in a good mood, Dad might lead us in a song. 'Oh, you take the high road and I'll take the low road, and I'll be in Scotland a'fore ye, but me and my true love will never meet again, on the bonnie, bonnie banks of Loch Lomond,' we sang at the top of our lungs, as we bounced over potholes, bumps and stones.

Despite its small population and lack of railway station, there was lots going on in Walcha in the 1950s, with its pubs, stores, garages, machinery and equipment suppliers, the picture theatre (there had been two, but one closed not long after our arrival) the cafes, the saddlery, two bakeries, a newsagent and bookshop, the police station, the courthouse, the library, the banks, the stock and station agents, pharmacies, doctor's surgeries, the cottage hospital, the showground, the sports field and its three churches: St Patrick's, St Andrew's and St Paul's – Catholic, Anglican and Presbyterian.

For the local farmers and graziers, the weekly social life revolved around sporting activities and the Sports Club (for the men) and the Tennis Club (for the women). So after the shopping and other errands were done, my father took himself to the cricket or football if there was a home game, or straight to the Sports Club. We children went with our mother to the Tennis Club.

But shopping was the first Saturday task, since the shops shut at noon. First stop was McRae's or Lovett's for Rinso, Ajax and other cleaning supplies, brown sugar, salt, tea, flour, coffee, custard powder, peanut butter, onions (which we did not grow), baked beans and canned spaghetti (was there any other kind?) and possibly a sack of potatoes. Everything was ordered over the counter and packed in string bags and cardboard cartons, since plastic bags barely existed then. In his constant quest for farm improvements, my father would have other things to buy or order: nails, fencing wire, machine oil, rabbit traps, bolts and washers, rope, sheep drench.

Once I had learned to read, however, town for me meant first and foremost a trip to the library, a small brick building on Derby Street presided over by my friend Mrs Brazel. Before entering the children's room, my first stop was at the desk to return the carton of books I already had, unloading them one by one onto the counter while Mrs Brazel told me about any new titles she thought I might like. There was usually a limit of three books per reader, but Mrs Brazel would let me take a whole box, because it might be weeks before we got to town again. It began with picture books, but before I turned eight I had read all the *Milly-Molly-Mandy* books and was starting on Enid Blyton's *The Secret Seven* and Eve Garnett's *The Family from One End Street* books. Soon I discovered Richmal Crompton's *William* books and then Evadne Price's *Jane* books, which I loved as much as the William books. But there was a whole world to discover in that small room, and over the years discover it I did, writer by writer, book by book.

It was at the Apsley Tennis Club that my mother made and consolidated her wider circle of friends. The club was on the corner of Hamilton and North Streets, a short walk from Derby Street. The women played tennis on the courts, but the highlight of the day was the Tennis Club lunch, when the committee and various rostered members contributed dishes to the buffet. Hectic activity in the club's kitchen preceded the lunch, and sometimes the older girls were delegated to gather napkins and cutlery, slice bread or chop salad, which they didn't mind because there was always interesting gossip to be had this way.

The tables in the main club room groaned under the weight of casseroles, curries, shepherd's pies, meatloaves, cauliflower cheeses, green beans, boiled potatoes and salads, bread rolls and butter. Then there were the puddings: rice pudding, crumbles, steamed puddings, custards, flummeries, jellies and junkets. There was a small fee per adult and a smaller one per child, which covered some club expenses, and for us it was a banquet.

Often some of the men would come around from the sports ground for lunch, disappearing back to the cricket match or football game for the afternoon, before rounding out their day back at the Club (as we always called it) with some card playing, snooker and drinking.

The population of the district was overwhelmingly white, and frequently northern English and Scots. Names like Fenwicke, Gill, Borthwick, Fletcher, Nivison, Wauch, Eliott, Turton, Weber, Goodwin, Laurie and Blomfield filled the region, and many families had lived in Walcha for generations. These families were the children with whom we played on the lawn at the Tennis Club, whose birthday parties we went to, and with whom we went to the pictures. Because, if we were lucky, on Saturday afternoons in town we might be allowed to go to the pictures. The Civic Theatre on Derby Street put on a weekly matinee, sometimes (but sadly not always) suitable for families and children. The theatre was run by the Lucas family, who were originally from Greece. The Greek families who ran the picture theatre and two of the cafes (one on each of the two main streets) were, aside from the local Aboriginal people, the closest Walcha could come to a show of cultural diversity.

It cost one and ninepence to go to the pictures upstairs. We girls were supposed to sit upstairs, as the boys and more rambunctious children from town sat downstairs, including the orphans from the Ohio Boys' Home. Many children we knew were given two shillings and sixpence, but our family were each given two shillings, which left threepence for a half scoop of ice cream at interval. A whole scoop cost sixpence.

The first half of the program was always cartoons, followed by some breathless newsreels and maybe a Laurel and Hardy or Abbott and Costello short. Then at interval there was a rush to the White Rose cafe and milk bar over the road. In lieu of the half scoop of ice cream, you could get three liquorice sticks or three musk sticks or a handful of boiled lollies. But if you had extra cash for some reason (such as a recent birthday) and you were a forward planner (like Katrina) you might have been to McRae's in Fitzroy Street before it shut at noon and spent time at their lavishly stocked lolly counter. Spread out in their display boxes were not just musk and liquorice sticks, but lollypops, Kit-Kats, and bags of sherbet with their liquorice straws. In big glass jars were all-day suckers, liquorice allsorts, barley sugars, creamy caramels, chocolate freckles, jelly beans or jelly babies, all for maybe two or three a penny. Then, in their own cardboard packets, were the expensive items: Minties, Fantales and Jaffas. We particularly coveted Fantales. They were a chocolate-covered caramel, and their wrappers had mini-biographies of film stars on them – Cary Grant, Rock Hudson, Doris Day, Elizabeth Taylor – eagerly swapped and shared by young movie-goers, but alas, they were way beyond our usual budgetary reach.

After the interval, the main feature could not begin until we had all stood for the national anthem, 'God Save the Queen'. But when we sat down and the MGM lion roared, or the Paramount lady with her flaming torch emerged from the clouds, or the J. Arthur Rank man in his loincloth began to strike his huge gong, a hush of expectation descended upon the audience. Flickering over the screen might come *Son of Paleface* or *Doctor in the House*, or *Anchors Aweigh*. Or a western, now long forgotten: *The Siege at Red River* or *Pony Express*, or *Escape from Fort Bravo*. Or a war movie: *The Sea Shall Not Have Them*, or *To Hell and Back*. The film I remember best from our early picture-going years was *Jedda*, an Australian drama that came closer to home than anything we had yet seen. We were excited and proud to see a story from our own country on the screen.

Downstairs, things occasionally got raucous. A careless person might let some Jaffas roll down the aisle and there would be a scramble to grab them before the original owner could claim them back. No-one would spill their Jaffas deliberately, since they came at too high a price, but sometimes a boy sitting next to someone with a box of Jaffas might give them a hefty nudge, causing a spill. Sometimes the town kids would pick on the orphans from the Ohio Boys' Home or the kids from the Aboriginal reserve, who would sit in the very front rows, and a scuffle would break out. A passionate screen kiss might cause some hearty heckling from the boys. But anyone caught causing a real disturbance would be tossed out and a note made. In a community as small as this it was hard to get away with too much.

Afterwards, when we trailed back along Hamilton Street, past the blacksmith shop and the tennis courts the Tennis Club was finishing up its afternoon tea. We fell upon what was left of it: scones, sponge cakes, pikelets, marshmallow slices, lemon bars, shortbread, chocolate crackles and a delicious confection known as white Christmas, made from Rice Bubbles, coconut and dried fruit in a Copha base.

But then the sun began to go down and the evening chill closed in and babies began to fret and people would start to pack up their cars. We retrieved my father's Sunday bacon and three pounds of sausages for dinner from the Tennis Club fridge before we all scrambled into the Austin, and Mum turned into Fitzroy Street to park the car outside the Sports Club. We took it in turns to go inside to ring the bell and send a message to Mr Wales that we were ready to go home. Other wives on the same mission were parked up and down the street with cars full of children. The Club was sacred to men: no woman or child could cross its threshold – under pain of what I don't know, because nobody ever dared.

Eventually, sometimes fairly soon, but sometimes after a long, cold wait, the men would stumble out and we'd set off on the rattling twenty miles home, my mother at the wheel. Frequently my father would have had a few drinks, so he would start a song.

> *There was wee cooper who lived in Fife*
> *Nickety nackety noo, noo, noo*
> *And he has taken a gentle wife*
> *Hey Willie Wallacky, hey John Dougal*
> *Alane quo rushety roo, roo, roo.*

If he had had enough to drink he might launch into 'There was an old man called Michael Finnegan'. We joined in until one of the boys fell asleep.

One would have thought, after all the Tennis Club food, that we would not be hungry for dinner. But we always were. Sausages were a deliciously comforting pleasure and a perfect end to a good day.

Chapter 12

The Show, The Geebungs And Other Amusements

The car churning up dust across the opposite hill turned out to be Clennell Fenwicke. He pulled up outside our gate, slamming his car door and scraping his boots at our back entrance.

'I'm killing a beast tomorrow,' he announced to my father. 'I'll need a hand, but if you want to come over, I'll give you a quarter, and John can take a quarter, and I owe Dick Blomfield a quarter, so that'll make me square with him.'

That was how it went. In the days before freezers, a family could not eat a whole steer before it spoiled, and so it was shared around. It was at these times that we got to eat steak, a treat, and a welcome change from lamb. My father kept a bottle of HP Sauce in the pantry for just such an occasion.

The larger community, spread out over the miles as we all were, depended on this kind of sharing, and on the goodwill and kindness of friends and neighbours both. Clennell Fenwicke often came the five or six miles over from Earsdon to help my father with some building or fencing, in return for my father's help when Clennell needed it. Sometimes Buddy Blomfield would come to help, or John Fenwicke would come the twelve or so miles from Waterloo. Sometimes, when he was sober, Mick Brien would give a hand.

Pas and Clennell Fenwicke had three or four pear trees, and they exchanged some of their pears for our apples. We also exchanged apples for surplus marrows or pumpkins from neighbouring gardens. The Cheyenne Blomfields were unfailingly generous with spare milk and vegetables. Mrs Brien had an apricot tree and a peach tree, and occasionally gave us a box of apricots in return for apples. Apricots were a luxury and we could get four or five large Vacola jars of apricots for the winter from a box. In later years we were invited to Brookmount, near Emu Creek, to pick as many peaches as we could take home.

Barbie and John Fenwicke kept an abundance of chickens, and frequently helped us with a few extra eggs, as well as with what were then strange and exotic vegetables, such as artichokes and zucchini, from their vast vegetable garden. John was a pioneer of exotic vegetables in the region.

One weekend when young Anne Fenwicke was staying with us, she announced, 'Dad's going to make honey. He's gone to Tamworth to buy beehives.' We knew that Mr Fenwicke never did anything by halves, and that this was going to be a massive undertaking. So a few months later we were sitting on the verandah at Waterloo watching him in his beekeeping outfit and big netted hat and gloves tending to his collection of half-a-dozen hives down the hill from their house. Escaped bees buzzed around us, darting and swooping and looping. We had to learn to sit still and not panic. When John decided he was ready to make some money by selling his honey to the local shops, my father helped design a label for him. In return, we received a four-gallon tin of honey, so we were supplied with all the honey we could use for some time.

For families with children, the usual form of social entertaining was an afternoon tea. We all looked forward to such events, our mother to the social companionship and we children to the scones, pikelets, jam-drop biscuits or shortbread we might reasonably expect. Who knew, there might even be lamingtons.

At such an early tea we met Peter and Rob Blomfield at Karori, boys close to our own age and second cousins to Bunky on Cheyenne. Snowy haired Rob, sporting a magnificent Indian headdress, lost no time in teaching Katrina how to use a bow and arrow. His older brother Peter, a good-looking boy in a cowboy outfit, was shy and offered to teach me no such skills, but the family friendship was to become important to us over the years.

~

The local newspaper, *The Walcha News*, came out every Thursday, and aside from the bush telegraph of local gossip, much of it circulated by Mr Grieve the mailman, it was the major source of community information. The paper had an office in Fitzroy Street, and the writer, photographer, editor, compositor and printer were all the same man: Erle Hogan. Erle was known to everyone as Blue, a nickname he had inherited from his father. We dropped into the office from time to time with a piece of news, and would find him ink-stained in his tennis visor, happy to leave his small printing press clunking away in the background to come and scribble down our news or advertisement. One frigid winter's day we found he had hung a couple of bar heaters from the ceiling to warm his press and keep the ink from freezing. Blue was also the community printer. He made fliers, brochures, posters, sale catalogues, wedding invitations, community notices, race and show programs and more.

WE WANT NEWS, ran a frequent item in the paper. *If you have died, eloped, been married, sold out, been born, caught cold, been robbed, been gypped, bought a car, been visited, had company, been courting, stolen anything, sold your house, been snake bitten, cut a new tooth, bobbed your hair, been evicted, had an operation, been arrested, been in a fight, been to a party, gone to church, or done anything at all, tell us. We want local news.*

The paper published, of course, marriage, birth, death and funeral information, but also news of livestock sales, wool prices, weather trends, upcoming field days, reports on balls and local debutantes, examination results and prize givings for the local schools, fetes, council meeting minutes, show and rodeo results, and community happenings. Local merchants took lots of advertising space: Erratt's, McRae's, Lovett's, Bowden's Garage, Robert's Store for Men and the Walcha Pharmacy all touted their wares. Even some outside interests, such as New South Wales Railways and Arnott's Biscuits, had a weekly quarter page. Arnott's advertised a different variety of biscuit each week: Jatz, Sao, Milk Arrowroot, Scotch Finger and Shredded Wheatmeal.

Walcha was immensely proud of its sporting history and prowess, and *The Walcha News* devoted as much of its space to local sporting activities as this pride would allow. Football and cricket games, horse races, the annual Walcha Cup, tennis, shooting and golf all attracted much interest. Indeed, Walcha produced more than its fair share of outstanding athletes: Bill Laycock, Andrew Laurie, Peter Fenwicke and later Sam Payne among them.

Many column inches were devoted to issues such as the aerial baiting of dingoes, the eradication of rabbits (was myxomatosis working?) and blackberry bushes, and whether New England should secede and become its own state. Snake bites were big news and so was the discovery of nests of deadly brown or tiger snakes and their precise location.

And then there was the Show.

Oh, the joys of a bright blue day at the Show! Held over two days in early autumn at the showground, it was one of the biggest community events of the year, and second only to Christmas for us. We loved every bit of it. Even the drive going in, with all its anticipation, was special. 'Speed bonnie boat, like a bird on the wing,' we sang as the trees and fence posts and sheep sped past us.

My parents were working hard to consolidate their place in the community and the Show was a good place to do it. The women gathered around the exhibits and tea tent, and the men at the crowded and noisy bar tent where they could have a beer before watching the sheepdog trials or prize bull parades. We children were given two shillings each and sent to roam free for the day.

The Show was a profusion of earthly pleasures. The long low pavilion that ran along one end of the showground held artistically arranged displays of local produce, apples, pears, peaches, corn, pumpkins, tomatoes, beans; special displays of local wool; and a couple of rooms of local arts and crafts, painting, flower arranging, dressmaking, embroidery, needlepoint, knitting, weaving and crochet. It was all very competitive. In another room were bottled fruit and vegetables, preserves, chutneys, jams, scones, biscuits, cakes and cake decorating. Oh, the cakes! There were castles, ships, English cottages, books, fairy princesses, footballs, tennis courts, even a large pink pig, all made from cake and icing.

A crackling loudspeaker in the stand beside the benches narrated the ring events: hacking, show jumping, campdrafting and tenting, as well as sheepdog and cattle dog trials. There were wood-chopping and sheep-shearing competitions, and on the second day, a grand parade including all the winners – prize sheep and cattle, pigs, poultry and their red, blue and yellow ribbons. We did not yet have a ram or ewe worthy of entry in the Show, but Dad promised that one day we might.

The ring events, however, were only of passing interest to us children. What we were there for was the jangle, the colour, the jubilation of sideshow alley. Spruikers with their megaphones exhorted us to enter their tents to see the Half Man-Half Woman or the Tattooed Lady. A magician promised to saw a lady in half, and a lady in gaudy costume invited the boys to witness a semi-striptease by risqué dancing girls. Be astounded in the Mirror Maze! Scare yourself senseless in the House of Horrors! A young man with a bullhorn invited other young men to try their fists in Sharman's Boxing Tent. There were laughing clowns with open mouths that you could feed with balls to win a stuffed bear or perhaps a kewpie doll. There was a shooting gallery where you could aim at a passing parade of scruffy yellow tin ducks, a coconut shy and a tin can alley game.

From the scattered food stalls wafted the spicy aromas of pies, sausage rolls, Pluto Pups and hot dogs. There were stands that sold toffee apples and fairy floss. Even just watching the fairy floss man spin the pink sugar into its fluffy clouds had its own special allure. But best of all were the rides: a small Ferris wheel, some dodgem cars, a merry-go-round, an octopus, a little train. With most attractions costing sixpence each, we had to choose our entertainment carefully. Two shillings meant three rides and a snack, or four rides and an empty stomach.

Driving home from the Show, we babbled about the highlights of the day and poured out our encounters. I was full of new ideas for cake decorating when someone had a birthday, or for fruit bottling, when the season came around. Our parents, too, might have picked up important tips, heard some useful advice, or made a valuable new friend.

We looked forward to attending at least one of the annual fetes, held in support of the hospital, or the Ohio Boys' Home, or perhaps the ambulance service. They usually took place at one of the more historic homesteads closer to town – Mirani or Langford or Yalgoo – and in addition to the stalls displaying baked goods, jams and relishes, or knitted or wooden craft items, there were treasure hunts, a pet parade, pony rides and games. We were allowed a lucky dip parcel each, and bought only the occasional jar of orange marmalade and possibly a winter beanie or two. Sometimes John Fenwicke organised a clay-pigeon shooting contest for the men. Often there was a pipe band and displays of highland dancing from Armidale. Katrina and I watched the band and the dancing with an almost religious fervour. After all, were we not half Scottish? Was not this our heritage?

But there was one annual social activity that eclipsed all the rest: the Geebungs, held each year on a spring Friday. The Geebung Picnic Race Club was very prestigious, and membership was by invitation only. Our parents initially went as the guests of Pat and Buddy Blomfield, and it was an important day for them when they were invited to join in their own right; it meant that they were finally becoming accepted.

The Geebungs ball was as grand an occasion as Walcha could pull off, and it was taken very seriously. 'What are you wearing?' my mother's friends would ask each other for weeks beforehand. The organising committee arranged for a band to come from Tamworth or Armidale, decorated the hall with garlands and flowers, and planned an elegant supper. We were usually farmed out to a couple of families in town for the weekend, and sent to St Patrick's school for the day.

The school was divided into two rooms: one for years one through three, and one for years four through six. One nun taught each room. A large faded map on the wall showed the British Empire in pink, including India and other countries which, even we knew, had left the Empire. It was the British Commonwealth now, not the Empire, but budgets didn't yet run to new maps. We had our Vegemite and lettuce sandwiches and green apples in a brown paper bag, and we were thankful we had each other to talk to at lunch and recess, because we didn't know anyone else there. The girl sitting next to me showed me how to write AMDG in the top right-hand corner of my exercise books, which stood, she explained, for All My Deeds for God.

'God asked Abraham to sacrifice his son Isaac, to kill him on the altar. Does anyone know what happened?' Sister Anthony asked one year.

Thanks to my compulsive reading habit and Grandma's books of bible stories, I knew the answer, so I waved my hand in the air. Sister Anthony ignored me.

'Well, does anyone else know?' she asked. No-one did, so she was forced to call on me. I hope I scored our supposedly heathen family a point.

Chapter 13

In Which We Do Not Get Rich

Because of Oskar, my mother had asked that the new vegetable garden have no gate, so access was via an old-fashioned stile in one corner. The garden was situated up the hill by the cow yards, so there was now much more space to plant things, although it meant extra work. My mother ranged everything neatly in rows. Here, rows of corn. There, the pumpkin patch. Here, marrow or broccoli. There, carrots and parsnips. Rhubarb here. On the back fence, tomatoes. Here the bean and pea trellises. Cabbage over there, lettuce here. Celery there. The herb patch (mostly parsley and chives) here. The more we could grow ourselves, the less we needed to spend.

As a sign of yet more progress, we were going to get new sheep yards. Having our own yards, instead of having to use Winterbourne's, was essential to our independence and future growth. My father had been planning ahead, and had already amassed quite a pile of logs, cutting down extra trees in the bush and dragging them back with his tractor. He spent backbreaking hours sawing them to size for the posts and rails.

At about this time, the first correspondence lessons came for Katrina. From the very beginning, Katrina and my mother were locked in battle over her academic education. Katrina did not want to be sitting at a desk, labouring over letters of the alphabet and one and one makes two. She could already count, anyway, and could tell how many sheep were in a mob at a glance.

Once the actual construction on the sheep yards began, she was up helping Dad with the yards for as much time as she could get away with. One day, while digging a posthole on the site of the new yards, he unearthed a shovelful of earth with what seemed to be bits of glitter running through it.

'Do we think this is gold?' he asked. They both examined this shovelful of earth, and then Katrina seized a golf ball-sized stone from the shovel and washed it with water from their canteen. Yes, it had threads running through it that glinted.

At lunch time, they burst into the kitchen full of excitement. My father spread a handful of the earth on a piece of newspaper on the table and Katrina handed the stone to my mother. We crowded around to inspect them carefully, and we all agreed – there were undeniable shiny flecks. Was it gold, or something else?

'Are we going to be rich?' asked Philomena.

Maybe this was it. Maybe we were going to be rich. All afternoon we children discussed what we would do with the money that was going to start flooding in (bride dolls, bicycles), and in the evening my father drove down to Winterbourne to consult with Old Bill, who helped him wash and sift further samples. Bill felt that it was probably mica, but they sent it off for analysis anyway. Gold was not unknown in the Walcha area; veins had been found here and there, but they had never come to anything.

In the meantime, Bill enthusiastically offered to help my father build the yards, in the hope of finding something more. Other people – Mick Brien, Clennell Fenwicke – came to help, a morning here, an afternoon there. The sheep yards were to have sorting races, various pens and a ramp for loading animals on and off a truck. My father also built a concrete dipping channel alongside the yards, so that we could do our own dipping on site.

The mineral analysis, weeks later, confirmed Bill's guess. It was mica. By then we had spent the imagined riches in our heads, many times over, but the promised trip to Scotland by ocean liner would have to wait.

~

Grandma had handed down to her daughters the usual store of proverbs and aphorisms. Many of them went something like 'waste not want not', or 'take care of the pennies and the pounds will take care of themselves', or 'a penny saved is a penny earned'. Every now and then my mother would expand upon this particular subject and pronounce, as Mr Micawber had done before her, 'Annual income twenty pounds, annual expenditure nineteen nineteen and six, result happiness. Annual income twenty pounds, annual expenditure twenty pounds ought and six, result misery.' She had read *David Copperfield* at school.

The shortages and privations of the Depression and war years might have been easing a bit for some people by the 1950's, but not for us. We were still struggling to get ahead. Making ends meet, as my mother put it, meant never spending money on anything that we could grow, make, cook or fix for ourselves, using everything to its maximum capacity and reusing every item that could possibly be reused. It also involved never spending money on anything that we did not seriously need. We used every single part of a sheep when we killed it: brains, liver, kidneys, roasts, chops, stews, mince and, finally, fritters. Using recipes from Betsy Borthwick, Tony Blomfield's mother, we made fruit chutneys, blackberry and plum jams, and tomato sauce to add to the bottled vegetables from the garden, using recycled jars and bottles. We used old Vegemite jars as drinking glasses. We saved and reused string, bags, rubber bands, gift wrap and paper, buttons, zippers and fasteners from worn-out clothes, and we mended, patched and darned. We saved nails and screws, turned sheets and collars.

Originally, we had tried to grow our own potatoes in the paddock downhill from the house. But when two years in a row we dug up nothing but blighted, undersized specimens, we ended up having our potatoes delivered from town in large hessian sacks on Mr Grieve's Monday truck, along with bulk sacks of sugar, flour and rolled oats for our porridge.

One summer afternoon, Mrs Bloo pulled up in front of the house with a sack in her hand. Popcorn. She showed us how to pop it on the stove and we liked it. Mr Bloo liked popcorn, because of his American childhood, and Mrs Bloo had found someone in Armidale who sold it. It was even cheaper than rolled oats were, and we began to eat it in summer for breakfast. We became expert at popping up a batch in the same pot that in the winter was used for the porridge, and we ate it just like cornflakes, with sugar and milk. It was always skim milk, because the cream was saved for butter. Once we had milked the cows in the morning, the milk was left to stand until most of the cream rose to the top. We then skimmed the cream off and left it to stand for a day or two before churning it for butter. The rest of the milk was what we drank, but it wasn't the watery skim milk we think of today; there was still a little cream in it.

When my mother told me that I was old enough to learn how to make the butter, I was proud and pleased. But the pleasure was short-lived. Our butter churn was a makeshift affair, a small cylinder set in a cradle, with a clip-sealed top and a handle that you had to crank. And crank. And keep cranking. It seemed to me to take hours and leave me with a very sore arm before the cream would curdle. *Crank, crank, crank, slosh, slosh, slosh.* Would it never thicken? When it finally did curdle, however, you could strain off the buttermilk, wash the butter in cold water several times, add salt, knead it to remove as much of the buttermilk as possible, and then pat it into shape.

Big blue and yellow boxes of yellow Sunlight bars came from town too. We used the soap for everything, including to wash our hair. When Mum had a birthday, we saved our pocket money to buy her a bottle of shampoo, which we all knew to be a treasured luxury. Towards the end of the bottle's life she put a little water in it to take advantage of every drop, in the same way that she would thin down the tomato sauce or my father's HP Sauce.

All food scraps, vegetable peels and all, went to the dogs, or cats or chooks (or, during the period we kept them, the pigs). No food scrap was ever, ever thrown away.

We were almost always short of eggs, so if a cake was called for we often used a recipe called the One-Egg Sandwich, from the *Country Women's Association Cookbook*, the only cooking manual I ever remember being in the house. Over the years the book became grease-stained and dog-eared. The One-Egg Sandwich was not a great cake, but filled with plum jam and covered with icing, it frequently rose to the occasion.

If we were expecting visitors we often relied on scones, which did not use an egg, or Anzac biscuits, which also did not use an egg, and which Mum kept in a tin on the highest shelf of the pantry. Anzac biscuits would keep for months if tightly sealed. Mum always knew how many biscuits were in the tin, and she knew if one was missing. The culprit was punished with the wooden spoon.

In the storeroom off the back courtyard were several bolts of cloth, including a large bolt of blue denim and another large one of red and white striped jersey, with the red stripe sporting a thin black zig-zag along its edge. Another, smaller bolt of jersey had yellow and green stripes. There was also a bolt of pale blue cotton. From these bolts my mother made almost all our clothes, cutting them out on the kitchen table, her Singer pedal sewing machine rattling and clattering in the evening firelight while my father sat in his armchair with his pipe. Shorts, jeans and overalls for us and shirts for my father from the denim; T-shirts from the two bolts of jersey; and nightgowns and pyjamas from the cotton. For years all five of us wore identical red and white striped T-shirts, summer in and summer out.

There were old shoeboxes full of patterns – Simplicity, Butterick, McCall's – which my mother would use and reuse. But every now and then, if there was an occasion coming up, she might send off for a new pattern and have Grandma send some fabric and matching thread and trim from Sydney so that she could make herself a dress. The dressmaking leftovers were used for patching or for doll's clothes or table napkins or potholders, or to be given to those of my mother's friends who made patchwork quilts.

Clothes were of course passed down from child to child, but anything with some decent wear left in it after it no longer fitted anyone went into a special bag. When the bag was full we dropped it at the gate of the Aboriginal reserve on our way into town. 'But why don't we go in and give it to them?' we asked my mother the first time we did this. She said that they would be too proud to accept charity from us face to face, but if we just left the clothes there they would be able to take them when we had gone. And sure enough, when we drove by on our way home the bag had always disappeared.

Our father fixed anything that broke with glue, nails, his soldering iron or makeshift spare parts. There were, however, two luxuries he allowed himself: the after-dinner pipe, and two rashers of bacon each week for his Sunday breakfast. The maddening smell of the bacon cooking on a Sunday morning wafted about the kitchen, and we sat and watched him eat his bacon with envy and bitterness in our hearts. Sometimes afterwards he cut any leftover rind into pieces so that we could all have a bit to chew on.

Despite his residual chest problems, Dad smoked Temple Bar tobacco, which visiting friends or relatives would bring or sometimes send from Sydney. It had its own special aroma.

My mother's big indulgence was a jar of Pond's Cold Cream. It sat on her dressing table, and she eked it out a little at a time so that it would last. But sometimes times were so tight that she could not even afford that, so in the evenings after a day in the garden she would take some rendered lamb fat or occasionally some butter, the nearest thing she had to hand lotion, and rub it into her overworked hands. She had not forgotten Aunt Phil's cautions.

In the summer we mostly went barefoot, even in the bindis, and in the winter wore hand-me-down boots, but every now and then there would be no help for it – someone would require a new pair of good shoes. So when the David Jones mail-order catalogue arrived, my mother would draw around at least one person's feet and send the drawing off to David Jones with her order. It was always practical brown lace-ups, which we wore with (often darned) white socks. No black patent leather Mary Janes for us. When the shoes arrived, they would be a little big, to allow our feet room to grow. We all had one 'good' pair of shoes each, for wearing to town or social occasions. We passed shoes down in the family, and we took great care with the good ones, to make the most of their useful lives. They were carefully dried out with newspaper if wet, and polished each time they were to be worn. The same went for my father's boots.

Some evenings after dinner, my father would bring his shoemaker's last in from the shed, along with his tack hammer and box of supplies, to mend our shoes. He had pieces of rubber and leather from which he cut new soles and heels, a special hammer and tacks and glue. He put steel tips on the heels and toes to increase the wear.

And then, and then, and then – our lives changed a little. Eventually the powers that be finally agreed to grant a telephone line to the Arran homestead. This was a momentous event for us – lines were scarce and the waiting lists long. As it was, because our family had five children, we had been given priority, and some people were not pleased. Indeed, it set Clennell Fenwicke off. 'What makes you so special?' he fumed to my father. 'We've been on the bloody waiting list longer than you, and just because you've got five bloody kids you get to jump the queue. Where's the justice in that?'

We finally had the telephone. It was a party line, which we shared with Winterbourne and Cheyenne. Everyone had their own ring: one long ring, two shorts and a long, a long-short-long, and so on. You turned a handle to call neighbours, but dialled calls or calls made through the Walcha exchange cost money and we kept them to a minimum. No-one ever dreamed of making a long-distance telephone call, not even at Christmas – trunk calls were immensely expensive. If there was an urgent piece of news, a birth or a death, for instance, it would come by telegram to Walcha, and then be read over the phone by the operator. But even the party line meant we were far less isolated than we had been up to that point.

Letters and parcels to Scotland and to our aunt Nessie, now married and living in South Africa, came and went by sea mail, because air mail was a great extravagance, although as the years went by, people started using cheaper aerogrammes.

～

One can hardly talk about all this now without it sounding like something out of a Monty Python sketch, but the truth is, it wasn't just us; following the Depression and war years, even those who were prospering were careful, and waste was simply a cultural sin. Everyone understood that this was the way things were. Our family just had to try that little bit harder.

Chapter 14

We Get Lucky

'What do we think?' asked my father one autumn evening at dinner. 'What do we think about getting a piglet? Maybe we could make our own bacon.'

The acquisition of a pig had been suggested by John Fenwicke, who also kept pigs. Dad didn't usually ask our opinion, and we were intrigued. Perhaps he was looking to us for support, in view of some potential resistance from my mother.

We were enthusiastic. Bacon? Oh, yes. A piglet? What fun.

'Well,' said my mother, seeing how the land lay, 'I suppose it could help the horse with the rotten apples.'

As it happened Mr Grieve, the mailman, was selling some piglets cheap, so we agreed to buy a young sow. It seemed like a good idea at the time. We named our piglet Lucky, and although she was still quite small, Dad built a large pen for her, with a trough and a shelter from the elements, but after a few weeks of confinement she was mostly allowed to roam free about the place during the day, with the idea that she would get fat. She became a member of the family, following us around and joining us children as we sat on the edge of verandah to while away some time.

She grew bigger quite quickly. For a while she grew bigger generally, and then at some point she really did get fat. And fatter. And fatter. Her teats began to enlarge. Observing this, Katrina pointed out that she thought Lucky might be pregnant.

'She couldn't be,' said Dad. 'Not possibly.' Because who would the father be?

But like Miranda before her, Lucky had found a secret suitor, which implied that there was at least one feral boar somewhere out there in the bush, and although we had never seen him, he had got Lucky.

Eventually her time came. Dad was away, but the boys came to tell us that Lucky seemed to be in labour, and we all congregated around the pigsty to watch. Mum had brought a bucket of water and rubber gloves in case help was needed, but none was. We watched in awe and fascination as Lucky gave birth not to three or four, but to ten, eleven, twelve piglets. That was going to be a lot of bacon.

My mother gave Lucky some carrots and some overripe marrow from the garden to eat, and after the novelty wore off, we left the pig to suckle her swarming, squealing little brood alone.

But it was only half an hour later that Philomena came bursting into the kitchen. 'Come quick, come quick!' she said, gasping for breath. 'Lucky is eating one of her piglets!'

We scrambled to remove the remaining piglets until we figured out what to do. Consulted by telephone, John Fenwicke advised that we crate the piglets in a box overnight, give Lucky some meat to eat (iron deficiency may have been the cause of her decidedly unmaternal behaviour) and for the next day only allow her offspring to feed under supervision. By then the danger should have passed.

Soon, of course, we were swarming with little pigs. More pigs than we knew what to do with. They wandered around the orchard snuffling up fallen apples and eating the cows' grass, as well as all the food scraps the dogs or chooks couldn't eat. The local butcher already being well supplied (presumably by John Fenwicke and Mr Grieve) we began to give the piglets away. The Briens took one, the Blomfields another, the Earsdon Fenwickes another. When our remaining ones were nearly full grown, my father killed one for meat. We loved the novel taste of the pork to begin with, but we tired of it quite quickly, even though we had split the carcass with the Blomfields and Pas and Clennell Fenwicke.

Lucky thought herself a member of the family. Sometimes she would wander inside the house and have to be chased out. She became so over-familiar that one afternoon we came home from town to find her lying full length on our parents' bed, her head on the pillow, snoring gently. She had nosed open the back door and made herself at home.

'Off, Lucky, off!' we shouted, but she only opened an eye halfway and closed it again. We slapped her rump. Still no response. We tweaked her ear, but that didn't work either. We pushed from one side and pulled her legs, but she was heavy, and quite comfortable where she was. Each attempt seemed only to exasperate her. 'Why are you bothering me?' her look seemed to say, as she flicked her tail. Eventually we managed to get her to move, and annoyed, she found the floor. With a last baleful look she stalked through the back verandah and out the back door. Then we discovered she was expecting again.

It had been a nice idea, and occasional pork was fine, but I don't recall any attempts to smoke bacon, and eventually the butcher agreed to take some young pigs and that was the end of the second litter. But our parents worried about the wild boar and the ultimate possibility of an unmanageable wild pig community down in the gorge. So eventually Lucky was sent off too, to become someone else's bacon, and that was the end of the pig experiment.

One autumn, as the leaves in the orchard began to turn and fall, and the evenings began to cool, our parents prepared to go to Sydney for a friend's wedding. They had hired a young woman to come and take care of us for the five or six days they would be away. I will call her Patsy, since sadly, I don't remember her name now. Patsy lived on the Aboriginal reserve just outside of town. My father drove into the reserve to pick her up, and she spent a day with Mum learning the ropes before Mum and Dad took off down the track in a flurry of dust.

The original people of the district were a branch of the Dunghutti, and so I suppose Patsy was one of them, although she told us her father was white and lived in the town. She announced that she would take us walkabout, and we liked the sound of that, so the morning after our parents left we set off to walk in the bush. Patsy had found some rabbit traps in the storeroom, and she put some in a hessian bag to take with us, setting the traps at the head of some burrows. The rabbits were diminishing now, because of myxomatosis, but there were still some about.

Although the twins were still quite little, she took us on three big walks while she stayed with us: first uphill along the Millbank boundary fence, all the way to the top of the hill, above the spring, where we imagined we could see to Karori and over to Earsdon and other properties; then along the Winterbourne boundary fence below the house into thick scrub, towards the gorge; and finally, part way up the mysterious and majestic Trig Hill. During these adventures, Patsy showed us how to tell where we were and how to find our way home if we were lost. Pay attention to your surroundings. Look out for distinguishing features and landmarks. Leave little markers – a broken twig, a scratch on the bark. Keep track of the sun.

As we crunched through the twigs, bark and dead leaves of the bush floor, we saw a blue-tongued lizard, his tongue bluer than the sky, and then a goanna, large and ugly.

'We could catch him and eat him, if you like,' teased Patsy, but we were horrified.

She pulled some bark off a tree and showed us how to find witchetty grubs. 'They're delicious,' Patsy said, teasing us again, but we preferred to think of our sandwiches, safely packed in her rucksack.

We had never travelled so far afield from the homestead on foot, and all these adventures were an exhilarating novelty for us, although we were footsore and tired by the evenings. Perhaps that was Patsy's intention. But there was a new culinary experience, too: Patsy had caught some rabbits in her traps, and she skinned, gutted and cooked them for us, soaking them overnight in milk first. The flavour was rather bland, we thought, but we ate it without complaint At least it wasn't witchetty grub.

Our parents returned to find us all happy and intact, but with a house full of unmade beds and piles of dirty laundry – Patsy had been too busy keeping us out of mischief. But we had loved her stay and thought we had learned a lot. As far as we were concerned, she was the best babysitter we ever had.

I was eight now, and I had a new friend: her name was Helen Thorold. Helen was my age, and her parents lived on Table Top, close to the Blomfields at Karori. One afternoon at the Tennis Club I had seen a girl reading an Enid Blyton book and I introduced myself. It seemed we were both familiar with Mrs Brazel at the library, and we became instant friends. We swapped stories and book titles for hours. Helen also loved going to the pictures, so when we could, we sat together upstairs at the Civic and watched *The*

Living Desert, *The Seven Little Foys* and *Three Coins in the Fountain*. We resolved to go to Rome when we grew up.

I was invited to stay at Table Top for a few days. At night Helen and I lay together in her bedroom listening to the wind in the trees.

'Have you ever seen a bunyip?' she asked.

I hadn't.

'Well, it's enormous, gigantic. It has great big red eyes and the biggest, sharpest teeth, you've ever, ever seen, bigger than a shark's. It has nasty red and purple and blue scales and massive long sharp horns and it roars worse than a lion. It can eat you in one huge gobble.'

This was a little unsettling. 'Have you ever seen one?'

'No,' she said, 'but we have them, you know, out there in the creek. They come out at night, like the banshees. I heard a banshee once.'

'What's a banshee?'

'A banshee is a sort of ghost. She wails and screeches at night when someone is going to die. She wrings her hands in the creek, all covered in blood. Her screams are just bloodcurdling.' She rolled her tongue around this alarming word.

This was even more unnerving than the bunyip. 'Does she come up from the gorge?' I asked. Helen agreed that she probably did.

She told me that the wild family down in the gorge, the Brennans, had long hair and beards, and lots of dogs and guns. Old Man Brennan, she said, had a white beard down to his waist. She claimed she had once seen them. I didn't know what parts of this story to believe, although a part of the Thorold property, like ours, bordered the gorge. I couldn't wait to get back to Arran and frighten my younger brothers and sisters with tales of a more grotesque bunyip than we ourselves had ever managed to imagine, and stories of banshees and Brennans and tiger cats as well.

One winter morning when I was staying at the Thorolds', we were in the kitchen dressing by the stove. I picked up my hairbrush to brush my hair when Helen said, shocked, 'My mother says the best people don't brush their hair in the kitchen.'

I was taken aback but said, with some genuine curiosity, 'So who are the best people?'

'You know, the *best* people,' was all she could say.

When I went home I told my mother about Helen's statement and asked her who the best people were, and without missing a beat, she said, 'We are.'

Although I remained friendly with Helen for a while, I was never again invited back to Table Top to stay. Perhaps Mrs Thorold didn't approve of little girls who brushed their hair in the kitchen.

~

One weekend Katrina, Philomena and I went to stay at Cheyenne for a couple of nights while the boys went to the Fenwickes at Earsdon, so that our parents could go into town and see a production of a new Australian play, *The Summer of the Seventeenth Doll*, by Ray Lawler. The Australian Elizabethan Theatre Trust and the Arts Council were touring the play around New South Wales country towns. Someone had bought our parents the tickets as a gift. They were elated, because an Australian play was an almost unheard-of phenomenon then, except on the radio. They were even more excited when they got to talk to the cast afterwards.

For me the weekend was memorable because in the kids' house at Cheyenne early one morning as the magpies carolled, I found a paperback copy of a book called *The Diary of Anne Frank* and began to read it. It was a little old for me, but I was shocked and profoundly dismayed to read the blurb on the back; why did I not know about these terrible events that had happened only twelve or thirteen years before? I could not wait to ask my mother about it when we got home, and when she told me the story of Hitler and his attempt to exterminate the Jews, I was aghast. We had had several Jewish neighbours in Bondi. It was almost impossible to believe that such things could happen. It was a lesson, Mum said, as to where bigotry and hatred could lead. 'Never think you're the ant's pants,' she said, 'because you're not. The best people are the people who only think of themselves as equal to everyone else and treat everyone else as equals too.'

Since I was by now becoming aware of the stratified nature of even our small community – Catholic versus Protestant, old families versus new, white versus black – this was not in accord with my observations to date of general human behaviour, but I took Mum at her word for now.

~

When the wattle trees were in bloom and the sun shining, danger could sometimes appear out of the clear blue sky – a sudden bomb of thrashing black and white fury diving at our blond heads. Our screams and waving arms were of no help as the magpies swooped again and again. Once one actually drew blood, and we had to run up to the house for first aid and to grab hats, hands over our heads.

The magpies were also thieves; once we caught one stealing an earring from our mother's dressing table, which was under the window in our parents' bedroom. When nesting season came around she had to remember to keep their bedroom window shut.

The magpies may have been fiercely protective of their nests, but they woke us every spring and summer morning and into the autumn, chortling and carolling as the day began. By mid-morning the air might be full of the sounds of chattering birds – currawongs, butcher birds, plovers, noisy miners, apostle birds or warblers, depending on the season. A family of kookaburras nested in the gum tree that sat alongside the track leading down to the mailbox, and their raucous laughter burst into the quiet of a tranquil spring morning.

My mother told us the birds talked to each other. Sometimes Katrina and I would sit with our legs dangling from the verandah, trying to figure out what the birds were saying. 'Probably it's "Breakfast at the Arran Homestead!"' said Dad, walking by with his bridle on his way to catch the Old Grey Mare.

Wherever we went, whatever we did, the background echo to our lives was that of the crows croaking and wailing overhead, the long dying fall of their cry fading into the sky. A throng of circling crows almost always meant trouble – an animal wounded or dead. If the crow was a soaring reminder of our fragile place in the world, the willie wagtail was the familiar close-up reassurance of home comforts. We had willie wagtails everywhere. *Sweet pretty creature, sweet pretty creature*, they tweeted outside the kitchen window and along the front fence. They nested in the pine trees around the house, and in the spring we stood at the kitchen sink and watched the little nestlings learning to fly a few feet from the window.

An invitation came for me with my correspondence lessons to join the Gould League of Bird Lovers. I joined, and for a time wrote down the birds in a little notebook. *Flame robins,* I wrote, *yellow robins* and *blue wren family*. I carefully noted soldier birds, diamond swallows and butcherbirds as they perched on the fence posts or along the phone line, and white-winged choughs as they pecked around in the gully. After a summer rainfall I earnestly noted the koels, or rain birds as we called them, announcing the wet in their sonorous tones. Brilliant flocks of parrots, black cockatoos and rosellas came and went, sometimes settling to pick at the grass in the front yard, sometimes gathering in the trees around the house.

On forays into the bush with our father, looking for a lost animal perhaps, we sometimes came upon lyrebird mounds, and occasionally even the lyrebird himself, fanning out his beautiful tail as though to mark his territory. We could hear the whipbirds and woodpeckers there, but hardly ever saw them. And down in Kitty's Gully, which was bordered on one side by a deep ravine with a creek and a waterfall that ran into the gorge, we could hear the *tink, tink, tink* of the bellbirds.

The Blomfields had built a brick barbecue in their backyard, and to celebrate our mother's 30th birthday they invited us over for a party. We left at about 5:30pm, and on the way home through the tree-lined track we saw ahead of us a large mob of eastern grey kangaroos in a clearing beside the road, all standing in a circle. 'Wait! Stop the car, Daddy, stop the car,' we begged, and he did, turning off the engine.

In the centre of the road were two old man kangaroos having a boxing match. The kangaroo spectators were apparently so intent on the drama before them that they had not heard us coming and scattered. We all watched in silence, probably for about ten minutes. We, too, were mesmerised. Every now and then one of the boxers would stand on one leg, balancing on his tail, and try to rip the other's throat with the claws of his foot. Eventually one of them seemed to have had enough, and turned around and hopped into the bush. The mob parted to let him through, and some began to follow him. The rest of them hopped away with the victor in the opposite direction. 'Just for my birthday!' exclaimed Mum, clapping her hands. 'That was marvellous, wasn't it?' And indeed, this incident remains embedded in family lore.

Although the kangaroos and wallabies usually steered clear of the house, we often saw a mob of them somewhere in the distance, especially at dusk. The kangaroos grazed on the pastures intended for the sheep, so most years the local graziers would get up a roo drive, to try to cull the numbers. As they did for the dingo drives, the men rode on the back of utes with their rifles, setting out at dusk and returning late, the utes laden with kangaroo carcasses.

One evening my father returned from a roo drive with a small bundle wrapped in a hessian sack. It was a joey, who had been found curled up in its dead mother's pouch. My father had put it in a canvas rucksack and brought it home. We put it in a hessian-lined box with a makeshift pouch by the kitchen stove, and fed it watered-down cow's milk from a bottle. Sometimes we would let the joey hop around the yard, but soon it would return to its warm spot near the stove. We could tell it was not thriving. Nevertheless, the Mirani fete was coming up, and they were holding a 'Best Pet' competition and parade, so Katrina took our little joey and won first prize in the Unusual Pets section.

The joey lasted a few more weeks, but it eventually wasted away and died. We were full of sorrow. It was too young to leave its mother, and we didn't know the right formula with which to feed it, anyway. That was guesswork on our part, and sadly, we got it wrong.

We were constantly on the lookout for wombats and koalas, but we never saw them. My father said he sometimes saw them deep in the bush when riding the boundary. But they are shy, nocturnal creatures, the koalas sleeping in the foliage by day while the wombats dozed in their burrows. But incessant land clearing for sheep, combined with the foxes – introduced to Australia by misguided Englishmen more than a hundred years before – had very probably disposed of most of the Arran wombats and koalas long ago.

One cold winter's night, while the wind howled and moaned

around the house and we sat around the table finishing dinner, there was an unfamiliar yowling sound outside the back door to the inside verandah.

We all stopped talking and sat still. 'What is it?' asked Philomena.

'I'll go and look,' volunteered Aidan. 'Maybe one of the cats is hurt.' He ran outside, leaving both back doors open.

Then a wild beast streaked into the kitchen, shrieking and snarling as it raced in frantic circles round our feet. We hastily leapt onto our chairs, flattening ourselves against the wall. Then the creature flew up onto the kitchen bench, knocking over pots and pans and making a leap to the sink, flinging itself at the kitchen window with a crash. We stood transfixed while it continued to hurl itself around the kitchen, screeching and yowling in panic. A plate and glass toppled to the kitchen floor and smashed. Finally, the animal realised that there was an open back door and out it tore, as rapidly as it had come.

We hastened to slam both doors behind it and stood quite still, aghast. For several seconds, no-one spoke. The whole event had probably only lasted half a minute, but it seemed a mighty long half-minute while it was happening. Then everyone started talking at once.

'Was it a bunyip?' asked Robert.

'No, a banshee,' said Aidan, who had sheltered behind the kitchen door but seen everything. 'It was screeching.'

'A tiger cat, a tiger cat!' we girls cried.

'No, no, it was probably just a wild cat, a feral cat,' said Dad, lifting a twin down from the table.

It took a while to sweep up the broken plate and glass and to calm us all down since we were so shaken, but my father said it probably solved the mystery of who was fathering Miranda's kittens.

We were not bothered too much by venomous red-back or funnel web spiders, as our place was too cold for them (although an occasional red-back hitched a ride from town in a load of timber), but sometimes a huntsman spider the size of a hand would scurry across our bedroom wall. We knew it was harmless and would eat the flies and other insects, so although it would alarm city visitors, we would leave it alone.

Our resident kookaburras kept the goannas and blue-tongue lizards lying low in the bush, their preferred habitat anyway, but in the summer there were always plenty of smaller lizards about, frilled-necks, jacky dragons and penny lizards, sunning themselves on the front steps or scuttling across the front verandah, keeping one step ahead of the cats and the kookaburras.

Chapter 15

Work, School And Play – A Child's Life

My teacher in second class was Miss Howard. Miss Howard seemed to take a genuine interest in me, and was very encouraging in her comments. This made me eager to please her, and I put extra effort into my small compositions. So taken with Miss Howard was I that when we visited Sydney that summer I talked my mother into taking a bus to Blackfriars so that we could visit her. Blackfriars Correspondence School was a rather forbidding but impressive blackened old Gothic building set back in a narrow street somewhere beyond Central Station. The visit was a bit late of course, because the following year I would have another teacher, no more Miss Howard, but it did mean that I could picture the building from which our OHMS lessons came and went. Miss Howard was very nice, and had reddish hair. She wasn't the glamorous young person I had imagined, but she may not have been all that old, either.

Katrina finally deigned to learn how to read and write, presumably so that she could read the labels on a can of sheep drench, and write up notes on merino breeding for Dad, but after that she became an exasperating student. For my own part, I had figured out that with luck it was possible to get through the week's lessons by the end of a long day on Tuesday, but certainly always by lunchtime on Wednesday.

We took to writing in the front of our notebooks. We wrote our name and then:

Arran

Walcha

NSW

Australia

Earth

The Solar System

The Universe.

There seemed nowhere to go after that.

Our education lay not just in the correspondence lessons. So that we could be a help to her, our mother was schooling us in needlework, darning, mending and ironing, as well as continuing with kitchen skills and laundry folding. I was eager to please, and quite proud to darn my father's socks for him. When he taught me to polish his boots, applying the polish with one side of the double-sided brush and brushing to the best shine I could manage with the other, he instructed, 'I want to be able to see my face in them.' But try as I might, this was something I could somehow never manage.

I revelled in the privilege of being allowed to use the pedal Singer sewing machine, and my mother let me make dolls' clothes on the machine for practice before she put me to basic mending.

And then I made a discovery: Arthur Mee's *Children's Encyclopaedia*. This ten-volume red-bound set with its gold lettering had been sitting on the bookshelves by the fireplace in the living room all this time without my really noticing it. But one day I opened a random volume, and whole new worlds revealed themselves to me. Again I began to spend precious spare moments creeping into the living room and curling up in my new position under the desk in there with a volume of Arthur Mee. As the hours ticked by I became more and more absorbed in the story of Pompeii, the building of the London Underground, or Horatius defending the bridge, and my mother's calls for me faded into the background. There was so much more to discover: the story of Queen Boadicea (as she was called then), Grace Darling saving shipwrecked passengers, stories of medieval pilgrims heading for Canterbury, Dr Livingstone finding Victoria Falls, the wonder of the giant California redwoods, the story of Elizabeth and Robert Browning and the sad story of children forced to work in the factories.

~

'You have six thousand acres to play in. Why do you have to build a cubby house right under my feet?'

My mother was right, of course. We did. And yet here we were, building a cubby house under the kitchen table, or along the walkway to the laundry. There were still plenty of chores, yet we somehow managed to find time to play. During the summer, when there were no lessons to clutter our day, and no more tasks to worry about until evening, we might be gone, out of sight of the house all day, and no-one would care or notice. Barefoot and ragged, we were free to roam where we might. And it was just us, our exclusive little band of five. Only occasional visitors from the outside, and only occasional forays into the world at large. Simply us.

So, mostly barefoot around the paddocks and into the bush we chased, leapfrogged, squabbled, pirouetted, and cartwheeled. We spun ourselves round until we fell down dizzy. We rolled downhill from the house until we reached the edge of the gully. We sat in the lower branches of the apple trees, signalling to each other in code. We wheeled around in the wheelbarrows meant for carting wood for the kitchen until we had to stop, gasping for breath. We played hide and seek in the scrub or around the house. We knew to stay away from our father when he was ringbarking or chopping down trees, as he didn't want us anywhere near his axe or chainsaw, but there was still plenty of bush to explore.

'I'm the king of the castle, and you're the dirty rascal!' cried the first one to reach the top of a boulder, for the paddocks around the house and the scrub uphill from the house were scattered with clusters of rocks and boulders. Rounded smooth by time and weather, each set of rocks was filled with its own special mystique for us, and there were specific games we played only there. For a while we favoured a small cluster of boulders in the corner of our front paddock, not far from a small grove of wattle and bottlebrush trees. There was a tall gumtree nearby for shade. At this corner, our boundary bordered with both Winterbourne and Millbank. We were playing cowboys and Indians there one day when Big Chief Sitting Bull, that is to say Aidan, pushed Hopalong Cassidy, that is to say Katrina, off his tribe's rock, hurting her arm. When we got her back to the house Mum decided it was probably just a sprain, and bound it up, but when Katrina was still fretting with the pain two days later, we all went to town and took her to the doctor. An X-ray at the hospital showed that she had a greenstick fracture, and so we brought her home with her arm in plaster.

This was how things usually went. It almost always was just a sprain, or a bruise, and would clear up in its own good time. We were not encouraged to feel sorry for ourselves and we were taught to soldier on, no matter how bad we felt. 'Don't make a mountain out of a molehill,' Dad would say, and 'The less you think about it, the sooner it will mend,' said Mum. We often had so many cuts and bruises that in summer, Mum had a regular evening clinic at the kitchen table before bedtime. Her arsenal was basic: iodine, Dettol, bandaids, Vicks VapoRub, gauze, calamine lotion and long rolls of elasticised bandage.

But there was another problem with that corner spot. Sometimes, when we were playing there, Old Eric Blake would suddenly appear on his horse, as though he'd been scouting us out. Then one day he showed up in his truck. 'Girlie! Yes, you!' he called to Philomena over the fence. 'I have sweeties. How about a ride in my truck?' We retreated home in alarm, and stopped playing in that corner.

Our fairy glen sat above the flat at the head of the gully. It was a small grassy clearing surrounded by tall white gums and with its own group of rounded boulders. In the summer it was cool and shady, and we were sure the fairies gathered there at night. We conjured up wishful scenarios from our story books and built cubby houses with eucalyptus and tea-tree branches, furnishing them with cracked teacups and hessian sacks and wooden boxes from the shed.

Hidden in the bush, further up the hill not far from the spring, sat a tall cluster of more dramatic rocks. These rocks had a slightly menacing aspect, and we only played there when we were feeling brave. There was a narrow fissure between them, and a steep fall on the downhill side. We played bushrangers there, someone pretending to be Captain Thunderbolt, others pretending to be passengers in a coach, his hold-up victims. Here it was Robert's turn to be injured. He returned from his trip to town with his leg in plaster. I felt guilty that I had allowed the boys to climb those higher rocks. But to my surprise I wasn't blamed.

Our greatest delight was to splash around in the small waterhole at the bottom of the gully. In summer rain we slid gleefully through the wet clay down the slope into the water, our clothes becoming stiff with clay and mud, but Mum was not amused. She made us rinse them out in the backyard under the tap fed by the uphill spring. This was such hard work that it finally gave me an inkling of the challenges my mother faced every day.

One day Philomena jumped into the water and cut her foot

on a piece of broken glass buried just under the surface. It was presumably there from before our time. The gash was very deep, and bled profusely. We got her up to the house and Dad, who had fortunately been working in the shed that day, drove as fast as he dared into Dr Dodd's surgery on Fitzroy Street; Dr Morgan had semi-retired. The blood had soaked through two towels, but the wound was stitched up. Philomena was given a tetanus injection and had an excuse to get out of her chores for a couple of weeks. Undeterred, we continued to frolic in the waterhole each summer, until the weather got too cold, and when it iced up in the winter, we dared each other to walk on the ice at the edge, to test its thickness.

As children will, we knew and loved every rock, every tree, every little clearing and every little sheep trail on the place. The rolling hills, the bush, the apple orchard, the little dam below the house, the wide arc of blue sky, these were our territory, our domain, our kingdom. Sometimes when there were visiting children we played a game of rudimentary cricket in the yard, under the plum tree, mostly using a tennis ball instead of the real thing. Once some visitors brought with them hula hoops, the latest craze in Sydney, and we spent hours trying to master the movements.

We looked forward to our birthdays for months, anticipating presents and a special dinner, and a One-Egg Sandwich cake with candles afterwards. Occasionally we had a small party, but not often; we were too remote for most people, and our amenities somewhat bare. Once, however, when we had a birthday party for Katrina, it was so cold a day that the entire group, maybe twelve in all, had to squeeze into the kitchen for Smith's Crisps and cordial, chocolate crackles and fairy bread – buttered white bread sprinkled with hundreds and thousands. We pushed the table against the wall, found some wooden boxes for extra chairs, and Dad orchestrated games of pass the parcel, musical chairs and pin the tail on the donkey. He drew the donkey himself.

There was great joy when Mr Grieve delivered a birthday invitation in the mail. We didn't receive many, because the host, in inviting one of us, would be saddled with all five, but we did go to two or three parties a year. We looked forward to these events, most especially to the sausage rolls, the cocktail frankfurts, lamingtons, jam tarts and other treats we did not get at home.

For my eighth birthday, I had received a book of games and crafts. One of the things you could make was a kite. I talked Dad into helping me make one from brown paper and saved-up pieces of string, spreading the frame out on the kitchen table as we cut and glued and taped. He took a morning off his weed spraying so that we could take it out to the cow paddock to fly it, running back and forth with the string and the kite trailing behind us. When a gust of wind finally caught the kite and it sailed up in the air, our elated hearts went with it. Up and down we ran in exhilaration until the kite took a sudden dive and crashed into the paddock.

Our birthday presents were always modest, but we lived in hope. For my ninth birthday I received a paperback atlas, which I needed for schoolwork, two new hair ribbons and a patterned drinking glass. That was all. It took a while to recover from my deep disappointment, and it was a lesson in moderating expectations.

~

After Easter, after the fruit and vegetable bottling, and before the winter proper set in, our kitchen table would be strewn with cardboard, glitter, scissors, crepe paper, paints and glue as the annual P & C Juvenile Ball at the Civic Theatre in town approached. The ball was fancy dress, and there were prizes for Best Nursery Rhyme, Best National Dress, Most Comical, Most Original, Prettiest and

Cheapest.

Mum pedalled away at the sewing machine, its foot rat-tatting away, making a fairy costume for Philomena from one of her old petticoats. 'I need wings, Mum, and a tiara. And where's my wand?' We made good use of our copy of *Alice's Adventures in Wonderland*, because I went as Alice more than once, in a costume handed down from Bunky Blomfield and a blue headband. The boys' first appearance, complete with large white paper collars and little bow ties, was as Tweedledum and Tweedledee. Katrina variously went as a Christmas cracker, a hula dancer and the Red Queen, and it was her costume that always seemed to require the most work.

The Civic Theatre would be cleared of its cinema seating, and Ken Hoy's Orchestra tuned up on stage. An adult at the microphone began to call out the steps for the dances, including the barn dance and the Gay Gordons. Round and round we twirled, emboldened by our costumes.

After the category parades, the judges watching from the stage with their notebooks, there was a small supper of sandwiches, cocktail frankfurts, sausage rolls and biscuits, washed down with lemon or orange cordial. But before we had eaten quite enough, the supper was cleared and the prizes announced. We were always disappointed if we didn't win anything but sometimes we did. Tweedledum and Tweedledee got an Honourable Mention.

Then the best part: the Hokey Pokey. 'You put your left leg in, you put your left leg out ...' Finally a conga line, with a lot of shrieking and silliness. One year during the conga some uncouth town boy pulled the fronds from Katrina's crepe paper Hawaiian grass skirt and left bits of her knickers exposed, which meant we had to go and sit down until Mum came to pick us up.

Empire Day, or, as it was more famously known, Cracker Night, always came on 24th May and every now and then it was at our place. We looked forward to this event for weeks, saving pennies to buy penny and twopenny bungers and collecting spare bits of wood and rubbish to burn on our bonfire. In the kitchen, my mother and I set to making sandwiches, lemon slice and Anzac biscuits.

As the sun began to go down people started to arrive: the Blomfields, Pas and Clennell Fenwicke with Anthony and Alistair, John and Barbie Fenwicke with Anne and Buster and their baby Thomas. We had built up a pyre in the orchard paddock, and now the fathers lit it and fanned the flames into a great blaze. We stood as close to the fire as we dared, warming ourselves in the winter chill. We had only bungers and Tom Thumbs and Catherine Wheels and some modest-sized rockets, plus a few Roman candles, but the rockets were the best, shooting into the sky and sending showers of coloured sparks into the dark night. The bungers, which simply made a loud bang, were only for throwing, and the Tom Thumbs were only good for their rat-a-tat sparks, but we loved them anyway. As the cold grew deeper we wrapped ourselves in blankets, the parents sharing tea from a thermos and passing around tins of biscuits. The only ones who didn't like Cracker Night were the dogs, who spent the evening cowering miserably in their kennels.

~

On Saturdays in town when there was no money for the pictures or the movie was considered too grown-up ('No, you can't see *From Here to Eternity* – it's not suitable') we played games with other children on the lawn at the Tennis Club: 'Here We Go Round the Mulberry Bush' or 'Ring a Ring a Rosy' or 'London Bridge' or 'Oranges and Lemons'. The irony of such very ancient English games and songs celebrating a London that even most of our parents had never seen, being played deep in the Australian bush would have been lost on us then, but they certainly indicate a marvellous kind of cultural tenacity.

Often there were skipping games. Some rhymes reflected prejudices of the time: 'My mother said, I never should … play with the gypsies in the wood. If I did, she would say, naughty girl to run away.' Others were old standbys: 'Jack be nimble, Jack be quick, Jack jumpover the candlestick …' Skipping games take a lot of practice, and I never really became competent at them, because they require a good deal of time in a school playground.

In the mid-50s there was a big Davy Crockett craze, and some people even had raccoon hats. Although nobody had television, we all knew the song. 'Davy, Davy Crockett, king of the wild frontier!' we sang, and 'See you later, alligator!' or 'The yellow rose of Texas.'

We had a few modest dolls, but we did not have very much in the way of toys other than those occasionally sent by Sydney relatives. Mum taught us to make rudimentary dolls using clothes pegs, cotton reels, pipe cleaners and scraps of cloth, but they never seemed to turn out the way we wanted them to, and a dressed-up clothes peg is no substitute for a bride doll, you can take it from me.

As time went by the twins began to spend hours making weapons – bows and arrows and slingshots – using eucalyptus branches, string and rubber bands. They sharpened the points of their arrows with the cheap penknives someone had given them for Christmas. We girls knew to stay out of the way and got very good at dodging. 'Someone's going to get their eye poked out if you're not careful,' warned our mother, but somehow this never happened.

We saved the knuckle bones from slaughtered sheep so that we could play jacks. You would toss up five in the air to see how many you could catch on the back of your hand, and then flip your hand over to toss and catch them in your palm.

But perhaps on a hot summer's day, with the cicadas thrilling down in the gully, we might not play at all, but simply lie on our backs and chew grass or blow dandelion clocks in the front yard, looking up at the broad blue sky. When we had Lucky she might come and lie down with us, rolling on her back in a patch of dust. We would watch the slowly moving clouds and amuse each other with the fantastical creatures their shifting shapes might suggest. Here's an Indian chief. There's an elephant. Oh, a seahorse! Over there – a castle!

Every day at lunchtime a single plane flew high overhead, its silver wings glinting in the sun, possibly on its way to Brisbane, but perhaps just to Armidale. None of us of course, except my father during the war, had ever flown anywhere, and I longed to be on that plane. Every day I dreamed that someday this plane would land in our front paddock and we could climb up a ladder and look around inside and then it would take off, high in the sky, carrying us on an enchanted journey to London, say, to see the changing guards at Buckingham Palace, or the Isle of Skye where Bonnie Prince Charlie fled, or the Colosseum in Rome where Christians were long ago thrown to the lions. Anywhere, somewhere that wasn't the middle of nowhere. My nose was pressed against the window that was the world, but I was shut off from it, and so very far away.

Chapter 16

Shifting Fortunes

It had been raining for days, and it seemed like weeks. We had wet, sloppy fun sloshing through the flat above the gully, which had turned into an ankle-deep marsh. Everything was green, as far as the eye could see through the mist of rain, but the sheep were soggy and unhappy, banding together in sorrowful little huddles.

At night, the sound of the frogs croaking in the gully competed with the sound of the rain battering our corrugated iron roof, and when the rain stopped for a moment, the frogs took up the slack.

A day or two before, on a frog egg-collecting trip into the gully, we had come upon one of our milk cows, Polly, lying down beside some wild rose bushes at the gully's edge with her feet in the air, her belly enormous and swollen. Dad said that she had died of bloat, from eating too much green grass after a dry spell. It was another setback for our parents. It meant we now had only Molly to supply us with our milk and butter; we couldn't afford to buy another cow.

The first red plums were out on the cherry plum tree and in my eagerness to bring some of them in to my mother for lunch I climbed the barbed wire fence that had been designed to keep Oskar away from the house and gashed my leg. There was a huge, gaping hole at the top of my calf. Dad was in for lunch and he and Mum inspected the wound with alarm; although it wasn't bleeding too much, they could see it needed stitches. In silence they walked to the sink to look out the window, hoping for a miracle.

But there was no miracle. Just a long silver streak at the bottom of the hill, the same streak that had been there earlier in the day, but higher now. Fed by its surrounding creeks and gullies, including ours, the Winterbourne Creek was up. More than just up – it was a raging torrent of water and there was no chance of getting to town. We knew to expect the creek to rise during heavy rain, but heavy falls upstream might send the creek rising even though the falls were light at our end. Occasionally we would come home from town and find the creek unfordable. Then we would have two options: to struggle over the footbridge and walk the half-mile uphill to the house, or backtrack to Pas and Clennell Fenwicke at Earsdon, where they would have to find beds for us all, tucking children in end to end, throwing cushions on the living room floor, and rushing in the pouring rain to put up camp beds in the leaky shed. 'I could sew it up myself,' offered Dad. I had not howled before, but I did now.

Mum staunched the blood, swabbed Dettol around the wound and bound up my leg with sticking plaster and bandages as best she could. 'She might have a scar there for the rest of her life,' she lamented.

She was right. The scar is still there, but it's quite faded now, and barely noticeable. The week of my gashed leg we learned from the radio that the rain had flooded the entire Hunter Valley, in some of the worst floods in Australian history. A few days later, the house paddock was full of mushroom circles. Mum took us out – me with my bandaged leg – with buckets to collect them, showing us how to tell the difference between poisonous toadstools and edible mushrooms. Then she sliced and cooked them up in the kitchen with some butter and parsley from the garden. None of the other children would eat them, but Katrina and I were willing to try, and declared them delicious.

Ranged along the kitchen bench under the window were the jars of frog spawn we'd collected from the gully, and we watched the little black globules grow into tadpoles and then little frogs. Then it was time to throw them back into the waterhole, and my leg was nearly mended.

The tanks were all full, and there was no risk of the uphill spring drying out – for the foreseeable future, at least.

~

One very hot day later that summer, when there was plenty of water in the creek, Mr Brien invited us to come down and swim in his billabong. This was a waterhole adjoining the creek, further west from the Winterbourne homestead. We had nothing to swim in but our underpants, but we packed a picnic lunch and blankets, and my father found some old inner tubes he had perhaps been saving for the purpose, and off we went in the Austin, bumping along an old sheep trail through the tall grass to the pool's edge. The waterhole, surrounded by rushes, was not that big, maybe twenty feet across, but it was quite deep. Mr Brien's truck was already there in the long grass, and so was Mr Brien, with his dogs and his carton of beer. Our parents began to unpack the tartan picnic rugs and sandwiches, telling us to wait for them before we went into the water.

But I couldn't. I tore off my clothes and charged in. Instead of the gradual deepening I had been expecting, all at once the stones gave way beneath my feet and I was in over my head. My feet struggled to find a footing, but there was none. I could see only water and weeds, and then a snake swimming by. There were snakes here? Not only was I going to drown, but I'd be bitten by a snake as well? I considered this for a second, but my predicament was too urgent. I couldn't breathe. My heart was racing. My arms flailed wildly above my head. Was I going to die? What would my mother say? Should I pray? Which would work best, an Our Father or a Hail Mary? I went for a direct approach.

'Dear God, please save me! I'll be good, I promise! I won't answer my mother back any more. I'll do all my chores on time, I promise!'

The hand that grabbed my wrist was not the hand of God, but of my father. He hauled me over his shoulder and carried me, coughing and spluttering, to shore. As he threw me on the rug he slapped me on the back, hard, and both he and my mother began to shout at me for not being more careful.

'What were you thinking? How could you do that? Where is your sense?'

'I saw a snake,' I gasped, shaking and shivering, trying to distract attention from myself. 'There are snakes in the water!'

'Oh,' said Mr Brien, waving his bottle of beer, 'those are eels. Plenty of eels in there.'

Despite the eels, over the summer we went to the billabong several times and it was there that my mother taught me and Katrina to swim, or at least to tread water and dog paddle, enough to stay afloat in an emergency. The others, deemed too young yet to learn, stayed in their rubber tyre tubes.

We were also allowed to swim, or at least cool off, in the creek near the Winterbourne house, where the water was clean and clear, and you could see the stones shimmering on the bottom. The creek was wide in places, but usually relatively shallow. It was safe. There were two big old willow trees set a little back from the creek just at the base of the hill, and these provided pleasant shade on hot days, although we sometimes shared the shade with some of Mr Brien's cattle.

The footbridge spanning the creek was rudimentary but impressive. Since it was intended as an emergency crossing for when the creek was flooded, it was perched quite high up, at least six or eight feet above the normal water level. We practised crossing it from time to time, just for fun. It felt like tightrope walking and we children worried that we might lose our footing and fall between the logs at any moment.

When we swam in the creek we sometimes also scampered up the steep hill beside it to play around the Old Stone House. It was there we occasionally found Mr Brien's secret stashes of beer and whisky hidden in the weeds in overgrown corners. And the occasional snake. Venomous red-bellied black snakes slithered quietly through all our springs and summers, an unwelcome surprise in the long grass or in our own woodpile, under a log or in a roll of fencing wire. They were easily chased away, although if my father were around he would kill it. We did not have deadly brown or tiger snakes; we were either too far east or too cold.

Any kind of snake was frightening, and with any luck promptly dispatched, with a large stick or preferably a shovel. But although we knew several people each year who had ended up at the hospital with snake bite, we never knew anyone to die from one.

There are very few photographs of our activities. Developing photographs was expensive, and we couldn't afford it. What little pictorial record of our childhoods does exist, therefore, is thanks to various visitors. The lack of photos might be just as well, because although my father occasionally went to the barber in Walcha, none of the rest of us had professional haircuts. My father would cut the boys' hair, and Katrina's, since she did not like long hair. Philomena and I had plaits. I was proud of my long hair and plaits. I daydreamed that I was Rapunzel in the fairy story. I was sure a handsome young prince would someday come along and say, 'Rapunzel, Rapunzel, let down your hair.'

The winter that followed that wet summer, like many of our winters, seemed endless. At night, we shivered under our several layers of scratchy grey army blankets, unable to get warm, even with a kitten or a hot water bottle, which seemed to go cold all too soon. We pulled the sheets and blankets right up over our heads and tried to warm the top part of the bed with our breath. The bedroom I shared with Katrina and Philomena had a fireplace, but Dad said it was not safe for three such little girls to have a fire in their room. The wind howled around the house, and Annie, Baxter and Bluey, chained up outside, howled too. In the mornings, the condensation on the inside of the windows was iced up, and we scratched drawings in it with our fingernails.

We rose in the dark, scrabbled for our clothes and ran into the kitchen to huddle by the fireplace. We shivered as we pulled on our clothes by whatever flickering heat the fire could throw off until it got going. There was almost always a frost blanketing the paddocks and fences in white. Sometimes it was gone by mid-morning, but sometimes it lingered in the shade almost all day. Many mornings my father came back from checking the thermometer down on the front fence to report that it was 20 or 22 degrees Fahrenheit (−6 Celsius). Sometimes on a cold sunny morning the five of us might sit on the front verandah in our dressing gowns and have a competition to see who could run barefoot in the frost the longest, our feet making footprints in the white grass. 'One elephant, two elephant, three elephant …' we shouted as the hapless competitor raced around in circles. The record was about twenty seconds.

In the kitchen we spooned down our warm porridge and huddled back around the fire to make our toast, spiking pieces of bread on makeshift toasting forks made from wire coat hangers.

By day we gathered in the kitchen with the logs crackling in the grate, I with my lessons at the table (and sometimes under it) while the smaller ones played underfoot. Those who went out on errands, to collect kindling or feed the chooks, came back with fingers frozen, and had to coax them painfully back to life by the fire. Washing left out overnight froze solid on the line. A frozen tea towel might snap into pieces in your hand.

Those were the days when our beans or corn for dinner came from jars in the pantry. And sometimes the pipes would freeze, so the running water from the uphill spring dried up, and we needed to cart water from the tanks for the day.

Huddled in the kitchen together on a bleak frosty day, my mother sometimes amused us with a poem as she sewed or ironed. 'Piping down the valleys wild,' she would start, or 'In Xanadu did Kubla Khan, a stately pleasure dome decree,' or 'Lars Porsena of Clusium, by the nine gods he swore …'

One morning we awoke to a strange stillness. The birds were silent, and there was just a faint bleat from some sheep in the distance. We scratched the ice off the windows to see that the paddocks were a blinding white, not with frost, but with snow. Snow! We were delirious with excitement. We dressed hurriedly – never mind the fire – and charged outside to throw snowballs, roll around and make snow angels.

After our porridge we rushed out again with our plastic buckets and spades to build a snowman. We gave him pebbles for eyes, a carrot for a nose, and an old hat and scarf from the rag bag. We named him Trevor. He stood proudly looking out over the gully until, around lunchtime, he began to droop, sadly dissolving into a small pile of mush, rags and carrot.

But by then we had found some old cardboard cartons, and squashed them to sled down to the flat. We got four or five trips in before the sun rose too high and the snow began to melt, and the cardboard went soggy.

~

I had long wanted piano lessons. There was no piano, and no teacher either, but when I was about seven or eight my father ordered a recorder and a little book of instructions by mail. The recorder seemed a poor substitute for a piano, and I was still struggling with 'Twinkle, Twinkle Little Star', when Philomena, only four or five at the time, picked up the instrument, experimented a little, and played the nursery rhyme by ear. You could sing her a tune, 'The Skye Boat Song', say, or 'Waltzing Matilda', and she would play it. Using a sheet across the back hallway as a curtain, we put on plays and entertainments, with Philomena providing the musical accompaniment.

The nights were long, and the only warm place was the kitchen. Sometimes after dinner our father organised a talent quest, in which Philomena played the recorder, Katrina might do a magic trick or attempt a barefoot Highland Fling on the black and white linoleum, I read a story or poem I had written, and the boys sang a duet.

Roaming in the gloaming, on the bonnie banks of Clyde
Roaming in the gloaming with a lassie by your side,
When the sun has gone to rest, that's the time that I like best,
And oh, it's lovely roaming in the gloaming.

One night as they neared the end, we heard the generator splutter and then the lights flickered and went out, as they often did, leaving us with just the light from the fire. Mum lit one of the hurricane lamps kept on top of the fridge. Dad, noticing the shadow this made, said, 'Here, watch this!' And by the flickering lamplight he began to make shadow rabbits, snakes, deer and other animals on the kitchen wall with his hands. We were enchanted.

Every now and then in the evening he pulled out his easel and his oils and worked on a painting, sometimes a scene from memory – a flower seller at Covent Garden, the view along the Thames Embankment – or sometimes a still life. He could do anything, we thought, and we worshipped him.

~

We waited for spring. Even the yellow wattle came out late that year, but a tentative spring arrived as shearing time came around, and the hustle and bustle of shearing seemed like a turning point. Then the cherry plum tree, followed by the apple trees in the orchard, came out in glorious white blossom and yes, it was really spring.

Our shearing that year was quite late – in October, after Winterbourne finished theirs. We were still using the Winterbourne shed, my father on the Old Grey Mare driving our little flocks down through the creek and up the hill again, with the dogs nipping at their heels. We had some quality bales to send to market and our parents were hopeful of a good price, although we still weren't sending enough.

A day or so after shearing, we had the most severe frost of the winter yet. Overnight the temperature on the thermometer nailed to the back gate went down to about 5 degrees Fahrenheit (−15 Celsius). The morning dawned crisp and blue with the paddocks carpeted in a blinding white. As Dad slapped the milk bucket on the kitchen bench he said, 'Looks like we lost a few last night. Eagles and crows everywhere.' And turning to me he said, 'Come on, get your coat on. We'd better go out and see the damage.'

Our breath made clouds in the sharp air. As we crunched through the hard white frost we could see the sad little bundles dotted around the paddocks. There was no bleating, no sound other than the crows cawing incessantly overhead. Ewes, lambs, wethers, their newly shorn bodies frozen stiff. 'Keep count,' said Dad. After we reached a hundred, he said, 'That's enough,' although we could see that there were plenty more, and we tramped through the frost back to the kitchen, to where the fire crackled in the grate.

Mum's face was ashen. She could tell from Dad's expression that the news was bad.

'I need a whisky,' he said. But we didn't have any.

'More than two hundred, I think,' I said, proud of my counting skills.

But it was much more than that. We had lost more than half our sheep, maybe three-quarters, in just one night. This was catastrophe on a massive scale. A pall hung over the house as we went about our day. My parents were in shock. Only the boys seemed not to understand, buzzing around the back verandah with their Matchbox cars and toy aeroplanes.

The next day was Saturday. The fire was raked back and we all got dressed up, clambered into the car and drove to town, where my mother could commiserate with Pas and Barbie Fenwicke at the annual flower show, and my father got extremely drunk at the Sports Club. This was a disaster beyond their imaginings. As reality set in they were both distraught, my mother on the verge of tears for days. Why had she allowed him to bring her here? How could all that work be for nothing?

When the news reached Grandma she came to visit. She took pity and offered a loan to get us back on our feet; and bought train tickets so that Mum could bring us to Sydney for Christmas.

We arrived home after Christmas to a big surprise: not only

had he painted the outside walls of the house, but our father had replaced the rickety front gate with a ramp, buttressed on either side by two imposing dry-stone pillars. A ramp meant we could drive in and out without stopping to open and close the gate. And we had most of a new front fence, with mesh wire stretched between smart white posts, which gave our little house a whole new aspect. Now it didn't look nearly as ramshackle. This was his apology, and his Christmas present to our mother.

Chapter 17

Our Own Woolshed At Last

The sound of whirring and sawing and hammering filled the air, echoing across the hillside to the house. As the final piece of our critical infrastructure, and using some of the loan from Grandma, we were to get our own shearing shed. My father was cutting the logs for the foundations, overhead beams and corner posts. The shed, which was to be built beside the new sheep yards, up beside the road to Cheyenne, would not only simplify and streamline many tasks for my father, but would signify our total independence from Winterbourne. Sheets of corrugated iron for the roof and sides and lengths of timber for the flooring were delivered from town. A sorting table, some machinery, sorting cubicles, a press, a small outhouse and we would be in business – self-sufficient, moving forward.

My father hired a handyman from town to come and help. At first this handyman slept in the daybed on our inside verandah, but as the shed took shape he camped on site with his swag, boiling his billy in the morning for breakfast. Other people came to help, a day here, a day there: Clennell Fenwicke, Mick Brien, Old Bill. Katrina was anxious to play an active part, and she engaged in daily battle with my mother as to which was more important, school work or real work.

Finally, it was finished. There were three shearing stands with chutes to the pens below, built in the hope that we might one day have enough sheep and money for three shearers at once. The new shearing plant, the machine that powered the mechanical shears, was installed and a test run decided upon. My father and Old Bill switched it on. There was a great rattling and shaking. The entire shed began to sway. Something was wrong. This was a disaster. Four letter words rang through the air, and we were shocked.

Old Bill, however, was unfazed. 'Looks like a job for Ray Borthwick,' he said.

Ray Borthwick was the district's self-appointed all-round engineering consultant, and distant cousin to Old Bill. Ray, who was not in fact an engineer but an autodidact miracle worker, was summoned over from Myamba. He came, and after a few days of head scratching, intense discussion and more sawing and hammering, he and Bill and my father had the whole thing stabilised. The shed never gave any more trouble, and now we children had yet another place to play.

Around this time my father began to wake me up to accompany him on his early morning milking. We went out into the cold morning at first light, almost as soon as Andre had begun to crow from his perch in the chook yard. Dad taught me to settle the cow at her bale, tie her outside back leg to the fence so that she wouldn't kick the bucket over, position the bucket and then to perch on the little three-legged stool. We greased her teats with Vaseline and massaged the udder, then teased the milk into the bucket with a, supposedly, dextrous movement of the wrists and fingers. Even after much practice, however, my little fingers could only produce about a third of a bucket of milk to Dad's whole bucket.

Nevertheless, after a couple of weeks my father left this task to me. I made the crunching trek in the morning frost up the hill to the cow yard, my breath clouding in the still air, the stars shining in the thin light of dawn. The only consolations were Molly's warm flank against my face, and the occasional cat or kitten prowling around in the hope of a squirt in his or her direction.

In the summer, as the sun began to rise and the mist to clear from the valley below, the twins would sometimes come up, too, hoping for a warm squirt themselves. After six or nine months of inadequate family milk supply, my father began to teach Katrina to milk the cow. She had bigger and stronger hands than I did, and somehow had a better feel for it. She became a much better milker than I could possibly be.

Our first shearing in our new shed was an adventure. My father hired Lionel, one of the regular Winterbourne shearers, and he himself was the other shearer. A wool-classer came out from town and Katrina and I were now old enough to be roustabouts. We helped pick off sheep in the holding pen, so that as soon as one was finished we had a new one ready. One of us had to be the tarboy, holding a can of warm tar and a brush with which to paint any nicks or scratches in the skin. There weren't many, and they were rarely serious. My father showed us how to throw a fleece onto the sorting table in one piece, although we were still too young to make much of a fist of this. In the evenings Lionel stayed at the house, sharing a room with Aidan and Robert, who were bundled into one bunk for the duration. He had breakfast and dinner with us and my mother brought smoko snacks and lunches up to the shed.

A little while after the shearing, Mr Grieve brought an airmail letter from our Scottish aunt Nessie in South Africa, announcing the birth of her second son, Alastair – a new cousin, and younger brother to Colin, but half a world away.

~

A letter came from the government decreeing that all children were to be vaccinated for polio, so my mother took us to the Oddfellows Hall, a crusty old building with peeling paint on the outskirts of town, where we joined a long line out the door to await our turn. As we got inside, and closer to the white-coated nurse with her needle, Philomena took fright. She started to cry, and when that didn't work, she began to scream. Then she threw herself on the bare wooden floor and banged her fists and kicked her feet. I wanted to pretend I didn't know her. The boys looked on in amazement, or perhaps it was scorn. None of this did Philomena any good; she got her jab anyway, but it probably hurt her much more than mine did me.

By now Katrina and I had many chores. Chopping, washing up, weeding, sweeping, hanging and bringing in washing, ironing, darning, carrying water from the tanks to the kitchen, shaking out and folding the kitchen table cloth after dinner, carting firewood in the wheelbarrow from the shed down to the house, keeping the stove fed. When we occasionally complained to Mum about what we saw as a heavy workload, she would remind us about the children in the north of England, a hundred years ago, who were forced to work as slaves in the English factories from sunup to sundown. She said that in her opinion we had plenty of free time, and that we were most fortunate not to be one of these children. Then, as she loved to do, she would quote a poem.

Do ye hear the children weeping, O my brothers,
Ere the sorrow comes with years?
They are leaning their young heads against their mothers –
And that cannot stop their tears.

My mother herself never stopped working, day and night, since there was so much to do and no labour-saving devices to help, but we thought that was just the way things were. And it never occurred to us that our mother might not want to be there, that she might in fact be working her fingers to the bone in service to my father's dream. At least she had the consolation of knowing that his hacking cough was gone, and his health restored.

~

Once a month the mail brought the *Ladies' Home Journal*, sent as a gift to my mother from Aunt Phil in Sydney, and I had begun to read it. The magazine came from America and it seemed to me both sophisticated and mysterious. Through the advertisements, I learned of the existence of miracle machines that would both wash and dry the dishes or dry one's laundry, as well as baffling items like Kleenex tissues, which apparently could replace cloth handkerchiefs. There were glamorous fashions – suits, hats, stiletto heels, gloves – at which my poor mother could only sigh, and articles on dieting, makeup and health. Dr Spock dispensed advice on child rearing. Even he was not opposed to corporal punishment, not then. Through the 'Can This Marriage Be Saved?' section I learned about divorce. Divorce may have been a subject for discussion in America, but it was not a concept we ourselves were familiar with. Catholics didn't get divorced, and people in Walcha didn't get divorced. Sometimes one half of a marriage moved out to live elsewhere, but mostly they just 'put up with it'. Every now and then *The Walcha News* would run an item on the front page such as WALCHA MAN SUES FOR DIVORCE, but it was never anyone we knew.

For Christmas every year Mr and Mrs Brien gave our parents a subscription to *Reader's Digest*. When each issue arrived, I headed straight for the 'Humor in Uniform' and 'Laughter is the Best Medicine' sections. I also loved 'It Pays to Increase Your Word

Power', which did indeed increase my vocabulary exponentially (thank you, *Reader's Digest*, for that word). It seemed I was the main reader of this little magazine, as my parents had limited time and other priorities. Eventually the pages of the *Reader's Digest* ended up on a spike in the dunny, to be used as toilet paper.

At some point I suffered a run of sore throats. My mother took me to Dr Dodd on Fitzroy Street. 'I think we might take out her tonsils,' he said.

'But,' I protested, 'the *Reader's Digest* says that ninety per cent of tonsillectomies are unnecessary. The article said they should only be thought of as a last resort.'

Dr Dodd stared at me in surprise and then he nodded. 'All right,' he said, 'let's wait.' Thus, I was allowed (unlike my sisters, who had both lost theirs, as was the fashion then) to keep my tonsils. I still have them.

In October, 1956, not long after shearing, and with one or two poddy lambs still in the kitchen, the radio brought news of the Hungarian revolution. Then, somehow mixed in with that, came the Suez Crisis. In the evenings, our parents huddled beside the radio, their faces creased in frowns. Hot on the heels of the British capitulation over Suez, Russian troops invaded Hungary. We heard alarming stories of shootings and people fleeing across the border, some hidden under bales of hay in the backs of trucks. These were the first big political events coming from the far outside world that I remember absorbing and wondering about. It began to occur to me that the big world might be a scary place.

We relied almost entirely on ABC radio for all our news, for weather reports, for school broadcasts, for the Children's Hour and for entertainment. Although the radio was rationed to certain times of the day, it was the one luxury my parents allowed. Every day at 1pm the familiar theme music of the long-running serial *Blue Hills* drifted over the countryside, over paddocks and wheat fields and market gardens. People stopped what they were doing to listen to the trials and tribulations of Ethel and Granny, Rose and Hilda, Jerry and Ed, inhabitants of the fictional town of Tanimbla. On weekend evenings our parents listened to the plays, *The Goon Show* or *My Word*. We also tuned in occasionally to the commercial station 2AD in Armidale, for more detailed regional weather reports and for the weekly hit parade. We sang along to 'Walking in the Rain' and 'Que sera, sera'. But my mother didn't like the commercial station, because of all the ads – Aeroplane Jelly, the Flick Man, Vegemite. We children loved to sing the jingles.

I was a devoted listener to the ABC school broadcasts. Katrina and I especially enjoyed the singing lessons, in which, apart from the English, Scots and Irish songs we had already learned, they would teach songs from other lands. We learned 'Alouette', and 'Sur le Pont d' Avignon', the 'Canadian Boat Song', 'Once Upon a Time in Arkansas' and 'Skip to My Lou'. We would sing these songs, along with recent pop songs from the radio, around the house and to Molly the cow in the mornings.

Although we knew that television had come to Sydney, we also knew we had no hope of getting it in Walcha, much less on Arran, any time soon. It had been introduced just in time for the Olympic Games, due to be held in Melbourne in the late spring of 1956.

As the Games began, we crowded around the radio to listen to the account of Ron Clarke lighting the torch, and to the events in which young Australians were competing. We cheered as Australia won medal after medal, especially in swimming, where Dawn Fraser, Lorraine Crapp, Jon Henricks and Murray Rose ruled the pool. In field events, Shirley Strickland and Betty Cuthbert were stars. I was in love with Betty Cuthbert. I wanted to *be* Betty Cuthbert. We were Olympics mad, and all five of us practised running back and forth in front of the house, setting up imaginary starting blocks and finishing lines. We did long jumps and hurdles, too, and my father, who had had some gymnastic training at the Greenock Academy, brought out one of the old wooden saw horses from the shed, on which he usually stored his saddle, to show us backflips and vaults and pommel horse moves. We looked on in awe, but Mum worried that he might break his back or his neck.

However, we did not let the Olympics distract us from Christmas. Christmas, of course, was for us the highlight of the year, the point of everything, what it was all *for*.

The first frisson of anticipation in the run-up to the great event was the arrival of the David Jones Christmas catalogue in October. Although we never ordered Christmas items from David Jones, we all loved to pore over its colourful pages, examining the pretty dresses and the toys and decorations and the Christmas hampers.

The Walcha shops started putting up their Christmas decorations in early November, and from then it really was countdown time. Lovett's, the store where for a time we bought most of our provisions, had a giant Christmas stocking, full of toys and games prominently displayed at the store entrance, and customers received a free ticket for every ten shillings they spent. When Lovett's began this promotion, we urged our parents to spend as much of their non-existent money as possible there, and hoped we didn't win the canteen of cutlery, the other prize on offer. But two or three years went by and we didn't win the stocking, so we resigned ourselves to not winning, although the hope still lay buried deep in our little hearts.

As November rolled around, and with it warmer weather and longer days, it was time to help Mum make the Christmas pudding. This had to be done at least six weeks before Christmas, and she had been collecting threepenny and sixpenny pieces for the purpose. We all gathered round to have a stir ('For good luck,' said Mum) before she wrapped it in cloth and put it to boil, for hours, on the stove. Afterwards it sat, still in its cloth and swathed in extra tea towels, on a plate in the cupboard to await the big day.

We pulled out last year's Christmas cards and cut out decorations and motifs from them to stick on stiff paper to make new cards. Mum sent these to her family, and we sent some to cousins and neighbours. Parcels arrived from our Scottish grandparents, almost always books. Since they came by sea mail, often well ahead of Christmas, Mum hid them in her bedroom, at the back of her wardrobe. By Christmas I had surreptitiously read at least half of the *Girls Own Annual* they usually sent to me. Mr Grieve also delivered the Christmas cake from Grandma, wrapped in brown paper and old newspaper inside its tin, plus a bulk-size tin of Sao biscuits, to be carefully stored until Christmas Day.

Each year, a week or so before Christmas, we made a special trip to Tamworth or Armidale for our shopping. The trip to Armidale took about two hours, on largely unsealed roads, the one to Tamworth a little longer, on better, although steeper, roads. We all had our Commonwealth Bank square tin moneyboxes and had been saving all year for this. Although we didn't get regular pocket money, we sometimes got a shilling or a two-shilling piece for our birthday or another occasion and our mother sometimes paid us to do chores over and above the usual. I might get a shilling for cleaning the silver, for doing extra mending or for collecting extra buckets of cow manure for the garden. Then there was tooth money. The tooth fairy usually left sixpence a tooth, and in our house, she was kept quite busy. Usually Katrina and I had managed to save close to ten shillings by Christmas, after the money spent on each other's birthday presents.

The trip meant an early start. No lingering over breakfast but straight into the clothes we had picked out the night before. For us girls, this trip meant a dress. Our second-best dress, because the best one was kept for birthday parties and Christmas Day. This year we were going to Armidale. From the showground, instead of turning left into town, we continued straight ahead along the partly unsealed road to Uralla, a small town on the edge of the New England Highway, and then up the highway to Armidale. Uralla was famous for having been the haunt and eventual burial place of the bushranger Captain Thunderbolt, but he had spent quite a bit of time around Walcha, too.

Each of us had our list, and for me, this is how it went: Mum, a bottle of shampoo or perhaps a box of chocolate-covered almonds, of which she was fond; Dad, a handkerchief in a box or a bar of his favourite dark chocolate; Katrina, a little china box or a pack of cards or perhaps a book with the lyrics of the latest pop songs; Philomena, a Little Golden Book or maybe some hair ribbons; the boys, easy, a Matchbox car each for their collection. Most of this could be accomplished in Woolworths, with a side trip to the chemist, but we loved wandering around the shops, coveting the toys so prominently on display. Bride dolls. Hula hoops. Elaborate kitchen sets. Electric trains.

Mum brought a picnic lunch of baked bean or tinned spaghetti sandwiches, accompanied by a big flagon of lemon squash, which we consumed in the park, surrounded by Christmas beetles, before heading back for some more shopping. Then, laden with our parcels, we bundled back into the car for the journey home. Our parents had mysterious packages that they stacked in or on top of the wardrobe in their bedroom until the appointed time.

Our mother encouraged us to make our own Christmas presents: potholders, dolls' clothes, an apron, hand-hemmed handkerchiefs, little pots fashioned from clay dug from the waterhole in the gully and dried in the oven, knitted scarves, a bag for clothes pegs, papier-mâché trinket boxes. The handcrafting went both ways: one Christmas my father built the boys a plywood garage and service station for their collection of Matchbox cars, complete with little wooden petrol pumps, just as he had made us girls an elaborate wooden doll's house with a door and windows on its hinged front.

The day before Christmas Eve, as the excitement mounted, Dad took us bouncing over the paddocks on the back of the truck to select a Christmas tree. We had plenty of pines growing about the place, some native, some perhaps not, so the question was, which tree to pick? Every year it was an agonising decision.

'That one, that one!'

'No, this one over here – this one's best!'

We set up the tree in a bucket of sand in the living room, in front of the fireplace. Out from the back of a cupboard came the decoration box, and we all squabbled over the hanging of such ornaments and strings of tinsel as we had. There weren't many, and they became more tattered as the years went by. My mother reminded us frequently that money didn't grow on trees. It didn't grow on the Christmas tree, either – no twinkling Christmas lights for us. Mum supplied us with a roll of cotton wool, and we broke off little balls to look like snow, and we made garlands with string and crepe paper. Then we made a cardboard star for the top, smothering it with glue and glitter. Somehow the previous year's star never seemed to make it to the following year.

The tree up, we gathered to help Dad pick out a chook for Christmas dinner, one that wasn't laying much any more. He lay the chicken's head on the wood-chopping block and chopped it off with the axe. Sometimes when he did this the chook continued to run around the yard with its head cut off, so we waited to see. After the deed was done he hung the chicken for an hour or two. Then he dipped it in hot and then cold water, plucked it and gutted it. He kept the smaller and softer feathers in a bag to make a pillow or eiderdown later. It took us many Christmases and Easters to amass enough feathers for an eiderdown, but eventually we did. It seems hard to imagine now, but Christmas and Easter were the only times we ever ate chicken. For us it was a treat to be savoured. Dad also gave us the feet so that we could amuse ourselves by pulling on the tendons and pretending to make them walk.

By Christmas Eve we were in a complete fever of excitement, shooing each other away as we wrapped presents – recycling last year's wrapping – making and decorating place cards for Christmas lunch, gathering flowers from our scrappy garden for the table. Mum took us into Midnight Mass in Walcha, possibly in the hope that we would sleep in the next morning, but it was a vain hope. We lay awake, whispering to each other, wondering if it was daylight yet.

At Andre's very first crow, about 4am, we began to wonder whether it was light yet. Agreeing that it was, we tip-toed onto the verandah and into the living room, where our presents were under the tree. But we had miscalculated the time.

'Get back to bed,' Dad growled from his bed. 'It's not light yet.'

'But Andre crowed! That means it's light,' we protested.

'Just because the bloody rooster crowed doesn't mean it's light. Look out there. I can still see stars. Get back to bed or it's a hiding.'

So, we crept back to bed for another sleepless hour.

Instead of stockings, each of us had a pillowcase. And once we were let loose there came a frenzy of unwrapping. A new T-shirt, books, socks, a yo-yo, games or a spinning top for the girls, Dinky toys or cap guns or Meccano for the boys. We looked for a bride doll, but it was not there. Nor did the boys get the train set they craved. When the excitement subsided, we gathered up any decent wrapping to fold and put away for next year and wound ribbon into balls to use again.

And then for what was really the high point of the day: Christmas lunch. The least our mother could do for us, she felt, was to make it an Occasion, with a capital O.

The stuffed chicken went in the oven to roast, with a big pan of potatoes and carrots on the shelf below. On top of the stove, the pudding steamed away in its calico cloth, further warming the already overheated kitchen.

At noon, we set the table. Out from the sideboard in the living room came the white damask tablecloth, which Mum and I spread with great ceremony over the kitchen table, smoothing the wrinkles and spreading some tinsel down its length. Then we put out the best Noritake china plates and the Community Plate silver cutlery – which a week or so ago I had earned some extra money for polishing – along with the best linen napkins and two crystal-cut wine glasses for our parents. We distributed the place cards we had made, argued about the seating, and put a Christmas cracker at each place.

Finally, dressed in our good clothes, we gathered round to watch keenly as Dad carved the chicken. We were anxious to ensure that it was meted out fairly, that nobody's portion was bigger than anyone else's. Mum served the roast vegetables, along with tinned asparagus (a treat) and beetroot (not a treat).

Dad drew out and popped the cork of a bottle of wine with great ceremony. This was the only time of the year our parents ever drank wine, since, like their friends, they generally drank beer or whisky.

Then squeals and happy cries as we pulled our Christmas crackers and put on our hats. When the main course was done, we read each other the jokes or riddles from the crackers. We thought these were hilariously funny.

'What's black and white and red all over?'

'What, what?'

'A newspaper!'

'Why is six afraid of seven?'

'Why, why?'

'Because seven ate nine!'

Again we watched closely as Mum divided the hot, delicious Christmas pudding carefully. There was much jostling over who got the most threepences and sixpences.

After a massive load of washing and drying up, for which we used many tea towels, we were hustled off to our bedrooms to take what Dad called a siesta. We had been up rather early, after all. And somehow, we did fall asleep.

The coins from the pudding went into our new Commonwealth Bank moneyboxes to start the big save for next year's Christmas, and maybe, at least in my case, have enough left over to put away in my bank passbook, too. Later we pierced a hole in the bottom of the asparagus and beetroot cans and linked them together with lengths of string which we pulled taut to make primitive telephones, a game that kept us going, on and off, until New Year's Day rolled around.

Chapter 18

A Mars Bar And A Satellite

New Year's Day, 1957, dawned blisteringly hot, unusual for Walcha. The flies were out in force, buzzing and beating at the screen doors. Mum was making sandwiches, all the bread slices lined up along the workbench on a large piece of greaseproof paper, ready to butter and fill with cold lamb and chutney. The New Year shortbread nestled in more greaseproof paper in its tin. Philomena, with an armful of early plums from our tree, was at the back door.

'Someone let me in, let me in,' she said, and as one of the twins opened the outside flyscreen door, a large blowfly buzzed into the kitchen and made a dive for the platter of lamb.

'Shoo, fly, shoo!' we shouted as we chased it around the kitchen with the swatter.

'Got him,' shouted Katrina.

Dad appeared at the door, wearing his kilt and sporran, as he did every New Year.

'Oh, you handsome devil you,' said Mum, looking up, and we all paused to admire him.

We were off to the river at Waterloo, for a picnic with both the Fenwicke families. A shimmer hung over the hills as we rattled along the road, Philomena's new Christmas water wings and various inner tubes at the ready.

The Fenwickes had already chosen a grassy spot on the river bank to lay out the tartan picnic rugs, the food and the thermoses of tea. My father produced a bottle of whisky that he was given for Christmas.

'Keeps off the flies,' he said. Everyone laughed.

'We could do with some rain,' murmured John Fenwicke. The other adults agreed.

After lunch, the adults lay about on the picnic rugs in a kind of torpor, waiting for a breeze, listening to a sporting event on a portable radio. We children splashed happily in the river. Every time one of us left the water to join the adults for a gulp of lemon squash, our back was covered in flies. Some summers, especially after spring rain, the flies buzzed and thronged around the cows, the dogs, the sheep and around us. Our backs were black with them.

Before we packed up to leave, John Fenwicke proposed a toast. 'Here's to a great 1957, ladies and gentlemen! Plenty of rain and higher wool prices.' They all raised their glasses, nodding in assent.

~

There was other excitement in the family that summer, as Mr Grieve had delivered a happy letter from our aunt Anne, the oldest of my mother's three younger sisters. She was engaged to be married. Her fiancé was a wheat farmer from Yerong Creek, near Wagga Wagga, and his name was Bruce Gorman; everyone said he was a 'catch'. The wedding was set for March, and our parents began preparations to go to Sydney for the big event. My father got out his oils and painted and framed a still life for their wedding present. I carefully hand-stitched kitchen potholders for my own wedding present to them, and begged to be allowed to go to Sydney too, but no.

To take care of us in their absence, our parents engaged the services of Mrs Goodwin, who lived on a property called Allandale, which was on our route to town. We had never been to the Allandale homestead, but its green corrugated iron roof, set back from the road and surrounded by trees like ours, was a familiar landmark to us. Our new minder was to sleep in the day bed on the back verandah while she stayed with us.

Mrs Goodwin, who seemed rather old to us but very likely wasn't, told us to call her Goody. This may have been a mistake. The over-familiarity went to our heads somewhat, and we did not behave well. We were cheeky. We didn't make our beds. We left messes of clothes and toys everywhere and disregarded her pleas to clean them up. I sat high up in the plum tree reading *Little Women* and then *Little Men* most of the day, barely lifting a finger to help her, as I was supposed to do. One day the others climbed onto the roof and sat up there, something they would never dare to do when our parents were home, and ignored Goody's supplications to come down. But she knew they would come down when they got hungry, and they did. As it turned out, she was a kind and good-natured woman, and didn't punish us, even though we deserved it. She didn't even tell our parents how naughty we had been. But she never offered to look after us again either.

On their return our parents were full of the news that Anne and Bruce were planning to leave on the grand ocean liner called the *Southern Cross* for a six-month tour of Europe. Bruce had been saving for such a trip for years, and Anne was the lucky bride.

'They're going everywhere,' my mother sighed. 'England, Scotland, Ireland, France, Switzerland, Italy, Spain, Holland – just everywhere.' She herself had never been anywhere.

I was in awe. I took myself to the Arthur Mee encyclopaedia to read about the places they planned to visit. I knew about many of them not just from my lessons, but from my reading. The PL Travers *Mary Poppins* books, among many others, made me want to go to London, and the *Heidi* books by Johanna Spyri made me long to see the Swiss Alps. I wanted to see Vesuvius, Pompeii and Horatio's bridge in Rome.

Our parents had also brought back from the wedding pieces of the wedding cake, fruit cake with marzipan and fondant icing, in little tins that tradition dictated we put under our pillows to dream of whom we were going to marry. Katrina was going to marry Rob Blomfield, I was going to marry Peter, or perhaps Prince Charles, and Philomena was going to marry Prince Charming.

My mother also brought back for me a copy of Charles and Mary Lamb's *Tales from Shakespeare*. So now I learned the full stories of Desdemona and Othello, of Miranda, of Portia, and of Cassius.

Mum and Dad had only been back a week or so when a large trailer came to town and parked itself in Derby Street. By government edict, every member of the adult population of the district was to be tested for TB. Town that Saturday morning was as crowded as we had ever seen it. People jostled for parking spots. The pubs were overflowing. We waited outside the interesting van as our parents stood in line, chatting to friends and acquaintances from the district. Over a thousand people were X-rayed, and, it was later reported, two cases of TB and several other conditions were caught. It wasn't anyone we knew, fortunately.

Up until now we had been just managing to keep afloat with decent rainfall, loans from the bank and relatively adequate wool prices, even though our flock of sheep was still small, and the big freeze disaster of 1955 had been a major setback. In 1956 the railway station at Walcha Road shipped 20,563 bales of wool to market, though I'm guessing less than a dozen of them were ours. There had been complications over the purchase of the property, partly because of the terrible mess our Uncle Jack had made of things, but this had finally been sorted out; we were now the rightful owners, and by 1957 had set up the basic infrastructure – fences, yards, woolshed. We were getting a feel for the sheep business and despite falling wool and cattle prices, we were looking to the future.

It had rained a little in the spring, and then a few drops in January, but by the end of February, my father began to fret. Summer was our rainy season, and very little had come.

'Oh, don't be like Hanrahan,' said my mother, trying to jostle him out of his anxiety with one of her poems. 'We're not rooned yet.' Hanrahan the doomsayer was a creation of the bush poet John O'Brien, and my mother had grown up with his verses.

'If we don't get three inches, man,
Or four to break this drought,
We'll all be rooned,' said Hanrahan,
'Before the year is out.'

Yet she, too, was worried. When April rolled around and then May with not a drop more, anxiety began to turn to alarm. We were always conscious of the need to conserve water, but this time the lack of rain was becoming frightening. In June, there was some rain in some parts of Walcha, but it didn't come east so we didn't get any. We constantly watched the sky for clouds. Sometimes great banks of cumulus cloud collected behind Trig Hill, bringing hope but not rain. Every night we went to bed anxiously straining for the sound of drops on the roof. But they didn't come. Sometimes there were a few stray drips, but only enough to taunt us.

If you are a farmer or a grazier, water colours your every waking moment. And when rain doesn't come, there's a waiting game. Every morning as you watch your grass wither away and your sheep and cattle get thinner, you search the sky for clouds, examining each one that comes for a sign. Every day the family listens anxiously to the weather forecast on the radio. They scan the newspapers for more long-range predictions. They watch the anthills, birds and animals for signs. If they are religious, they pray. If not, they just worry.

In a drought, nobody can make plans. They don't know what their income is going to be, so they can't make improvements to the property, buy equipment or plant pasture. Will they have to borrow yet more money to pay for lucerne and hay to feed their stock? How will they pay the school fees? How long can they hold out before they must sell their animals (at rock-bottom prices in times of drought) and yet keep enough, emaciated and hungry, for future breeding? Or worse still, walk off their place and look for work in Armidale, Tamworth or even Sydney?

It's during drought times that you hear stories of farmers committing suicide, of families walking off their place, of people killed in vehicle accidents that should not have happened.

But for most, daily life must go on, whether you have green grass or no, water or no.

Our aunt Carmel came to stay to help my mother out for a little while. Carmel and my mother were very close, because my mother, almost twelve when Carmel was born, had stood in as her mother. Carmel loved a project. She brought with her on the train a large wooden box of Seville oranges, and she and my mother busied themselves making marmalade, a scheme that very much pleased my father. It was a welcome novelty to have something to put on our toast other than Vegemite or plum or blackberry jam.

We loved having Carmel with us. She was relaxed and indulgent, not strict and proper like Aunt Phil, and she was a good sport, willing to play and explore the bush with us. We showed her all the special trees and boulder clusters, the gullies, clearings and secret tracks through the bush that we knew so well and that we all loved so much. Better still, Carmel could do cartwheels. She showed us how to do them in the front yard, and it was fun trying until we started collecting bindis, a product of the dry weather, in our hands.

With a twin on her lap, Carmel squeezed into the car with us as we bumped into town and went to the football or the Tennis Club, and as she was young, charming and pretty, there were several young bachelors in the district who gave her more than a passing glance. It was the family's duty to find her a husband, and my parents were expected to assist.

~

Some of my father's friends had been talking about a polocrosse club. My father had learned to play polo with my mother's brothers in the early days of their marriage, and polocrosse, which is a cross between polo and lacrosse, is quite similar: two teams try to scoop a ball in a netted stick from the back of a horse and score a goal at the correct end of the field. When polocrosse was mooted in Walcha, my father was keen to participate. They needed twelve players, six to each side, and that May they managed to pull enough people together to make up the two sides.

In due course we began to go to Emu Creek on Sundays, or occasionally other properties, to watch my father play polocrosse. Other players included Clennell Fenwicke and Bob Gill, as well as Walcha's most handsome bachelor, Peter Nivison. In a rather complicated arrangement, Peter Nivison would pick up my father and the Old Grey Mare in his horse trailer at the Blue Mountains turnoff, and the rest of the family would proceed by car to Emu

Creek.

It was a fast game, requiring superior riding skills and a good horse, and it must be said that the Old Grey Mare acquitted herself very well, having had no previous experience at this sort of thing. Part of the idea was to have picnics, and sometimes we did, but the weather was usually so frigid that we squashed into someone's car, or another family squashed into ours, to eat our lunches in that steamed-up atmosphere, out of the wind and biting cold. The polocrosse period, for us, only lasted a couple of seasons – the effort became too much. But the club itself continued for years and went on to win the state championships.

~

One night I complained to my mother about an ache in my side. The next day it was worse, and when my mother touched the sore area I jumped with the pain. Suspecting appendicitis, she rang Dr Morgan, who was still practising part-time as a surgeon. Dr Morgan told her to bring me in immediately. After two minutes in his surgery he confirmed her suspicions and ordered us to meet him at the hospital. I was wheeled into the little operating theatre, and he removed my appendix within the hour.

'It was just as well you rang me when you did,' said Dr Morgan later. 'Had you waited another day it would have ruptured, and she might have died.'

That was the start of one of the most pleasurable adventures of my life so far. First, my mother asked Mrs Brazel at the library to put together some books for me. Propped up in bed in a bright and airy room, I was allowed to read all day for the whole time the hospital staff kept me in bed, which is what they did with surgery patients then. I gobbled down *Five Children and It* by E Nesbit, two *Pollyanna* books, *What Katy Did* by Susan Coolidge, and *The Children of Green Knowe* by LM Boston.

Word had got around the district and people came up to visit me. Pas Fenwicke came with advice about not too much running and jumping when I got home, and a copy of Enid Blyton's *Five on a Treasure Island*, which I devoured within hours. From then on, the Secret Seven were out – it was the Famous Five all the way. Barbie Fenwicke brought copies of *Biggles Learns to Fly* and *Biggles in Africa*, by WE Johns, battered relics from her husband John's own childhood. These, too, found an eager reader.

Then Mrs Bloo came and gave me my very own bar of chocolate. I had never had a bar of chocolate to myself before. I planned to give it to my father, who loved chocolate every bit as much as I did. What a nice surprise he would get when I gave it to him, I thought, but when I checked my little bedside locker just hours after I had put it there, it was gone. I was not allowed out of bed yet, so I begged the nurses to look for it. No, no sign of it. Could they ask around the hospital? No, no-one had seen it. To this day it remains one of the great mysteries. Did Matron think it wouldn't be good for me? Or did someone just take it?

The little cottage hospital on the hill had only about a dozen beds, and I was the youngest patient there, so I spent the week being fussed over and spoiled. The nurses in their starched uniforms and caps were cheerful and efficient and I loved them all, even Matron, a formidable figure who was very strict and whose every word was law. I told my mother I wanted to be a nurse when I grew up. 'Why just a nurse? Why not be a doctor?' she said. This was a surprise. I had not even known that women could be doctors. Well, if I couldn't be Betty Cuthbert, perhaps I could be a doctor.

After a few days, two of the nurses came to my bed, and, each taking an arm, lifted me carefully to the floor. I could barely stand.

My legs wobbled. What was this? But in an hour or so my legs had steadied and I was myself again, able to wander round, ask again about the missing chocolate bar, make friends with the other patients (all five or six of them) and staff, and make a special friend of the man who ran the accounts in the office. To make up for the missing chocolate he gave me a Mars Bar, a mystery to me – certainly I had never tasted one – and most pleased, I announced that I would give it to my father. 'No,' he said, 'Go on, eat it yourself.'

I did as I was told. As I sank my teeth into its chocolatey, caramelly deliciousness, eking it out a little at a time, it seemed to me that an exquisite pleasure invaded my senses, and that life could not get any better. Then came a just a little twinge of guilt: what would my mother, so strict about sweets, have said? And what about sharing it with my brothers and sisters? It was many years before I was to taste a Mars Bar again, but I believe the guilt was worth it.

This was in the days before Medicare. Even though they had health insurance, my week's stay in the hospital probably didn't do much to shore up my parent's finances, and with the drought getting worse, things were getting tighter. By now there was not enough feed in the paddocks for the sheep and cattle, and my father had to face the possibility of expensive hand-feeding until some rain should come. And it was not coming. Every day now, several times a day, we would tap the rings on the water tanks to see how much water was left. The tanks were getting lower and lower. And we had to eke out our drinking and cooking water bit by bit. Some evenings we sat on the verandah and watched the sky behind the hills flare up with lightning and hear the roll of distant thunder, but still no rain came our way.

And then the spring up the hill began to run dry. This was a disaster. We now had no water for washing and bathing, unless we used the drinking and cooking water in the tanks. But the tanks, too, were getting low. Mum took to standing us in the bath and sponging us down one by one using the same half-bucket of water. We went from brushing our teeth twice a day to once, using a mug, not running water. We left the sheets and towels an extra week before consigning them to the laundry. We wore our T-shirts one or two extra days. Some of the grey water from the washing went on the garden, but what the garden liked better was the water drained from cooked vegetables, so long as it wasn't too salty, and my mother saved it in a bucket. Our carefully cultivated flower beds down by the front ramp withered away.

It was a waiting game. Still we scanned the heavens for clouds, and still they mocked us. Sometimes a brief shower would blow our way and go as quickly as it came. In the meantime, my father finally had to borrow more from the bank for the purchase of bales of hay and lucerne to feed the stock, and even as he did so the price went up. Every afternoon towards sundown they would gather, the sheep and our small herd of cattle, around the shed, bleating and mooing while my father tossed down the fodder from the loft.

During all this, John Fenwicke fulfilled his Biggles fantasy and got his pilot's licence. Aerial spraying of superphosphate had been pioneered in the district several years before, and possibly Mr Fenwicke thought to supplement his income by aerial fertilising, although he did not own a plane. Mr Blake on Millbank had built a small landing strip, and we all went to watch John Fenwicke land a little Tiger Moth there and then take off again. To see this little plane up close was a dream come true. To fly in an aeroplane was the most intoxicating thing we children could think of.

There was no point in aerial spraying fertiliser over the paddocks if there was no rain, but now there was talk of seeding the clouds that hung around and taunted us to try to make them rain. Mick

Brien hired a plane to do exactly that. We watched as it flew back and forth in the unproductive clouds that hung over Winterbourne, Mr Brien on the ground yelling, 'Send it down, Hughie!' but it proved just as futile as our bedtime prayers to the Holy Infant of Prague, St Jude and whatever other saints might listen. None did.

Perhaps we really would be 'rooned'. The drought was the only thing anyone in the district could talk about. Well, almost the only thing. People were still excited that Peter Fenwicke had been selected to the Australian national rugby union team as a Wallaby. Walcha was also doing its bit for Hungary, by employing a Hungarian refugee as a farmhand. McRae's, Walcha's biggest general store, had joined the modern world and gone self-service. Instead of being served at a counter you could now wander the aisles to pick out packets of biscuits or cereal for yourself. This was an unheard-of development and it caused wonder and shaking of heads.

Several of our pine trees began to wilt, their usually green needles browning and falling in the gutters of the house, their trunks beginning to blacken. This seemed like an ominous sign.

Shearing came around, but without the usual bustle and excitement. The drought had cast a pall over every activity. The lack of water meant we had had to sell some of our sheep, and our clip was therefore depleted. In addition to this, the sheep that remained were not in top condition, and there were worries about the quality of the wool. This was only the second time we had used our own shed for shearing, and once again, we had only one shearer besides Dad – Lionel, who stayed with us in the house. Still, shearing is vigorous work, and shearers expect hot breakfasts and plenty of food, so we had the smell of bacon and eggs to torment us in the mornings and in addition to our roustabout duties, some extra baking and cooking to occupy our time.

And we waited. My father shook his fist at the Holy Infant, inscrutable on the kitchen mantelpiece, but to no avail.

After shearing we had to send all our cattle to graze at a place on the other side of Walcha, out past Nowendoc, which had had a little rain and still had some pasture. My father had to buy increasingly expensive bales of fodder for the sheep, and pile it up in the loft of the new shed. Things got so bad that when we went to town, our parents would duck around a corner if they saw the bank manager coming, and they were probably not the only ones.

One night my mother announced that we were going to say the Rosary after dinner – we were going to pray for rain, properly this time. Since we usually only said the Rosary when Grandma came, we were surprised. But after the washing up we all knelt down beside our chairs around the table, my father, too, and my mother began with Our Father, then ten Hail Marys, then Glory Be, and then all over again, five times.

'Daddy,' I said afterwards, when at last it was finished, 'you said the Rosary!'

'Listen,' he said, 'it made your mother happy, and we need rain. I'll try whatever works.' For him, this was very likely an admission of weakness, and certainly one of helplessness. He glanced again at the Infant of Prague on the mantelpiece and sighed.

As summer approached, Mum decided we should wear sandals or shoes all the time, not just when we had visitors, because there was not enough water to wash our dirty feet every day. By now the level of water in the tanks had become so low that my father had to take the truck to town to buy a small tank, which he filled up with water from Winterbourne Creek on his way home, siphoning the water into one of the house tanks. He left the new tank on the back of the truck in case he needed to do it again, and he did, two or three times more before the drought finally broke. But that meant we needed to boil all the water for drinking and cooking, because the creek water couldn't be trusted.

We had to drive our washing down the hill and wash it in the creek, too. This was hard work, and with the creek water being low, it was impossible to get things really clean, although the expedition had the added advantage of washing us while we were at it. We helped Mum beat the dirt out of towels and dungarees on the rocks at the edge of the creek and pack the wet loads in the car to bring back to hang on our line, but for us it was just a novelty, another adventure.

A little bit of rain fell, but just enough to put a few rungs in the tank and not enough to give us sufficient green grass to feed our cattle. The gods were mocking us.

~

We had heard on the radio that the Russians had launched a satellite into space, and that it was visible from earth. Our place, high on a hill, afforded a good view of the night sky, so our parents had invited friends for a Sputnik viewing party.

We lay on picnic rugs in our front yard, looking up at the night sky. Both Fenwicke families were there, and the Briens and the Cheyenne Blomfields. We had a small kerosene lamp to see by, so that we could locate our mugs of tea or cocoa and pass around the biscuit tin. The men filled glasses from the bottle of whisky Mr Brien had brought. We knew something of the night sky: Venus, the evening star, the Southern Cross, the Big Dipper and Orion's Belt. The Milky Way was clearly visible, but not as bright as on a crisp winter night.

Someone looked at their watch, and it was time, and we all strained to look. Where is it? No, not that, that's a shooting star.

'Look,' said Pas Fenwicke, pointing north, 'I see it. There it is!'

And yes, there, there, see there, there it went, blinking across the sky like a little star in its own right, moving slowly in a southerly direction, *blink, blink, blink*. Sputnik. Man's first object in space.

For many minutes we lay there, watching it on its journey across the sky, not speaking in our wonder. Then we children watched while the adults discussed the meaning of it all and how perturbing it was that the Russians were first, and whether America would be soon to follow.

Chapter 19

Fire, Smoke And Dust

It's hard to say what alerted us first: maybe the insistent ringing of various combinations on the party line, maybe the smoky haze over the hill or maybe even the distant whiff of burning eucalyptus. But the fire that had been burning down in the far eastern reaches of the gorge for some weeks now seemed to be moving in our direction. It had not rained since January and the dry conditions were perfect for a bushfire

When the alarm came, my father saddled up the Old Grey Mare, met Buddy Blomfield on his horse at the Cheyenne boundary and together they went to inspect the fire, because there was no road through the thick bush. What they saw startled them. When they came back they were immediately on the phone to town, and to the Briens and Fenwickes and Thorolds and Karori Blomfields.

Everyone knew what was at stake. Eucalyptus, with its heavy oil content, is highly combustible, and a fire in a eucalyptus forest is both fierce and terrifying. It can spread a kilometre in just minutes. Flames rise hundreds of feet into the air and spread quickly from tree to tree. Often in dry weather a tree will simply explode, like a firebomb. Red hot ash is borne by winds to ignite more fires nearby. The resulting conflagration can be devastating.

Within hours Arran was invaded. Trucks and cars bumped up the dusty track to our front yard and a circle of men, members of Walcha's volunteer firefighting brigade, unloaded axes, mattocks and shovels and held earnest discussions on our verandah. Someone brought a huge pile of large hessian bags that they had soaked in Winterbourne Creek. Off the men drove in convoy towards the Cheyenne border. As word spread, more and more people came to help.

There were winds coming up, and by the end of the day it was clear that the fire was gaining momentum, and the entire district was on the alert. In the critically dry conditions they knew it was only a matter of time before the fires roared out of control to engulf the properties surrounding the gorge and perhaps spread further. Of the several properties that were in immediate danger, our place, the Blomfields at Cheyenne, the Thorolds at Table Top and properties owned by John Campbell, one of the Borthwicks, and a Mr Monie, whom we did not know, were the most threatened.

Most of the first party of men fought the fires through the night, but more help was needed. By the next day a bulldozer had arrived, and more convoys of men. Our yard was full of dusty cars, as the men packed together on trucks and utes full of shovels, rakes, mattocks and water canteens to head towards Cheyenne.

The smoke hung heavily over the hills and the smell of it began to fill our nostrils, even back at the house, so our mother drove Philomena and the boys over to Pas Fenwicke at Earsdon. She put Katrina and me to work in the kitchen, which was soon full of women. Barbie Fenwicke arrived from town with a carton of loaves of bread, butter and big logs of Devon sausage, and we spent the morning making sandwiches and filling thermoses and water canteens, although we had little water to spare. We stoked the stove and made scones and biscuits to add to the ones Mrs Brien and Tony Blomfield had brought, and made up meal packets, which we packed in boxes. The women took turns to drive out to the

Cheyenne mailbox several times a day, where they dropped the boxes for the firefighters to pick up, and collected the empty tins, thermoses and boxes that had been left there.

As the sun came up on the third morning, my mother and I arrived at the Cheyenne boundary to deliver breakfast and found a group of men asleep in sleeping bags around an extinguished campfire under a large gum tree. Their faces and arms were black, and the whites of their eyes, when they opened them, bloodshot. But there was to be no rest; they gulped down the tea we had brought, gratefully bolted their sandwiches and piled into the back of a waiting ute to head back to the fire.

Without adequate firefighting equipment, the men had to make do with what they could. Apart from the wet hessian sacks used to beat back the flames, they had low-tech backpack contraptions that sprayed water onto the flames. The water came from Winterbourne Creek, so there were trips back and forth to refill the packs. Another tactic was to clear stretches of tall trees (thus the axes and mattocks) and bulldoze the debris to make a firebreak. They would also sweep swathes of other combustibles – wood, logs and undergrowth – towards the fire and burn controlled firebreaks to try to stop its progress.

In a few days, modern technology arrived in the form of a small plane, which flew over the vulnerable areas and was able to relay back which way the fires were heading, and where new outbreaks might have sprung up. We watched it fly past our house in the morning and back at night.

Everything in the house, lessons, gardening, washing, cleaning, was put on hold while we continued to organise food, water and supplies for the firefighters, and stood on the verandah trying to tell what was going on from the direction of the smoke. A pall hung over everything and the smell of smoke pervaded the house.

We prayed again for some rain to come, but there was no sign of it.

This state of dire emergency lasted for almost two weeks. Gradually, however, the flames came under control, and the men began to return to their homes. A small group of volunteer firefighters was rostered to stay and monitor the area for flare ups, and in late November, fires were still smouldering deep in the gorge, so nerves remained on edge for weeks afterwards, and indeed until the next rains came.

Altogether, over 140 men had taken part and we were grateful to them, none more so than Buddy and Pat Blomfield, whose homestead, perched on the edge of the gorge as it was, had been so closely threatened. Part of our land was burned but we had not lost any stock. Part of Table Top burned as well.

Philomena and the boys returned home at last, but they had their own story to tell. They had been playing in the yard at Earsdon when a strange man had ridden up to the house on an old brown horse, sending the Earsdon dogs into a frenzy of barking. He had a long beard, they said, right down to his waist, and his hair was tied up in a ponytail under his broad-brimmed hat. His stockwhip and several guns were slung over both his shoulder and his saddle, and four dusty, skinny dogs straggled behind him. He had raised his hat to Pas Fenwicke.

'Ma'am, can you perhaps spare some bread?'

But then he looked at all the children, by now standing in a goggle-eyed row beside Pas.

'On second thoughts, ma'am, I guess you've got enough on your plate,' he said. As an apparent afterthought he added, 'Not much to do around here, is there?' He turned around and rode off, the dogs trailing behind.

'We saw one of the Brennans from the gorge!' our little ones boasted in excitement when they arrived home, and so it must have been.

The cats were hungry. Their normal food sources, birds and rabbits, were disappearing. The birds had flown to more hospitable climes, and the rabbits had stopped breeding. But this did not stop Miranda from giving birth to a new litter of kittens, and as usual, my father took all but one to drown in the dam, despite Aidan's continuing protests. The kitten we kept, a pretty little marmalade creature whom we called Ginger, was naughty. As soon as she was big enough, she began to jump up on the kitchen table during breakfast and head straight for the milk jug. Day after day she would be shooed off, but she was persistent – up she would jump again. After dinner she would leap up by the sink and steal the leftovers from people's plates, leftovers intended for the dogs and chooks.

My father said to us, 'If you can't control that kitten, one day I'm going to take it out and shoot it.'

'Oh, don't be silly, Bob. Don't make threats you aren't prepared to carry out,' my mother said. To us, she said, 'Keep Ginger off the table or there'll be trouble.'

We knew it was coming. The only question was when. The radio had warned us it was heading our way, and we got busy trying to seal up windows and doors with rags and tape, bringing the dogs and cats inside the house, locking up the chooks, and protecting parts of the vegetable garden with old sheets weighed down with stones.

Then, there it was: we could see it. We watched from the verandah as the giant cloud of red dust rolled over the Blue Mountain hills towards us like an ocean wave. Then it rolled over Winterbourne and towards our boundary fence, and Mum hustled us inside. We could do nothing but wait until it passed. Mum felt we were safer in the living room, and we gathered there around the windows to watch as the house began to shake with the storm. We could see nothing outside but a blanket of swirling ochre. It seemed to go for an age, but perhaps it was only half an hour before the worst of it swept southwards.

Afterwards, a thick pall of red dust hung in the air for hours, and it was a full day before it began to settle. Worse than that was what it did inside the house. Despite our preparations, the dust had managed to seep into every corner. Each surface we touched had a fine layer of red. It even got into the sheets on our beds. It took us days and even weeks to get things clean, and there was still no water to wash things.

Christmas was a few weeks away and Mum was taking us to Sydney. But because of the drought and feeding animals, Dad would have to stay behind.

There was no room for us all at Rosemont, so we girls were farmed out to aunts and uncles. I went to stay with Uncle Ken and Aunt Libby, who lived in a flat on Ocean Street in Edgecliff, around the corner from Grandma. In pride of place in their living room stood a fascinating new cabinet – a television. Unlike at Grandma's, where such pleasures were not only unheard of but positively frowned upon, Uncle Ken and his family sat in the evenings to watch *Superman*, *Robin Hood*, *The Mickey Mouse Club*, *Lassie* and *Rin Tin Tin*, all in black and white. It was thrilling. The Robin Hood song had become famous: 'Robin Hood, Robin Hood, riding through the glen …' We even knew it in Walcha, although television was not to reach there for many more years.

Wearing our new best dresses – made by Aunt Phil as an early Christmas present – Mum took us to David Jones, so that we could look at the Christmas windows, with their glittering scenes of fairy tales or of Santa and his elves. The jostling crowds on the street, the women with their hats and gloves and the men with their ties and jackets, were both exciting and unnerving. Then we rattled up the wooden escalators to visit Santa Claus on his golden throne in the toy department. There in Santaland, together with the toy trains and Meccano sets, was a wondrous display of bride dolls. They were of all sizes, with names like Cindy and Debbie, and they were beautiful, with blue eyes that opened and shut and frills and pearly tiaras and tulle veils. Then it was our turn to see Santa, our chance to put in our request, and so we did. 'A bride doll, please Santa,' Philomena asked, careful to enunciate clearly and politely so that there would be no mistake about it. By now I felt a little old for a bride doll. The time had passed.

Through all this activity, we children only occasionally thought of our father, still feeding animals, struggling without water, waiting for rain, although our mother scanned the newspapers for the weather reports every day.

We loved the soft golden sands of Nielsen Park or Bondi or sometimes even Manly, but since we had no swimming costumes we were given little briefs, and that was humiliating, to me at least. I refused to go to the beach unless I had a proper swimming costume, so a shabby and faded hand-me-down was found, and I was somewhat, but not quite, mollified.

Grandma had arranged to take Katrina and me and some cousins to a pantomime at Her Majesty's Theatre in the city. We put on the new best dresses and were told to be on our most perfect behaviour. Her Majesty's, with its high, vaulted ceilings, gilded decorations, red velvet curtains with gold braid and velvet seats, seemed to us a magnificent place. The show was called *Goody Two-Shoes*, and Goody was played by an enormous fat man dressed in frilly women's clothes, which we thought was terribly funny. This was our introduction to live theatre.

Following Christmas morning Mass at St Joseph's, the family walked down Albert Street and around the corner to Grandma's, with all the uncles and aunts and cousins squeezing into the walnut-panelled lift and pouring into the apartment lobby. Aunt Anne and her husband Bruce, who had come steaming back into Sydney Harbour from their European honeymoon on the *Oronsay*, distributed gifts from the trunk they had brought back: Hummel figurines from Germany, leather handbags from Aden, hand-painted platters from Italy and Spain, souvenirs from Lourdes, knitted sweaters and Waterford crystal from Ireland and, from Austria, two pairs of Tyrolean lederhosen for our twins. The leather pants were a little on the roomy side to begin with (okay, more than a little), but from then until they were about ten or eleven, Aidan and Robert wore their lederhosen every time we went to town or to any social occasion in the district. And naturally, when the Juvenile Ball was coming, there was no need to forage around for a costume. The lederhosen must have saved my mother years of stitching, washing and ironing.

Anne and Bruce also had some interesting, but not really surprising, news. Anne was expecting a baby in June. That's just how it was then. Everyone we knew who got married always had a baby within the year.

The adults drank tea in the living room, and some even had a sherry or a beer, it being Christmas, but the children were offered one Monte Carlo biscuit each from a gold-rimmed plate that was passed around with great gravity. We cousins, many of whom did not know each other at all well, were instructed to behave quietly, not speak other than to politely thank someone, and above all, not touch anything. It was Aunt Phil's unshakeable conviction that 'children should be seen and not heard'. She had never married and had no children of her own. All the cousins were terrified of her. Every polished surface in Rosemont was covered with vases, lamps, porcelain bowls and china ornaments, and a sticky fingerprint was cause for a reprimand. So we stood together at the big bay window of Grandma's sunroom, looking out over the harbour at the ships anchored there, and discussed the various ocean liners that might come and go. The *Orcades*, the *Oronsay*, the *Orsova*, the *Southern Star*. The ships plied the routes from Australia to England, San Francisco and Auckland.

Even though she was a businesswoman, Grandma, helped by Aunt Phil, who worked part-time in the business and otherwise ran the household for her, had made a vast batch of both puddings and cakes for the family. On Christmas Day they sat piled on her dining room table in recycled tins and shopping bags, all neatly labelled, ready for her family to take home.

Grandma's Christmas pudding was full of sixpences and threepenny pieces. She saved up her threepences and sixpences all year for the puddings, keeping them in a jar in her pantry. Back in Ocean Street, Aunt Libby served the pudding with store-bought ice cream, another special treat. It occurred to me to wonder about my father, who was very probably drowning his sorrows with Mick Brien on the Winterbourne verandah.

Chapter 20

Miracles Big And Small

In the second week of January my father met us at Walcha Road station. He was in a buoyant mood. There had been a little rain, not enough, but there was more to come, the forecasters all said so. And as we drove out of town we saw a few hopeful patches of green tentatively creeping into the colourless brown earth that had become the local pastures.

We settled back into our daily chores. There was still a good deal of red dust everywhere from the storm, but we had too little water with which to wash it off. We just had to live with the grit of it.

But one morning we awoke early to the sound of heavy drops spattering on the corrugated iron roof. Could it be? Was it real? But the drops became heavier and heavier, gathering momentum.

'Is it raining?' shouted the twins, running into our room. 'Is it raining, is it real rain?' They could barely remember what rain looked like.

We rushed out into the front yard in our pyjamas. It was as though we had won a million pounds in the lottery. Even our parents came out and danced around the yard with us as we twirled, faces turned up to the sky, eyes squeezed tight, tongues out to collect the drops as they fell.

Deliverance.

'Here, help me clear the gutters,' yelled Dad over the din, and

Katrina and I scrambled onto the roof to clear out the pine needles to allow as much water as possible to flow into the tanks from the deluge. Then we rushed barefoot down the slope to the flat and sloshed through the cascades pouring through our fairy glen and into the gully. As the rain continued through the day and into the evening, we sat on the front verandah swinging our legs over the edge, allowing ourselves to remain gloriously, wondrously soaking wet.

'It's raining, it's pouring, the old man is snoring,' sang the twins, running up and down the verandah, waving their arms, 'he hit his head on the foot of the bed and he couldn't get up in the morning!'

The land, too, rejoiced. A day or two later the paddocks were shooting green everywhere, the birds were coming back, the frogs were once again croaking in the gully, there were mushrooms sprouting in the front paddock, and while the tanks were still not completely full, we were saved – for now. In another week there were dandelions lining the track up to the house, and the view from our front verandah might have been in England, so lush was it. 'Look, Mum,' I said, channelling her beloved Wordsworth, 'a host of golden dandelions!' For which I received a hug.

It was time for Philomena to start school, and now she, too, had her own packet of lessons arriving with Mr Grieve's Monday deliveries, and my mother was supervising lessons for three children. In the meantime, we, the Fenwickes, and the Hamels over at Blue Mountain were lobbying the council for a school bus to come close enough to take us and other children in our area into Walcha to attend school. But the wheels of the Walcha Council ground exceeding slow.

By this time, I was learning cursive script, what we called 'running writing', and was learning to write with a pen. There were copperplate style sheets for me to copy. 'The quick brown fox jumped over the lazy dog,' I wrote, tongue between my teeth. The pen had a wooden handle with a nib that you could replace. The nib required refreshing every few words with Parker's blue ink. Still, it made me feel grown-up and very important. My parents both had fountain pens. We had never heard of a ballpoint pen.

In February more rain came, the creek came up, right up, and the tanks filled to the brim. The grass was the greenest it had ever been, our thin, brave sheep were plumping out, and we were able to bring home the cattle that had been grazing on agistment to the south of Walcha.

As the dams filled up and the stock returned to their rightful homes, the bank managers extended loans so the graziers and farmers could pay some of their bills, and boarding school headmasters and headmistresses in Armidale and Sydney alike breathed a sigh of relief as the delayed tuition fees once again began to trickle in.

It was the miracle everyone had been waiting for, but 1957, it turned out, had been one of the driest years in Walcha's history.

But for us the question was had it come in time? Our grand venture was teetering on the brink. The wool cheque, when it came, was a blow, even though we knew it would be small. Not nearly enough to cover our extensive loans, let alone our living expenses. My mother sold some shares she had, and my father sold his golf clubs and his bagpipes to the local policeman, which brought in a tiny bit extra. I was old enough now to be aware of our difficulties and began to lie awake at night, worrying.

~

Bang, squeak, bang. There we all were, one Wednesday afternoon, the five of us bunched together on the swing seat on the Winterbourne verandah, swinging against the wall. *Bang, squeak, bang.* We were there with my father to pick up the mail, which Mr Brien had collected from the Blue Mountain mailbox. Mrs Brien had gone to town to play bridge, and Mr Brien and my father were settled into armchairs on the verandah with a bottle of Scotch. We children, however, were bored and wanted to go home.

Mr Brien had already foraged in the kitchen cupboards for biscuits and ginger ale but had come up short. And then a brainwave struck him. 'Go and catch a goose,' he said. 'If you can catch a goose and bring it back here you can take it home for dinner.'

'If we catch the goose then can we go home?' I asked. I was anxious not to miss the Children's Hour and the Argonauts on the radio at five o'clock.

'Yes, yes, you can, now go on, buzz off.'

But Katrina was cannier. 'Mr Brien,' she asked, fixing him with her big brown eyes, 'if we catch the goose can we have that pony?'

Mr Brien had been promising us a pony for some time. His stepson, Andrew Laurie, had two ponies on his place that were not being used, and Mr Brien had long intended to bring at least one of them over to us, or so he said, only he had not yet got around to it.

'Stone the crows, you bloody kids drive a hard bargain. All right, yes!' said Mr Brien.

We were a bit taken aback that he had used the word 'bloody' in front of us, but we let it pass.

'You mean we can have the pony?' Katrina drove home the point.

'Struth! You can have the pony!'

Mr Brien turned to my father and poured him a dram. 'They've got two chances of catching a goose,' he said. 'Buckley's and none.'

We hurried away, past the old slab huts and yards and big sheds full of rolls of wire and hay and bags of seed, down to the small creek that fed into the main one and where the geese liked to gather in the green grass and rushes. We knew from prior experience that these geese could be vicious, so we realised that some care was required. Still, we planned our stalking carefully, and spread out in a circle around our victim, waiting patiently until the goose was not only well positioned but comfortable with our presence, and then Katrina and I pounced. The startled bird didn't have a chance.

Holding the struggling creature under our arms between us, with the others following, we marched triumphantly back to where the two men were sitting on the verandah. The whole operation had taken about twenty minutes.

Mr Brien was, for once, speechless. But he had to keep his promise to let us go home, and we all got into the car still holding tightly to the goose. Goodness knew whether Mr Brien would come good on his other promise, but we were exhilarated in our triumph.

Sunday arrived, and we were to have the goose for our Sunday lunch. Its corpse had been hanging in the safe for a few days. The battered old CWA Cookbook had some rather imprecise instructions for cooking a goose, and since my father was the only one of us who had ever eaten it before, he suggested a stuffing with dried fruit in it and an accompaniment of apple sauce, which we always had in abundance. We made an extra special meal of it. We enjoyed the novel taste and the extra crispy baked potatoes that came with it, and there were some good feathers for the eiderdown bag.

Then, as we lazed around on the verandah after lunch, a truck trailing a horse float rattled up the track and over the ramp. What was this? When the float door was opened out were coaxed not one, but two, small, fat ponies. A pile of tackle was thrown to the ground – two little saddles and bridles. Mr Brien, a man of honour, had been as good as his word. We rushed to inspect these new marvels.

What a Sunday! Roast goose! Ponies!

But it was Mr Brien who had the last laugh. Once the ponies had taken stock of their new surroundings and the retreating float's dust had settled, it became clear that our excitement had been somewhat premature.

My father looked these two gift horses square in the mouth. 'A bit long in the tooth,' he said. Not only that, the ponies were so docile as to be almost immovable. Flicka and Thunderhead they were not.

It's hard to say which pony was older – Sandy, the bay one, or Susie, the grey. They were Shetlands. Dad took the opportunity to explain to the twins how you measure horses in hands. Sandy would have stood something over nine hands, or three and a half feet high, and Susie would have stood a scarce foot higher. Since they had been the Laurie children's ponies when they were young, and Doug, Mary and Andrew were by now well into their thirties, Sandy and Susie probably were too.

If Katrina and I had had dreams of galloping over the paddocks with the wind at our backs, or riding to collect the mail at the Blue Mountain turnoff, or even of winning prizes at the pony club, those dreams were now dust. It wasn't just that these ponies were small. Nor was it that they were too fat for the saddles. No, it proved simply impossible to coax either of them into a brisk walk, let alone a trot or a canter. They were not interested in any form of exercise other than munching grass. Sandy steadfastly refused to budge at all. An attempt to prod him into action would provoke nothing more than an irritated turn of the head, a scornful curl of the upper lip and a return to munching.

For a few months thereafter, we would line Susie, the slightly sprightlier one, up against a fence and drop onto her back, and with no saddle or reins, poke her into a twenty-second trot. Beyond that she would not deign to oblige. And for a while Philomena and the boys liked to sit on Sandy's back and pretend they were going somewhere, until the novelty wore off, and Sandy and Susie were left to serve out their remaining years in peace in our front paddock.

~

Now that the drought was over, the Briens took a trip to Foster on the coast, snaking down the steep, winding road through the mountains to Port Macquarie. They returned with fresh fish and a large box of oysters nesting in some iced-up hessian bags for my father. Mr Brien delivered these gifts personally, together with a carton of beer, which he planned to drink while he and my father opened and consumed the oysters at our kitchen table, as my mother cooked the fish, a rare treat.

Oysters are an acquired taste, but it didn't take me too long to acquire it, especially with the cocktail sauce my father had improvised with some chopped onion and a mix of tomato and Worcestershire sauces. The other children wouldn't touch the oysters, thinking they looked disgusting, but anything my father dared me to try I would try, such was my worship.

Aunt Carmel came to stay again, and this time her project was ginger beer. We thought this very special and grown-up and were most curious to taste it. She and my mother mixed up a potion, which had to ferment, and then they made a 'starter', which sat in jars on the windowsill and which they had to feed every day for a week. This was all before they could make the actual beer, but finally Carmel and my mother washed and boiled a bunch of the old beer bottles waiting out the back to be recycled in town, filled them with their concoction, and carefully lined the bottles up in the pantry.

Carmel had brought me a copy of *The Secret Garden* by Frances Hodgson Burnett, and I read it in hours. But I chafed a little as I wondered why were we stuck in the dusty Australian bush, instead of verdant England, where stories like that could happen. It didn't seem fair.

Then one Friday a truck rattled up the track and pulled up outside our house. On the back of the truck, wrapped in a sheet and lengths of hessian, was what was clearly an upright piano. A piano? For us? Just for a moment I was giddy with excitement. No, no, not for us, my mother explained, but for a party.

It seemed our parents were throwing a party. They had never had a big party before, at least not since we moved to Walcha. I have no idea what the occasion was, but there was much work to do before the big night. It was to be a buffet, laid out on a trestle table at one end of the living room. Some of the women were bringing desserts – pavlova, apple pie, flummery – but it fell to my mother and Carmel to provide the main course. In the end, they settled on chili con carne, a recipe my mother had found in a magazine, possibly the *Ladies' Home Journal*, and which Carmel assured her was the latest thing in Sydney. This was a daring and novel choice for the time, but it was inexpensive, we could find the basic ingredients, it could be prepared in advance, and it was good for a crowd. Now the search was on for the right spices. Where to find cumin and chilli powder? In the end Pas Fenwicke, who was going to Tamworth, found the spices. Times were changing, but not that fast.

We girls were intensely interested in these proceedings. People came and went, delivering flowers or extra chairs. Boxes of plates, glasses and cutlery were delivered from Mrs Brien and Mrs Bloo, to supplement our own supply. My father spent time practising various popular songs on the piano. This was the most exciting thing that had happened to us for months.

Cooking began the day before. We watched the beans soak and swell. Katrina and I helped chop copious amounts of onion, our eyes stinging and weeping into the afternoon. We browned pounds and pounds of lamb mince and opened jars of bottled tomato from the pantry. Whenever we could we sneaked into the living room when our father was not there to try to pick out tunes on the piano. What a thing, to have a piano in the house. I still longed for lessons.

As the pace intensified on the day of the big event, and my mother and Carmel bustled about, Katrina and I rolled knives and forks in linen napkins and piled them neatly on the table with the plates. My father had collected a keg of beer from town, and set it up on the front verandah, to be poured into jugs as needed. Several bottles of the newly made ginger beer were stacked in the refrigerator. A fire was laid in the living room fireplace and a supply of logs set by the front door. The chili bubbled away in a big pot on the stove. There were to be side bowls of chopped raw onion, grated cheese and sour cream, which struck me as the very height of sophistication, especially since they were to be served in the cut-crystal bowls from the sideboard that my mother had received as a wedding present and had never, to our knowledge, used.

We children had chili and rice, without the accompaniments, for our dinner, and it received a mixed reception. I liked it, but not so some of the others.

And now my father was lighting the living room fire, and headlights were threading across the opposite hillside. The party was about to begin.

Excited, Katrina and I asked Mum what we should wear. But after all the work we had put in, it seemed that we were not invited, not even for half an hour to say hello to the guests. Our breasts heavy with disappointment, we took ourselves to bed. We leaned around the dressing table at our bedroom window and peered through the curtains as car after car pulled up into our yard. We didn't even see many of the guests, as we were forced by the autumn chill to take to our beds. We lay there in the dark, listening to the clink of cutlery and plates and glasses and convivial chatter, and fell asleep.

At some point during the night we awoke to the sounds through the wall of the piano and raucous singing. 'Some enchanted evening,' they crooned. 'There is nothing like a dame,' they roared. Later, I could hear: 'Oklahoma, okay!' And finally, when it might have been towards dawn: 'There's a track winding back, to an old-fashioned shack, along the road to Gundagai.'

In the morning, we got up to find our parents and Carmel still asleep. Katrina took the bucket and went to milk the cow and I went to inspect the living room. Overflowing ashtrays and empty bottles lay everywhere. The smell of stale beer and cigarettes stung the air. Half-empty glasses of beer and gin teetered on the mantelpiece. I took a sip of one, to see what it tasted like, and spat it into the ashes of the fireplace.

After a couple of days of cleaning, the borrowed plates and glasses were boxed up, the chairs were stacked on the verandah, and the piano was taken away, as mysteriously as it had come. A piece of magic had left the house. Life resumed its normal course.

Our parents never had another party. Not on Arran at least.

Chapter 21

More Than One Sharp Turn

My father took Carmel to Walcha Road a few days later to get the night train to Sydney, and on the way back through town he stopped in at the Sports Club for a drink. Fellow polocrosse player Bob Gill was there, and my father accepted an invitation to go back to Emu Creek for another drink. Or two. After all, it was on his way home.

We children had gone to bed, but around nine or ten, the headlights of a strange car pulled up outside the house, and we heard voices. Katrina and I went to our bedroom door, which opened on to the verandah, to find Bob Gill helping my father up the steps and my mother in her dressing-gown exclaiming with horror at the front door. My father was bruised, bloodied and very muddy. What had happened?

'It's a miracle he's alive, Joan,' said Bob Gill, accepting a cup of tea in the kitchen while my mother tended my father's wounds, 'let alone nothing broken.'

What was broken, however, was the car. It seemed that my father had taken a shortcut on an unfamiliar track through Emu Creek, which joined the Winterbourne Road. We had taken this track once or twice in daylight on the way back from polocrosse, but parts of it had been washed out in the recent rains, and in the dark, my father had rolled the car into a gully. Our trusty little Austin Seven was completely written off. Now we had no transport except the truck, which was not registered, and which could not be driven on public roads.

For several weeks, we stayed at home. No trips to town, no social events.

And then, as autumn sharpened its grip, an unfamiliar car pulled up outside the house, and to our surprise, out stepped Grandma. She had taken it upon herself to choose us a new car, and the loan to purchase it was another debt. It was a pale blue Holden ute, which had a removable canopy on the back and a back seat that folded down. With the very best of intentions, Grandma had probably thought this would be a convenient vehicle for working the farm, as well as converting into a passenger vehicle for going to town. It turned out to serve neither purpose well, especially as the canopy was annoying to remove and refit, and the back-seat arrangement was uncomfortable for all of us. Still, we declared ourselves pleased, and were grateful that we could now go to town again.

The first journey into town in our brand-new Holden was to take Grandma to Mass in town on Sunday. The following night found us kneeling in the kitchen saying the Rosary that always came with Grandma's visit. We were into the fourth decade, another decade still to go, and the time to the finish seemed interminable. Then, jolting us out of our torpor, came the sound of a loud blast in the pantry next door. Grandma doggedly kept on with her Hail Marys while we children scrambled out the door and into the pantry to investigate.

One of the bottles of ginger beer had exploded.

Grandma sternly insisted that we deal with it later and finish the Rosary first. But it was all we could do to control our giggles. The incident seemed to us a sign from God that He didn't care about the Rosary much, which agreed with our own secret sentiments. Grandma, however, saw it differently. To her it was a test of our piety, which we had spectacularly failed. As far as she was concerned, we were turning into a bunch of little heathens.

This belief had consequences, for me at least. Grandma stayed several more days, but shortly before she was due to leave, my mother called me inside from loading up the woodpile at the kitchen back door.

'Grandma has made a very generous offer,' she said. 'It's time you made your First Holy Communion and Grandma has invited you to stay with her in Sydney while you go to school and take some religious instruction and make your First Communion there.'

The announcement came as a shock, and I had mixed feelings about it. On the one hand, it would be exciting to go to a real school and make friends with other girls my own age. Bunky Blomfield and Helen Thorold, along with the Blomfield boys and many others, had already been shipped off to boarding school in Armidale or Sydney. On the other hand, I was not sure if I was ready to leave Arran and my family, especially Katrina.

Still, the plan was set, and we put Grandma on the train back to Sydney. Soon a letter came announcing that the nuns could fit me in at Barat Burn, at Rose Bay Convent, probably in early June. My mother measured me up for uniforms and drew an outline of my feet for shoes, and posted the lot to Grandma.

~

A few mornings before I was to leave, Dad came into the kitchen and told us that Mum was not feeling well and that we were to get breakfast ourselves. We were surprised, and a little troubled. My mother was never sick, or at least if she was, she soldiered on, as we were all taught to do. But we set all the breakfast things on the table, and I stoked the stove and made the porridge and served everyone. Ginger, the naughty kitten, who was in fact a young cat by now, took advantage of my mother's absence and jumped onto the table.

My father threatened, yet again, 'If that cat jumps on the table one more time, I swear to God I'm going to shoot it.'

We shooed the cat down, as we always did, and were halfway through our toast when we heard my mother calling out. She had managed to get herself up, although she was still in her nightgown, and was staggering towards the back door. My father leapt from the table and rushed from the kitchen. We heard the flyscreen door slam, some retching and then a cry. We scrambled out into the back courtyard just in time to see Dad catch Mum as she collapsed in a dead faint.

He managed to help her back to bed and returned to the kitchen, ordering us to finish our breakfasts. But there was Ginger on the table, licking the milk from the milk jug.

My father didn't say a word. He picked up the cat by the scruff of her neck and tossed her out the back door. Then he went to the pantry and unlocked his rifle, loading it with several bullets, before marching outside.

We couldn't believe he was really going to do it. Apart from the drowning of the kittens, we had never known him to harm a healthy, innocent animal before.

'No, Daddy, no!' we begged, tugging at his shirttails. 'Please don't, Daddy, please don't!'

The little cat was sitting by the back gate, the one that led out to the dunny, licking her paws, content, complacent, her golden fur glinting in the morning sun. She didn't even look up, as *crack!* my father's bullet found its mark. Her body twisted in the air, fell to the ground, and then she was no more. We stood there in shock.

'Get dressed and put on your shoes,' he ordered. 'I'm taking your mother to the hospital.'

In fright as we all were, we did not ask questions.

As we passed Winterbourne, Dad pulled in at Old Bill's hut and, thrusting a loaf of bread and a jar of peanut butter into Old Bill's hands, asked if he could watch us for the day, since Mr and Mrs Brien were away visiting Mrs Brien's grandchildren. Bill agreed, and so out we tumbled before Dad spun the car wheels in his haste to get away.

I had been reading *Lorna Doone*, and had it with me, so I sat on Bill's steps and read. The younger children, however, did not seem to be worried. Having exhausted the possibilities of the surrounding sheds and yards and having broken quite a few rotten eggs that they had missed on our previous visits, they climbed up on Bill's roof, and despite the cold weather, one of the boys even got in his water tank. It was then that I was obliged to intervene, because to our great surprise, Bill did not. He seemed to have no idea that children need boundaries, and that they will test them to the limit of one's patience.

At lunchtime Bill stoked up his fire and made a large billy of sweet tea for us to have with the slabs of bread and peanut butter that Katrina and I had prepared for everyone. There weren't enough mugs, so we had to share, but we didn't mind. The younger ones thought it was very grown-up to sit around and drink tea, and even better from a billy, just like the jolly swagman.

In the afternoon, I finished the book. The last chapters were shocking to me and emotionally wrenching, and I wanted my mother. What was the matter with her? Would she be all right?

My father arrived to pick us up towards dusk. Mum was not with him. She was in the hospital, he explained, and it was a subdued little party that arrived home to our dark, cold house, looking forward to some dinner. We were ravenous.

Dinner? Dad had planned to kill a sheep that very day, so there was no meat in the house. There was only some leftover cooked cabbage in the fridge. 'Get the stove and fire going and peel some extra potatoes,' he instructed, walking up the hill, and so I did that, and put the potatoes on to boil, while we all waited expectantly for him to come back with something. What he came back with was a handful of parsley and some chives from the vegetable garden. He warmed the cabbage, mashed the potatoes more carefully than usual (that was the one domestic task he generally deigned to undertake, since he didn't like lumps), stirred in the cabbage and chopped herbs, dolloped a serving on each plate and made a little well in each heaping pile, into which he put a piece of butter. That was our dinner.

'Potatoes Colcannon,' he said. 'That's what they eat for dinner in Ireland, and if it's good enough for the Irish, it's good enough for you.'

We eyed him sceptically, then looked down at our plates and began to eat. No-one spoke. There was no jostling, no jesting, no high-spirited questions. After all, Ginger was dead and our mother in the hospital. We washed our plates and took ourselves off to bed.

The next day after breakfast we went into town to collect Mum from the hospital. She had been given a diagnosis of acute hepatitis. She was very weak, and still didn't seem well. The doctor said she needed complete rest.

At first, she tried to direct the household activities from her bed, but that was a plan doomed to fail. I could not get Katrina and Philomena to sit down at their lessons, and since Dad had not yet killed the sheep, there was very little food in the house. My father said I could try to make potato pancakes from last night's leftover potatoes. This required getting the stove hot enough, but while distracted I had let it almost go out. So, although I had been forbidden to do this myself, I did what I had seen my mother do a hundred times – I loaded in some wood and threw a little kerosene on top.

The resulting explosion, just as my father walked in, came right at me. Flames singed my hair, my eyelashes and eyebrows. They also blackened my face. The smell of singed hair was sickening.

My father grabbed me by the scruff of the neck and hauled me out the back door with one hand, while loosening his belt with the other.

He beat me so hard that I could hardly sit down for days afterwards. I was humiliated and outraged. I had not been given the belt for some time now and quite thought myself above it. I was so angry that I refused to take my place back in the kitchen for hours, until Katrina persuaded me to. The family needed to be fed, and she and I were it. Although I knew that I had transgressed – the lingering smell of singed hair reminded me of that every minute – I was still humiliated.

Sometime in the afternoon, Mrs Bloo pulled up in her Land Rover. 'I'm taking your mother out to Cheyenne to recuperate,' she said. 'She'll never get better if she can't get complete rest. Now come along, chickadees, pack yourselves a bag each. Don't forget socks and underpants.' She crammed clothes into a bag for my mother. As I was due to go to Sydney in a day or two, I had to pack a full suitcase for myself.

Next morning, while the frost still sat upon the fence wires, my father drove Aidan and Robert over to Earsdon to stay with Pas and Clennell Fenwicke. The following day he was taking me to the train, and on the way to the station he dropped Katrina and Philomena at Winterbourne, to stay with Mr and Mrs Brien.

As my father and I stood blowing warm air into our freezing

cupped hands on the platform at Walcha Road, waiting for the great steam engine to come puffing round the bend, we did not speak. I still had bruises and I was still angry with him. Then the engine churned into the station and to a stop at the platform's end.

'Behave yourself for your grandmother,' my father said, as he opened the door and helped me in with my suitcase, and then the whistle went, and he jumped off the train onto the platform.

A sudden wave of dismay swept over me. Just like that, I was ready to forgive him everything. I wanted him to hug me, but then the station master slammed all the doors and the train gave a lurch as it pulled out of the station. I put my head out the window and saw that my father was walking down the platform towards the car. He did not look back.

Soon we were at Woolbrook, filling up with water. As the lump in my throat started to subside, I allowed myself to get just a little excited. It felt very grown-up to be going all the way to Sydney on the train by myself. I mentally ticked off each station as it came and went. We stopped for half an hour at Werris Creek and lots of people got on. There was a busy refreshment room there where people were eating sausages and mashed potato at wooden tables and drinking tea from silver pots, and I bought myself a meat pie from the counter, a hot salty treat we were not normally allowed. Then all the stops to Wyong and the beautiful still silver waters of the Hawkesbury; and then, as the light started to fade, Gosford, Hornsby, Strathfield and through twinkling city lights to Central. It was dark now, but there was the still-terrifying Aunt Phil, waiting for me on the platform, prim in her hat and gloves.

Next day we boarded the tram to Queen's Square and went to David Jones to pick up my school uniform and to buy a pair of school shoes and a school suitcase for my books and homework. A visit to David Jones, with its big wooden escalators and the man playing the piano on the marbled ground floor, was always awe-inspiring, and the novelty that day was that we had lunch in the restaurant up on the sixth floor, ordering sandwiches from a menu, just like in the movies. I had never ordered from a printed menu before.

After lunch, we boarded the tram again and rattled all the way out to the school to take some tests. A nun took me into a room off the front parlour and gave me some leaflets, together with an exercise book in which to write my answers. The tests would determine into which class I was to be placed.

At Rosemont, I was to sleep in the spare bed in Grandma's room. Aunt Phil had her own small room at the back, but in the other front room slept my aunts Carmel and Christine. In the gloom of my grandmother's room I stared up at the patterns on the ceiling created by the light of the street lamps shining through the Venetian blinds and listened to the trams whining and switching gears as they laboured up the hill from Double Bay, the swish of the cars speeding up and down Edgecliff Road, and the pigeons cooing on the red-brick ledges of the building. Such different sounds from those I was used to, of the wind in the pine trees, the occasional dog barking or howling and the distant moo of Molly's calf – would I ever be able to get used to sleeping here? And what was happening to my mother?

Grandma drove me to school for my first day and presented me in my new uniform, too big for me since I was supposed to grow into it, together with my new Globite case containing nothing but a paper bag lunch, to Mother Dorothy. Mother Dorothy was a kind woman who was to teach my class and give me instruction for Holy Communion, two days a week after school. While she chatted to my grandmother, she sent me down into the courtyard, where the other girls were playing a ball game against the wall. I had no idea what the game was, or what the rules were, so I stood back, uncomfortable and bewildered. Then somewhere inside a handbell began to clang, and a nun came out of a doorway and made a loud clicking sound with a kind of rectangular wooden castanet she had taken from her voluminous front pocket. Everyone quickly fell into two lines, one on each side of the courtyard. I joined one of the lines and a girl hissed at me, 'Are you a Red or a White?' I had no idea what I should answer to this question other than that I didn't know.

Mother Dorothy took me aside and told me I was to be in Year 5. This was a promotion – I was going up a grade. I was also told I was to be a White, since the school was divided into two houses, Red and White, which competed in sporting and other activities. In the afternoon, the Reds played the Whites in a game called rounders, using a tennis ball and an old tennis racquet.

I was still anxious about my mother, but there were major excitements at Rosemont to distract us all. Aunt Christine was soon to have her 21st birthday party, and Aunt Anne arrived from Wagga, ready to give birth to her new baby. I was temporarily moved to the daybed in the sunroom while Anne slept in my bed in Grandma's room. She had her little hospital bag all packed and ready to go.

On the morning of Christine's birthday, only a few days after my arrival in Sydney, Anne went into labour. Bruce was called (on the telephone, no less!) and Grandma drove Anne to the hospital. When I came home from school that evening there was a joyous announcement – Anne had had a baby girl, to be called Alexandra.

But there was hardly time to digest this news, since now there was all the excitement and jostling over the bathroom mirror as Christine and Carmel plunged into a flurry of bras, petticoats and mascara for Christine's big party at the Pickwick Club, then a prestigious social club and private library in the city. 'Oh, you look so swooningly glamorous,' I said to them as they wiggled into their ballerina-style party dresses and high heels and elbow length gloves and put on their red lipstick. They all laughed, even Grandma, who had bought a new shot-silk mauve suit for the occasion. But I wasn't there to see them leave – by then Phil's friend Peggy had picked me up in her Morris Minor to spend the night with her and her son Basil at their house in Bellevue Hill. (Basil was the original owner of the Harris Tweed coat.)

The next day I came home from school to find Aunt Phil bustling around and Grandma packing a suitcase.

'Where are you going?' I asked her in some surprise.

'To Tamworth,' she said.

My suspicions immediately aroused, I said, 'Is it Mum? Is she back in the hospital?'

'Never you mind,' she said. 'Don't ask questions. I just have business there.'

In Grandma and Phil's view, children should be told as little as possible. In fact, that was very likely the prevailing view at the time. They probably thought they were being kind, and sparing us misery, but in fact the reverse was true. I was in a panic. There was something terrible going on, but despite my desperate pleas, neither she nor Phil would tell me anything. And whom else could I ask? A long-distance phone call was out of the question, and in any event, if my mother was in the hospital, whom could I call?

Not having been told anything, I was thrown into an agony of anxiety. I couldn't eat my dinner. Then at bedtime, Phil told me we needed to say special prayers for my mother.

'Why?' I begged, but more, she would not say.

I lay awake all night, past the time when the trams went silent, and through the morning's first grind up the hill, but after breakfast Phil packed me off to the tram with my red-rimmed eyes anyway and no reassurance of any kind. The knot in my chest was growing bigger and tighter.

I rushed home at the end of the day anxious for news, but there was none.

'We need to say a Rosary,' said Aunt Phil, and she and I knelt in the living room while I choked back sobs with every Hail Mary, every Our Father, every Glory Be. Was my mother dead? When was someone going to tell me something? Carmel and Christine, when they came home, would not say anything either.

My anxiety gathered for three more days, until I could hardly swallow. Then I came home from school to find Grandma back. The crisis, she said, had passed, and my mother would live. Would live? Had she nearly died? Why had no-one said anything? There were no details given and there was nothing more to be said, except another Rosary in thanksgiving.

It's taken a lifetime to piece the story together. Although they knew that our mother had been taken to Tamworth Hospital (which I in Sydney did not know but could only guess) my brothers and sisters were not told any more than I was. But it seems that while apparently convalescing at Cheyenne from her illness, my mother was only getting worse. On the second evening there she had suffered another collapse, and the district ambulance had been called. It was a stormy night, and the Blomfields did not want to risk transporting her into town in the Land Rover.

Katrina at Winterbourne had also been in a wretched state of anxiety. She and Philomena would not have seen the ambulance pick its unfamiliar way down the hill in the rain, ford the creek and head past the Winterbourne house up towards Cheyenne, its lights receding into the lonely distance. Nor would they have seen its lights return to ford the now-swollen creek, carrying our unconscious mother, with my father following in the blue Holden. But in the morning, Katrina overheard Mrs Brien on the phone saying, 'Oh dear, poor Bob. What on earth is he going to do with all those children?' She knew then that something was very wrong. She plied Mrs Brien with questions, but no-one would tell the two little girls anything. Mrs Brien did her best to keep them to a normal routine until alternative arrangements could be made for them.

The ultimate diagnosis, missed by the Walcha doctor and hospital, was an ectopic pregnancy, which had ruptured and then turned septic. My mother was, in fact, close to death. Grandma's first move on arriving in Tamworth had been to organise a priest to come and say the Last Rites for her daughter. Only massive doses of antibiotics had saved her, and her recovery had been little short of a miracle. It was almost thirty years later, on a long train journey, that my mother told me about the strange sensation of leaving her body and looking down at herself from the hospital room ceiling, and at my father, kneeling by the bed and begging, 'Don't leave us, please don't leave us.' She felt quite peaceful, she said, but it was his pleas, in the end, that had brought her back.

She was in the hospital for several weeks, and so Katrina and Philomena were reshuffled – Katrina to the Blomfields at Karori and Philomena to family friends Clive and Molly Laurence, on the other side of Walcha. Aidan and Robert remained with Pas and Clennell Fenwicke.

Katrina later related that on Saturday, while she and Philomena were still at Winterbourne, the Briens had taken them into town, and Mrs Brien took the girls to the Tennis Club while Mr Brien went to the Sports Club. In the evening, they waited, cold and hungry, in the car for Mr Brien to come out of the club. He didn't come. Mrs Brien went back to the front door and rang the bell, again, loudly and insistently. Yes, they would give Mick the message. Yes, he says he'll be out in a minute. He still didn't come. Finally, a furious Mrs Brien began throwing stones on the roof of the clubhouse. This had no effect, and finally, she got back in the car, started the engine, and drove home to Winterbourne without Mick.

It was my father, stopping in at the Sports Club on his way home from Tamworth Hospital, who dropped Mick at the Winterbourne front gate before he headed home to feed the dogs. And on Mick's arrival home a spectacular domestic quarrel occurred, which the two girls still remember to this day. It began with Mr Brien lurching from wall to wall down the long Winterbourne hallway. It ended with Mrs Brien throwing a large glass vase at Mr Brien, which missed, but which smashed against a wardrobe mirror behind him, sending glass scattering everywhere. The girls were glad to move on to the care of other families.

My father was thankful for modern medicine, but to Grandma and Aunt Phil, my mother's miraculous recovery was proof of the power of prayer. So, perhaps in gratitude, Grandma began attending 6.30am Mass every morning at St Joseph's before going off to run the Australian Cotton Manufacturing Company. This was a practice she continued for the rest of her life.

Chapter 22

City Life

A week or so after Grandma returned, a letter came to Rosemont for me from my mother to tell me that she was getting better and that I was not to worry and that she knew I would be a good girl for Grandma and Aunt Phil. I was to study hard for my First Communion. These were the first words I had heard from her for weeks. I had travelled on the train to Sydney without even saying goodbye to her, and I had been miserable and despondent ever since the crisis began. What would we do without our beloved mother? The remains of the tight ball that had sat in my chest began to disappear, but I longed to see her and feel her arms around me.

I took the tram to and from school. On Tuesday and Thursday afternoons and occasional Wednesday mornings for over a month, Mother Dorothy met me in the polished wooden parlour of the big school for my First Communion preparations. It was a momentous occasion, one's First Holy Communion. A few weeks before the big day, Grandma took me to David Jones to buy the white dress and new shoes that would be required. I did not come away with the outfit I would have chosen for myself, but just to have a new dress and patent leather black shoes made it special.

First Confession over, the big day arrived. I was to make my First Communion at Sunday Mass in the beautiful Gothic sandstone chapel at the Rose Bay main school, in front of the entire school. I was to walk up the aisle to communion alone, like a bride, in my white dress and veil and new shoes, and kneel on a special white satin cushion at the altar while the choir sang Mozart's hauntingly beautiful 'Ave Verum Corpus'. Although I had not expected her to come, my mother had written to say she was sorry she could not be there but that things were too difficult.

I did my dutiful best to feel mystical and ecstatic when the priest placed the host on my outstretched tongue. Disappointingly, nothing happened, and nothing changed.

Grandma had committed me to Rose Bay for the term, so I was to stay on until the next school holidays. Even though life was physically very comfortable at Rosemont, with its high ceilings, large rooms, two bathrooms, thick carpet and elegant recessed lighting, it was hard not to feel like a prisoner there. There were crystal vases, elegant clocks and mirrors and china ornaments on mantelpieces and side tables everywhere, all of which I was forbidden to touch or examine. Phil would not allow me to play with other children out in the street. She warned me not to linger at the Edgecliff shops on my way home. My reading material was carefully censored. I missed the wide open skies, the view of Trig Hill and the benign chaos of home, my *real* home.

Moreover, Grandma and Aunt Phil had taken me on as a project. Their commitment to God and the Church was almost equalled by their sense of familial duty, and they determined to make both a pious Catholic and a young lady out of the rough-edged larrikin they had been sent. They took over where my mother had left off. Table manners, introductions, letter-writing, deportment, all came under their eagle-eyed scrutiny. To improve what she saw as a slouch, Phil stood with her arms folded while I walked around the living room with books on my head. I was not the first granddaughter to suffer a prolonged stay with Grandma and Phil for the purposes of being ironed out, and I would not be the last.

My mother wrote regularly with news of another snowfall, a dingo scare, an outing to visit their friends Molly and Clive Laurence on their property near Nowendoc, where Philomena had stayed during the crisis. She was slowly getting better, she said, but hoped to be fully back on her feet by my return home.

On my way home from school, on Phil's approved route from the tram stop, I had discovered a small lending library on Ocean Street. They would lend you one book (*Swallows and Amazons*!) for sixpence or three (*Nancy Drew*!) for a shilling. The pocket money Phil gave me was spent on borrowing books. When Phil discovered these books by my bed she introduced me to the much bigger and very beautiful Woollahra Library, a rambling old house and garden on New South Head Road, where I could borrow books for free.

To her young nieces and nephews, the Aunt Phil of the 1950s and 60s was a daunting person, strict and full of rules. It was only years later that we all began to realise that there was great kindness and generosity beneath her stern exterior. She had worked for years as a nurse at St Vincent's Hospital, but now she managed the office at Grandma's factory in Alexandria, as well as running the house for Grandma. At first, she came home early so that she could be there when I arrived home from school, but soon she gave me a key to the front door and returned to her regular hours at the factory.

Grandma, who in every sense defined the word matriarch, ruled over the entire family with a rod of iron. She was a formidable woman to all of us. She had long ago won a power struggle over the family business with her eldest son, Jack, and the rest of the family had taken note – her word was law. She kept a close eye on all her children and their doings, and on her ever-increasing tribe of grandchildren, too. But although I shared a bedroom with her, to me she remained enigmatic and distant, very involved with both her pieties and her spiky hair curlers, with which she tortured herself every night. Perhaps she offered up the discomfort for the souls in Purgatory. Curlers in, she knelt and said a nightly Rosary before going to bed.

Perhaps having eleven children to wrangle gives you administrative and managerial skills by default, but Grandma had become an able and astute businesswoman. She had made a considerable success of Australian Cotton, the fledgling business into which she had been thrust after her husband's premature death, and by now she was quite comfortably situated. She and Phil did no housework. A woman came in once a week to clean. All laundry except for underwear was sent out every Monday to the Parisian Laundry, whose emissaries came to the door to collect it. It arrived back the following week wrapped in brown paper packages, the sheets beautifully ironed and starched, the towels soft and fluffy.

The butcher, down a narrow lane just off Ocean Street, delivered a week's supply of lamb chops, sausages and steak. The milkman trudged up the back stairs three days a week and left glass bottles with gold and silver foil tops in an alcove by the back door, where the baker left the bread. On Fridays, the fishmonger delivered a standing order of mullet or flathead, whichever was in that week. The greengrocer, from the corner of the same lane in Edgecliff as the butcher, delivered a cardboard box of fruit and vegetables, which had been ordered by telephone. There was always a bunch of green parsley on the top, thrown in for free. The order usually included a large paper bag of peas, which it fell to me to shell.

A few weeks after my First Communion, Aunt Phil put me on the train at Central to return home to Walcha, where Christine, sent up by Grandma, was trying to cope with my brothers and sisters. This time it was the Glen Innes Mail, a night train, and I had a sleeper compartment to myself. Phil gave the guard a ten-shilling note to take care of me, and to my very great astonishment he brought me a cup of tea and an extra biscuit in my little sleeper compartment at 6.30am. By the time we puffed out of Werris Creek it was full daylight, and in my joy, I stuck my head and shoulders out of the window to breathe in the air of my beloved bush, just in time to get a huge piece of soot in my eye. It smarted and stung for hours, but it didn't matter – I was going home to the little homestead and the rocks and trees and paddocks that I loved.

My mother met me at the station, but she was thin and pale and for a moment I didn't quite recognise her. 'You're going to have to help,' she said, 'there's a lot to do. The foxes got a lot of the of the chooks while I was sick, and I wasn't there to tend the vegetable garden, so things are a bit of a mess. But we can get back on our feet if we all pull together.' The spring planting was behind schedule, and she was working around the clock to set things to rights. Even before I had unpacked my suitcase I was up in the vegetable garden helping Katrina, who had been weeding for weeks, to hoe the earth and plant seedlings.

My father, too, had fallen behind in his tasks and was struggling to catch up. There was fence-mending and drenching to see to. At dinner I could see that the atmosphere was subdued.

But there was one big improvement. To lighten her workload, Grandma and Aunt Phil had conspired to buy Mum a washing machine. It was a relatively primitive affair, but it had a spin cycle, and it saved hours of work.

Christine stayed on for a few days, then we put her on the train to Sydney. It had been agreed that I, too, was to return to Sydney and continue to attend school for the final term, since Christine was going to Darwin to begin her Qantas career and I could have her bed. I didn't really want to go. With my First Communion out of the way, wouldn't I be more useful on the place?

'I could take over the vegetable garden for you,' I pleaded with my mother.

'You'll be coming home for good at Christmas,' she said, 'and we'll see about it then.'

I adapted back to Barat Burn as best I could, but still felt like an outsider. The girls had all been there together since they were five or six, and they had not only developed relationships and their own cliques, but also social mechanisms and skills at which I could only fumble. Still, I muddled through, reading all of LM Montgomery's *Anne of Green Gables* books and all the Mary Grant Bruce's *Billabong* books I could lay my hands on, and looked forward to the weekly letters from my mother.

At Rosemont, where despite the relatively luxury, I still chafed at the restrictions and the confinement imposed by the Phil/Grandma regime, rescue came from an unexpected source. Carmel had recently met a young doctor from Royal Prince Alfred Hospital, Neil Gallagher, who was beginning to show up at Rosemont for dinner a good deal of the time, sometimes with his friend Peter Evans, otherwise known to us all as Prof. Indeed, they all attended my First Communion. After Carmel and Neil announced their engagement, they (and Prof) adopted me. As the flashing of the ring and the plans for a January wedding began to occupy everyone's attention, I spent a lot of time with them when Phil and Grandma were busy, and they seemed happy to include me on various outings: to the zoo, to the pictures at the Vogue Cinema, and afterwards, coffee at George's in Double Bay.

School broke up in early December, and Phil put me on the Glen Innes Mail at Central, again tipping the porter to keep an eye on me. This time I was careful not to lean out the window and get more soot in my eye.

Chapter 23

Christmas Up The Creek

A few days after my arrival home we were to drive to Tamworth for our Christmas shopping. Our father had sold a painting to a local grazier and decided that half the money would go on Christmas. With the nine and sixpence I had managed to save from the pocket money Phil had given me and the ten shillings or so stored in my money box, I would have nearly a whole pound to spend on Christmas presents. I was looking forward to seeing my mother's reaction when she opened the Yardley hand lotion that I planned to buy for her, so that she wouldn't have to use lamb fat any more.

On a hot summer morning we packed our tinned spaghetti sandwiches and put on our dresses and lederhosen and good shoes and set off on our long drive. As was usual for a visit to the great metropolis of Tamworth, Mum wore a dress and stockings, and Dad a shirt and tie and his good hat. I had spent nearly an hour the previous evening polishing his best elastic-sided boots. 'There's rain in the forecast,' said our father as we forded the creek, 'so you'd better all pray the creek doesn't rise.' We could see that the Blomfields had left their Land Rover parked on the rise below the Winterbourne homestead, on our side of the creek, so they could get home from town if they had to leave their other car behind because the creek was too high. They were clearly not taking any chances.

As we passed through Walcha, we dropped in at Lovett's to pay our bill there, and Katrina and I made sure Dad got the tickets for their Christmas stocking raffle and put them in the box. This was by now a Christmas ritual. Lovett's had two Christmas stockings that year, both six feet high, propped against the front verandah posts to encourage customers. We had inspected them thoroughly, lovingly fingering the ping-pong bats, plastic water pistols, yo-yos, marbles and Kit-Kat bars held taut behind the nylon mesh.

We spent a good day in Tamworth, up and down Peel Street, in and out of Woolworths and Penney's and Treloar's, with a stop to inspect the beautifully gift-wrapped toiletries in Cohen's Chemist. At lunch time, we drove to a picnic spot down by the river to eat our sandwiches. It was so hot and humid that the boys stripped down and went for a swim in the river, and we girls hiked up our dresses and went paddling. Then more shopping, and a visit by Dad to the tobacconist to get his Temple Bar tobacco and supplies for his pipe. As we passed the music shop we saw the just-out LP recording of *My Fair Lady* in the window. We knew all the songs. 'Buy it for Mum, buy it, buy it! Please, Dad, please,' we begged. To our surprise, he did, even though it was expensive.

Black clouds gathered in the distance as we drove north on the New England Highway towards Walcha. Distant flashes of lightning lit up the dark sky as the car laboured up the steep Moonbi Range, but that didn't stop us from begging Dad to stop at Moonbi Lookout, from which there were rumoured to be great views of Tamworth and the plains on which it sat. Every time we went to Tamworth we begged him to do this, but he never did.

At Woolbrook big heavy drops of rain began to fall among the rumbling thunder. By the time we got to Walcha Road the rain was pouring down, and the windscreen wipers on the blue Holden were working overtime.

The thunder crashed and rumbled through town and most of the way home, but as we approached Winterbourne in the late afternoon the violence had faded, leaving a steady patter in its wake.

And then we came to the top of the Winterbourne hill, beside the Old Stone House, looked down and stopped.

Through the rain we could see that the creek below was a raging torrent, taking tree branches, logs and the occasional fence post with it. There was no way we could get the car across; we would simply be swept away. We couldn't turn back to the Fenwickes', because my father had had one of his fallings out with Clennell, and although Pas might welcome us, her husband would not.

Someone, probably the Blomfields, had roped a heavy ladder to the footbridge, and its bottom rung was just short of the waters.

'There's nothing for it,' said my father, 'we're going to have to get across the footbridge and walk home.'

'But Daddy,' I said, anxious as always, 'what about all our presents?'

'Well, if you're so worried, we can take some of them over in a bag and leave them in the Land Rover. We can get them in the morning, when we come to get the car.'

We couldn't pack everything, just the important things, and we watched in fear as my father slung the bag over his shoulder and negotiated the bridge, testing as he went. Then he came back for us. By now, my heart was pounding in my chest.

The footbridge was made up of three long, round, slippery logs with gaps between them, through which a small child could easily slip. For us children, crossing the bridge was akin to walking a tightrope. Just in case, my father tied a rope he kept in the car around my waist, since I was to go first.

'Don't look down, don't look down!' shouted my father through the roar of rain and rushing water. And then, one by one, through the pouring rain and gathering darkness, my father got the others across, the smaller ones on his back, picking his way over the bridge for the next one as soon as he had deposited each on high ground and into Katrina's and my care.

My mother came last, wading up to her waist to grab the ladder, just as the creek seemed to rise another foot, and darkness fell. To preserve her precious nylon stockings, she had taken them off and stuffed them in her bra.

We were soaked and miserable. We threw our sack of parcels in the back of the Blomfields' Land Rover, and began the half-mile trek up the hill in the dark, carrying our shoes and letting the mud squelch between our toes. The boys seemed to think it was an adventure, but my heart was still racing.

The next day dawned bright and sunny, although we could see from the streak of silver in the dip of the valley that the creek was still up. We walked down the hill through the mud to see what was happening and to retrieve our shopping.

The creek had risen so high that there was grass and debris clinging to the top of the footbridge. Our car was still perched safely on the opposite hill, although for now we could not get to it. But the Land Rover was not there.

Then we saw it, half submerged, fifty yards down the creek. It seemed that by the time the Blomfields had returned from their own shopping the creek was too high for them to cross, and they had turned around to go to their cousins at Karori for the night. By morning the Land Rover had been washed down the creek, together with all our Christmas shopping, including the Yardley hand lotion and the expensive *My Fair Lady* LP.

The Blomfields recovered their Land Rover, but we never recovered our parcels, despite a search expedition downstream through the battered grasses and rushes when the waters receded.

'Everything would be in Woop Woop by now,' Mum said.

But she came up trumps, and Christmas Day was not lost. A few small presents had survived in the back of our own car, and there were still those that had come earlier by mail from Sydney and Greenock, but on a trip to town on Christmas Eve Mum had a brainwave. She bought each of us two rashers of bacon and a bottle of usually forbidden fizzy lemonade for our pillowcases. It was unimaginable luxury. We thought the bacon was the best Christmas present we had ever had.

Later, as we sat on the verandah drinking our lemonade, we noticed the dust from a truck streaking across the opposite hill. Someone was coming, but who? The truck descended into the Winterbourne dip and then came up the other side. Was it for us or the Blomfields? Then the truck crossed the boundary ramp and instead of veering left towards Cheyenne, it rattled over our homestead ramp and pulled up in front of the verandah. LOVETT'S, said a sign painted on the side.

'It's the stocking, we won the stocking!' shouted Philomena as she ran inside.

'Does Robert Wales live here?' asked the driver.

'Yes, yes!' we cried.

He and his young son lifted the huge Christmas stocking from the back of the truck onto the verandah and propped it against a post. My mother invited them in for a cup of tea, but they said no, they had Christmas dinner waiting at home.

We ripped open the nylon mesh and flung debris everywhere. The stocking was full of cheap made-in-Hong-Kong items – flimsy cardboard Snakes and Ladders games and yo-yos and plastic water pistols – but we could not have been happier. Our faith in the world was restored.

Chapter 24

In Which Katrina Goes To School, And The Belts Get Ever Tighter

A new Australian film, *Smiley*, came to the Civic in January, and Katrina and I were desperate to see it, but our parents were saving money by not going to town so often and so we missed it. We were deeply disappointed. To see ourselves on screen was a novelty and a proud thrill for Australians then, and it was an all-too-rare event. We were just an outpost of the empire, a backwater where nothing ever happened. Everything important or interesting in the world happened somewhere else – mostly in England, as far as we could tell.

Carmel and Neil were to be married at the end of January, and our parents prepared to go to Sydney for yet another wedding. This time, we were all farmed out – Katrina, Philomena and I to Cheyenne, and the boys again to Pas and Clennell Fenwicke. Since we loved going to Cheyenne this was no hardship, and Mrs Bloo demonstrated another miraculous product: Saran Wrap, a stretchy plastic you could use instead of cloth or a plate to cover leftover food. Buddy's parents had sent it from Canada, and we had never seen it before. This time I managed to read to the end the tattered copy of *The Diary of Anne Frank* that I had put aside two years before. The book had a profound effect on me. I was one with Anne; she was my temporary best friend. Many years later, when I visited the house in Amsterdam where the family had hidden from the Nazis and saw the magazine and newspaper cuttings that Anne had pasted on the wall all those years before, I burst into tears and had to leave.

At our first family dinner after their return, our parents had an announcement to make. Grandma had decided that it was Katrina's turn to make her First Holy Communion and to spend some time being civilised at Rosemont, and furthermore, she was to stay the entire year. She could use my uniform, my Globite case and my textbooks. My mother was grateful for the offer; she had had a difficult time teaching Katrina, who was resistant to poetry and history (although quite good at maths) and only wanted to be out in the paddocks with my father. But we would all miss her, I most of all.

We put Katrina on the train only a week or so later. I went with my father to Walcha Road to see her off, and I remember her earnest little nine-year-old face pressed to the window as the train began to pull out of the station, a slight frown of anxiety creasing her brow. I knew what she was thinking, and I was thinking it too. Who was going to milk the cow and make the butter now? Who was going to be our father's right-hand man?

Since it was time for Aidan and Robert to start correspondence lessons, our mother now had a little school room going on the back verandah, yet more work for her in addition to the laundry, the gardening, the preserving, the housekeeping and the cooking. Even though she no longer had Katrina's stubbornness to deal with, adding the boys to the school roll proved to be a challenge. Every time Mum went to attend to the washing, or answer the telephone, a scuffle broke out. Or one of the twins disappeared.

'Where's Robert?' she would say when she returned. 'Turn my back for a minute and he's shot through like a Bondi tram.'

In the end, I moved myself and my lessons permanently to the kitchen table, so that I would not have the distractions they created, since I was still determined to get most of my week's work done by Wednesday.

I felt the loss of Katrina keenly. She had been my friend, companion and confidante. Now that she was gone, I took my refuge more and more in books. My mother scolded me for hiding away and reading when I should have been weeding the garden, or sweeping the kitchen floor, or bringing in washing or firewood, because by now my reading habit was almost a compulsion. I was demolishing *A Traveller in Time* by Alison Uttley, *The Wool-pack* by Cynthia Harnett, *The Ark* and *Rowan Farm* by Margot Benary-Isbert, anything I could lay my hands on by Geoffrey Trease or Malcolm Saville and more. Mrs Brazel at the library kept me informed of new books coming in by my favourite authors. I read *My Family and Other Animals* by Gerald Durrell, which made me want to go to Greece. I read Ethel Turner's *Seven Little Australians*, and after the last page I threw myself into my mother's arms and wept inconsolably.

Finances were tighter than ever. Not only had our numbers of sheep and cattle been reduced since the drought, our 1958 clip had again been small and the price we received for it barely sufficient to pay the shopkeepers and merchants to whom we owed money, let alone the bank and Grandma. Wool prices were now only a small fraction of what they had been in the early 50s and the loans caused by our various catastrophes were by now crippling. Nevertheless, my father was determined to press on. What else was there to do?

One day at Winterbourne I noticed a straight row of stones set into the ground outside the front gate. My mother said that they must be what remained of a wall from the original convict-built settlement there more than a hundred years before. A wall, here?

Had there been another house here? Who had lived in it? What had happened to them? My mind raced with curiosity. Could we dig this wall up and see what we could find? No, said my mother, and that was that. My archaeological inclinations would have to wait.

~

'Heave away, haul away,' the boys and I shouted, as we glided over the water. 'Land ahoy!' we yelled. Balanced precariously in our little flat-bottomed boat, we paddled with all our might, the skull and crossbones flag fluttering in the breeze. The *Hispaniola*, an old sea-trunk turned boat, was newly painted green, her name spelled out in decorative gold lettering on her stern. Our father had installed wooden seats, a mast and even a wooden prow with a carved mermaid. Sometimes it paid to have a father who was a frustrated artist. We pushed on into the centre of the dam's muddy brown water, where no man had been before, and then to the opposite shore, where he had. When I hopped out to pull the boat ashore in the way my father had shown us, the twins continued to sit there, disappointed there was not more. So I pushed them back in and they paddled happily round in more circles.

With the drought scare of 1957 fresh in his mind, my father had decided to build a new dam in the front paddock, on the other side of the Cheyenne road, not too far from the sheep yards and shearing shed. With some help from Buddy Blomfield, he began this task himself, fitting a blade to the tractor, and a grader came out from Walcha to finish the job, which took another few days. The dam was to hold perhaps 250,000 gallons of water and would help shore us up against another dry spell.

Miraculously, at the next rains the dam did indeed fill with water, and we could even swim in it, although the water was muddy, the banks were gravelly and there was no nearby shade. But we had our new boat, the *Hispaniola*, to take us to imaginary far-away places, if we screwed up our eyes hard enough. We were to take the *Hispaniola* to the river at Waterloo and to holiday picnics beside various dams around the district for several years, where it was to delight dozens of other Walcha children.

About this time, a leaflet from the government came through the mail. It seemed we were under threat and the Russians might drop a nuclear bomb on us at any time. The leaflet advised that the nuclear fallout could spread for thousands of miles, and that no-one was immune. It said we should take a supply of food and water, go into a room with no windows and wait there for three days.

'What will we do?' I asked my mother. 'We don't have a room without windows, unless you count the hallway outside the bathroom. How can we save ourselves?'

Her reply was philosophical. 'We'll worry about it when the time comes. Just now we have bigger things to worry about.'

Clearly, if my parents weren't worried about nuclear fallout, then it would be up to me to help keep the family safe. I spent several sleepless nights figuring out how to rig up a curtain of wet blankets across the small hallway outside the bathroom, how to make sure there was enough water and food, and otherwise worrying about what we would all do in the event of an attack.

~

In March, during a visit to the library, Mrs Brazel pulled me aside.

'Look at this leaflet,' she said. 'The Namoi Regional Library is holding an essay competition for school children. I think you ought to enter.'

The topic was 'The Benefits to the Public of the Namoi Regional

Library System', which seemed rather dry and boring, but since Mrs Brazel seemed to think I could do it, I would try. With my mother's encouragement, I worked away at my little essay and mailed it in. Not with much hope, because in the past I had mailed several drawings and stories in to the Argonauts program on the radio, hoping that my pen name, Philomela 19, would be mentioned in their weekly commendations, but it never was, so after three or four tries I had given up.

Now that we could all pitch in a little more, and were becoming more competent, life perhaps became a tiny bit easier for my mother, although probably not much. Looking back on those days, I don't remember ever hearing her complain, although she expressed many anxieties. Would we all be 'rooned', as Hanrahan predicted? Good wives were taught to accept the burdens God and their husbands gave them, and so she did, scrimping, saving and making the best of things, day after week after month. It's possible that, as her mother would have advised, she offered up her trials and sufferings to help the poor souls in Purgatory, but whether this gave her any consolation, I don't know. Years later, when she read *The Feminine Mystique* and *The Female Eunuch*, Mum became angry at the pup she felt she had been sold, but not then.

I was eleven now, and my father was teaching me to wield an axe, so that I could split the wood for the stove. Soon I could split a short log in two in one chop. I had been worried that, with Katrina gone, Dad might have me back milking the cow, but usually he did it himself. Our days continued to be an endless round of chores and thankless tasks, collecting kindling and firewood, working in the garden, lessons, sweeping, cleaning, feeding the dogs, cooking, washing up, raking the pine needles from the front yard, and helping in the sheep yards, and it seemed to us that nothing ever happened. By now I knew better than to hope that the plane that flew overhead daily might land in our front paddock.

And then one Monday, Mr Grieve brought a letter for me from the Namoi Regional Library. He plucked it from our pile and handed it to me personally. It said that my essay was highly commended, and that I was invited to collect my ten-shilling prize at a special ceremony in Tamworth. The overall winner was from Tamworth or Armidale, but the following week *The Walcha News* reported that (perhaps thanks to Mrs Brazel) two or three other Walcha children had also been honoured with high commendations and it listed our names. So as not to waste a trip to Tamworth, my mother made appointments for us to get dental check-ups.

In Tamworth Town Hall, the mayor and the president of the Namoi Regional Library system gave speeches, and shook hands with each of us as we walked up to collect our prizes. Tea and Arnott's biscuits were served afterwards on trestle tables with white table cloths. I could not wait to get back to Walcha and put my cheque in my Commonwealth Savings Account, where the teller would write it up in my passbook. Added to my meagre savings, plus the ten shillings money order that our Scottish grandparents had sent for my birthday, I now had more than twenty-eight shillings in there, and felt armed against all eventualities.

As we drove back through Walcha town we saw signs for the coming visit of Bullen's Circus, but we knew better than to beg to go. Money was too tight.

~

The pine trees swayed and bent in the winds, and the needles fell on the roof like rain. It was going to be another cold winter, and in mid-June we were recording temperatures in the low 20s (say -6 Celsius), well below freezing. No amount of scratchy grey army surplus blankets would keep us warm, and the twins took to sleeping together in the same bunk, just for the extra body heat. In the mornings, we were scraping ice from the inside of the window panes, and the entire countryside was white with a thick, crisp frost, a frost that might not completely disappear from the south-facing surfaces for the entire day.

That winter I was given the task of being first up in the morning to light the kitchen fire and then get the stove going for the porridge. It was still dark, so I crept across the back courtyard with the lamp we had taken to bed the night before. First, the stove. The newspaper and kindling were there, in the box, but my fingers were so stiff from cold that it was hard to light the match – and I knew enough by now not to meddle with kerosene. Once the stove got going, I turned to the main fireplace, which, if one was lucky, might not have gone out completely overnight, although it usually had, which meant cleaning out yesterday's ashes first.

Sometimes the bucket of water we kept beside the sink for drinking and cooking water had a thick film of ice on it, so we would have to crack the ice before we could pour water into the kettle for the breakfast tea.

By the time there was a roaring blaze going in the fireplace, and I had braided my hair into its two long plaits, the others would begin to creep in, with their bundles of clothes and shoes, to dress in front of the fire. My father came in from having milked the cow, stamping his feet and blowing on his hands. After the warming comfort of our porridge, we huddled around the fire to make toast with our wire toasting forks. There was no bread to spare if you burnt your piece; it was a good scraping down or no toast. We became expert at toasting, from necessity.

Despite the fact that we were saving money by not going to town, one cold winter Saturday we did go, and *Boy on a Dolphin*, starring Sophia Loren and Alan Ladd, was showing at the Civic. Incredibly we were allowed to see it. This film, with its glorious images of a sun-drenched, whitewashed fishing village on a Greek island, and Sophia Loren diving in clear green waters seeking an ancient bronze statue, gave us a sudden out-of-this-world summer. As the underwater scenes flickered across the screen accompanied by the strains of ethereal music, we were borne away on a cloud of joy. We didn't care about the jeering and booing from the boys downstairs that greeted the final dramatic embraces. Philomena and I dreamed of the film for months, and it remains vivid in my mind. I was now officially in love with Greece. Gerald Durrell had started it, but *Boy on a Dolphin* decided the matter. That day I resolved to find that island. I resolved to learn Greek. Forget being Betty Cuthbert. Forget being a doctor. I was going to be an archaeologist.

Chapter 25

In Which My Future Is Decided

As the years had rolled by, visitors had come and gone: Carmel, Grandma and Aunt Phil sometimes, and various others, mostly aunts and cousins.

Our cousin Mark, a rather delicate child, came for several summers, and we were supposed to fatten him up and make him stronger. On one of Mark's stays, my father killed a sheep, sending poor little Mark scurrying from the laundry steps to hide under the kitchen table in fright. Mark did get a little bigger and tougher under our regime, however, and we usually sent him back to Sydney with more roses in his cheeks than he had arrived with.

My mother's friend Ursula White came two or three times with her children, who included Joanne, Jenny, Mary, Marguerite and Antony. Ursula was Swiss-Italian, and she entertained us by singing Italian songs – 'Santa Lucia' or 'Marina' or 'Funiculi Funicula'. She lined us up in the kitchen like a little choir and schooled us in the chorus of 'Marina' until we were word perfect.

Marina, Marina, Marina
Ti voglio al piu presto sposar ...

When these families came to visit there was much reapportioning of beds, with up to three children to a bed, two at one end and one at the other. A single adult could sleep on the daybed on the enclosed verandah at the back of the house where we did our lessons. A married couple might sleep in our parents' bed, while our parents slept on sheepskins on the living room floor. Once, when some neighbours from Bondi came to visit, they brought their own accommodation – a caravan. When Basil came to stay, which in our last years there he did often, he just took the top bunk in the boys' room while the boys together took the bottom. Peggy, Basil's mother, who had been left a widow when Basil was only two, was a close friend of Aunt Phil from her nursing days. Somehow, my father became a kind of father-substitute for him. Basil brought various enthusiasms with him – chemistry sets, a fancy camera, books on sailing and seafaring.

Visitors were not just a welcome break from our daily routines, but they frequently brought things – yo-yos, hula hoops, old tennis racquets, footballs, comic books – things that we leapt upon with joy and which brought hours of pleasure.

A memorable visitor was Anna Cohen. Anna, a year older than I, was the great-niece of our grandmother's friend Miss Murphy, and Miss Murphy for some reason was raising her. When she came to us she slept in Philomena's bed, while Philomena bundled in with Katrina. Anna was a born storyteller, with a flair for the dramatic. At night as we lay in the dark, Anna would tell us the story of films she had seen – *The White Feather* or *A Night to Remember* or, her personal favourite on one visit, *Trapeze*. One night Anna told us the story of the apparition of the Virgin to the three children at Fatima, and how eventually thousands of people had seen the sun roll around in the sky. The Virgin had given the children a letter, Anna said, which was to be opened by the Pope in 1960, and which would foretell the end of the world along with two other secrets, which were so darkly terrible that they could not be revealed until then. This revelation filled us with dread and anxiety, which lasted long beyond Anna's departure. It was much scarier than bunyips and banshees. 'The end of the world is coming? Really?' we asked, shivering under our scratchy grey blankets.

Not all visitors came to stay, however. Sometimes a travelling salesman would arrive, wanting to sell my mother a vacuum cleaner or encyclopaedias. Once a man came bringing brochures for the University of New England. Sometimes the bank manager would track our parents down in their lair. One evening a priest showed up. He was lost, but he was given dinner and ended up staying the night. In the morning he said Mass in our living room. My mother got us all up and dressed in our good clothes, and the priest instructed the twins how to serve as altar boys. This was so solemn and special an occasion that for once the rascal in them was subdued and they carried out their duties with dignity and grace.

But whoever came, a visitor never went away without a cup of tea and whatever refreshments we could provide, whether it be Anzac biscuits from the tin or freshly baked scones, for how could we allow someone to travel so far and not give them food and some rest? The minute we saw the dust across the opposite hill, my mother put the kettle on the stove, just in case. If the car came past Winterbourne, we would throw some extra wood in the stove. The tea meant settling in for a leisurely chat or a conversation– the weather, Mr Menzies, sports, gossip – at the kitchen table.

In 1959 Neil's friend Prof, that is to say Dr Peter Evans, came to stay. His visit was an honour. He stayed for two weeks, helping my father in the paddocks, and chatting deep into the night by the fire with our parents. They were surely glad of the company, but we children were just as fascinated by the fact that he had brought the biggest box of chocolates we had ever seen: four layers, housed in an elaborate plastic box that resembled a Chinese pagoda.

After Prof went back to Sydney he wrote to say that he had decided to become a Franciscan priest, and would be entering the seminary in 1960. Had he come to stay in order to wrestle with the decision away from the hectic pace of the city? Or did our large and chaotic family scare him off the idea of marriage and children? Who knows?

In August, we met Katrina, returning for school holidays, at Walcha Road station. It was only for a few brief weeks, but we were all happy to see her and by the next day it was as though she had never been away. She had spent some of the pocket money Phil had given her on songbooks with the lyrics of current pop songs, and we sang around the house as we went about our business. 'Lipstick on your collar,' we wailed as we made our beds. 'It was a one-eyed, one-horned flyin' purple people eater,' as we pulled weeds in the vegetable garden. 'Catch a falling star and put it in your pocket,' as we unpegged the washing from the line. 'Hang down your head, Tom Dooley,' as we peeled potatoes for dinner. Finally, my father declared that he had had enough of our caterwauling for the time being, so we were forced to take our talents outdoors.

But the nights were cold and, a massive fireguard having been found at an estate sale, our parents finally decided that we girls could have a fire in our bedroom. It meant Dad had to clean out the long disused chimney first, a dirty exercise indeed, but we were pleased and happy. For us this was unimaginable luxury, even if it did only happen when the temperature dropped below freezing.

Since I was now in the sixth and final year of primary school, various papers began to arrive from the Department of Education outlining choices for my future education. High school. This was important. The subjects I took from First Year (now Year 7) would determine my course through school, and hence my entire future. My parents hoped that I might be university material and didn't want to cut off my options.

The Education Department arranged for me to go into Walcha Central School one day during the holidays and take a test. Because my mother had errands to run, she dropped me off at the school with my copy of Esther Forbes's *Johnny Tremain* a little early, and so I spent some time chatting to the gentleman who was conducting the tests while other test takers arrived. Most of them were students at the school, but one, like me, was a correspondence student from outside town. Finally, about ten or twelve of us were sat in a classroom and handed a booklet, which we were instructed not to open until told. Finally, we heard the words, 'You may begin,' and off we went.

When the test was finished I waited on a bench in the corridor for my mother to come and pick me up, while the other students melted away and the gentleman sat in the office to grade our completed efforts. When he came out of the office I asked him, 'Well, how did I do? Did I get everything right?'

He looked at me, startled, and said, 'My, aren't we the little perfectionist?'

But it seems I got enough of the answers right for the Education Department to write to my parents and suggest I be put on a track for university. Since the options available from Walcha were very limited, this put them in a dilemma. Various possibilities were batted back and forth over some weeks. My mother wanted to apply to Grandma to send me back to Rose Bay. My father didn't want to be more beholden to his mother-in-law than he already was. I was alert to these tensions, and just as curious about my future as they were. However, there was no point in my having a preference of my own. I would have to do as my parents decided.

Finally, my father agreed that my mother could ask Grandma if I could live with her while I attended Sydney Girls High School.

We went on with our lives. The shearing came around, with again only one shearer, the colourful Lionel, and then the lambing. New plantings went into the vegetable garden to supply our summer table and beyond. We all did our lessons, shifting to the kitchen table on cold days. The Namoi Library announced a map-drawing contest – a map of New South Wales highlighting the Namoi region – and Philomena and I both laboured over our entries, encouraged by suggestions and criticisms from my father, and sent them in.

One day in town my mother and I ran into Father McKeown at the post office.

'Oh, Mrs Wales,' he said, 'we have Confirmation coming up in November. Do you want to have Angela confirmed?'

Cornered, my mother agreed. I had to get confirmed at some point, and she didn't need the expense of a new dress, with the First Communion one still hanging there in the wardrobe; it would likely still do. It was good to have another momentous occasion to look forward to, but by the time November came around, the dress was too tight and too short. It was a stifling hot day, and the whole family crammed in to the already crowded church for the long Mass and to watch the bishop pronounce at length on the importance of Catholic faith and the evils of the demon drink before conducting the drawn-out ceremony. When it was over we were glad to leave, and I had second thoughts about momentous occasions.

Grandma wrote back on the Sydney Girls High School question, expressing her horror. She probably didn't say so in so many words, but it was clear that no granddaughter of hers was going to a state school, full of Protestants, Jews and heathens in probably equal measure. We were to leave the problem in her hands.

A few weeks after we received Grandma's letter, Mr Grieve brought two more interesting missives. The first letter was to say that Philomena had won a prize in the Namoi Regional Library map-drawing contest, and although I had not won a cash prize, my effort had been commended, and I was to get a certificate. We were to go to Tamworth for another ceremony. We helped Mum choose some material and patterns in Walcha and she began to make us new dresses. In early December, we piled into the car, along with Anthony Fenwicke, who was staying with us, for the trip to Tamworth. We wore our crisp new dresses to collect our honours and to our very great surprise and excitement, my father agreed to stop at the Moonbi Lookout on the way back. My mother took photos, and so we have a precious record of the day. If only Katrina had been with us.

The second letter was from Grandma, and contained her decision regarding my high schooling. She had spoken to the nuns at Rose Bay, and they had agreed to take me as a boarder as soon as a place could be found. She would foot the bill. Boarding school! I could not think of anything more exciting. My head was full of Enid Blyton's *Malory Towers* series, and of stories with titles like *Phoebe of the Fourth* and *The Youngest Girl in the School*. Now I was going to be part of this exclusive, self-contained and exotic world.

Chapter 26

My New Friend, A Haircut And A Ten-Pound Bet

It had been decided that Katrina would continue to stay with Grandma and attend school in Sydney, where, away from the temptations of the paddocks, she had been doing well. We were both to live with Grandma and Phil until the nuns could find a boarding place for me. We had had a good Christmas at home, and Katrina had tumbled into her ragged jodhpurs and turned out into the paddocks with all her old enthusiasm intact. We were happy to have her with us for the holidays. The nuns had not managed to tame her tomboy tendencies, nor her passion for the work of the place, for the sheep, the dogs, the cows and our small herd of cattle. Though she never did take much interest in the chooks. They were Philomena's province.

We sewed our Cash's tape laundry numbers onto our school clothes and looked forward to this new phase in our lives. We understood and accepted that Grandma, Aunt Phil and the nuns were conspiring to mould us into young ladies, in training to be good Catholic wives: accomplished and well-educated enough to be efficient mothers and to be of potential service to the community, and obedient enough to make observant Catholics. But we knew we would miss the daily rhythms of the countryside, the changing seasons, the wide-open skies, the never-ending round of chores and daily tasks.

There were other changes afoot, too. The Walcha Council finally agreed to bring a school bus to the Blue Mountain turnoff, at the junction of Winterbourne and Blue Mountain roads, where the mailboxes were. Now Philomena and the boys could go to school at St Patrick's. This was no small matter. Although my mother had to make two return trips to the turnoff every day, the burden of teaching was lifted from her. And she now had several hours each day to 'get on with things', as she put it. Pas Fenwicke was the bus driver, earning some pin money to supplement Earsdon's seriously shrinking wool cheque.

I was getting to be an old hand at the train to Sydney, and this time Katrina and I were to travel together. There was a new train now – the old steam engine had gone, and a quieter, less impressive diesel engine had taken its place. We were sorry, though; even though the trip was faster, the great steam train, with its grinding, huffing and puffing, had a grandeur and excitement that a diesel engine could not match.

Katrina and I were not the only children at the Walcha Road station; several others were also lined up with their parents along the platform, many wearing their school uniforms. Most of the landed Walcha children went to school in Armidale, but some went to Sydney, and here they were. We knew all the schools: Shore, Scots, Kambala (which was next door to the convent at Rose Bay), PLC, SCEGS. These shorthand names held a wealth of symbolism for the New South Wales middle classes of the day. Most of our fellow travellers were older than we were, so a couple of them were told to keep an eye on us, including Brian Turton, an older boy whose parents, pillars of the Walcha community, were friendly with ours. Brian was a tall boy, and his first move on getting settled was to pull off his school tie and buy a beer from the buffet car.

We arrived in Sydney to the news that Carmel had given birth to a baby girl, to be named Clare. Both she and Neil were delighted, and Grandma took us to visit mother and baby in the hospital.

On my first day at school I was seated up the back of the classroom at a double desk. The other occupant of the desk was a skinny girl with blonde plaits. 'Hello,' she said, as soon as I sat down, cocking her head to one side. 'I'm Libby. Who are you?'

From that moment we were fast friends. Libby was one of two other day girls, living with her parents in Double Bay. She had been a boarder with the nuns at their junior school campus, Kerever Park, since she was eight. It was she who saved my life at school, who took me under her wing and protected me, initiating me into those rites and customs of the Sacred Heart order that I had yet to learn.

The trams, which Libby and I took together to and from school, and which rattled and shifted their cranky gears up the New South Head Road hills and whined their way down them, were soon to go. During that year they were phased out and were replaced by double-decker buses. I was sorry about this, as I had loved the trams, which had seemed to me to be the essence of Sydney, and far more romantic than the buses.

Libby and I were conscientious learners of French, because it was our intention to save up and go to Europe, including Paris, just as soon as we were old enough. Latin, too, could do us no harm. It would help us with Italian when we went to Rome and Venice.

'We will be bluestockings,' said Libby, 'and fascinating, well-travelled women with salons. We'll invite all the artists and writers for cocktails.' I could only agree, wide-eyed at such ideas. What was a cocktail?

Saturday at Rosemont was hair-washing day. I still had my long plaits, of which I was very proud, but it's true that my hair was slow to dry – we had never heard of a hairdryer. After our hair was washed, Aunt Phil would take Katrina and me to Lyne Park at Rose Bay in Grandma's car. She made us sit in the car for a while until she thought our hair was dry enough, because if it wasn't, she felt, there was a risk of our getting pneumonia. After what seemed like hours, she relented and let us go play on the swings while she read the newspaper.

I was still possessed of a small slouch, apparently, so on some Sundays there was more pulling back of shoulders and more walking around the living room with books on my head. Katrina, for her part, was thought to be pigeon-toed; she was made to walk up and down the living room in straight lines.

'How are you ever going to get a husband if you can't walk gracefully?' asked Aunt Phil.

'I don't need to look for a husband, I'm going to marry Robbie Blomfield,' protested Katrina.

'Nonsense, don't be ridiculous,' said Aunt Phil, poking Katrina between the shoulders. 'He's not even a Catholic.'

One morning I arrived at school feeling very tired and shivery. Mother Wittering, in the Infirmary, took my temperature and sent me home.

'It's pneumonia,' pronounced Dr Pierce at my Rosemont bedside, stuffing his stethoscope back into his bag.

'It's that long hair,' said Aunt Phil.

'Well, not necessarily. I'll prescribe antibiotics, and normally I would admit her to the hospital, but since you are a nurse I think we can safely trust her to your good offices. Just let me know if there's any change.'

Phil blamed herself. She should never have let me out of the car with damp hair. Grandma said it was God's will and said more Rosaries.

In the end, I was off school for about three weeks. A few times a week, Libby came after school and sat by my bed, bringing me the French and Latin lessons and vocabulary to learn, with a movie plot or two thrown in. And Carmel came by with her tattered copy of *Pride and Prejudice*. I fell in love with the book and was head over heels for Mr Darcy.

My mother wrote with news from home: our kelpie Baxter had swallowed some dingo bait and died. The family were all very upset, and she said that Dad had taken it very badly. This was a blow. Although we were not allowed to spoil the working dogs as pets, we loved them and they were part of the family. They were our father's constant companions when out in the paddocks or the bush. And they were expensive to replace and required a good deal of time to train.

Aunt Christine (just Christine by now) dropped by in her Qantas uniform. She was a fully-fledged air hostess, sharing a flat with some other hostesses, and jetting off to Singapore and Hong Kong and Europe. She gave Katrina and me advice about the importance of face cream and pushing back your cuticles. She seemed to us to be the height of glamour.

Once I was well enough to go back to school, there was a lot of catching up to do, mostly with the French and Latin, but things quickly settled back into their normal routine. I was taken unawares, therefore, when Grandma unexpectedly picked me up at school one afternoon and took me to a hairdresser on Oxford Street, near the top of Jersey Road.

'Take them off,' she commanded the hairdresser.

What? Take what off? But before I could muster a protest, the hairdresser had taken a huge pair of scissors and snipped off each plait, just like that. There they lay on the floor, my beautiful plaits, like two dead things. I sat there staring at them in shock.

Grandma and Aunt Phil had decided they were not going to risk another bout of pneumonia by allowing me to have wet hair streaming down my back every Saturday. They had not consulted me, nor my mother, who would have stood up for me, I was sure of it.

Because I tearfully asked to have them back, the hairdresser gave me my beautiful plaits in a paper bag, before giving my hair a bit of a tidy-up. Later I gave the plaits to my mother, who kept them in a drawer for years. My image of myself as a romantic heroine with long, flowing hair turned into one of a drab non-entity with a pudding basin haircut. No Mr Darcy would ever look at me now.

~

Katrina and I stepped off the train at Walcha Road station, home for the May holidays. There they were, Aidan and Robert, chasing the engine along the platform, wearing their lederhosen despite the chill. There was Philomena, twiddling the ribbon in her blonde hair.

We could see at once that things were not improving. My father had worn out the patches on the elbows of his jacket, and our mother was wearing a mended old dress, still too big for her since her illness. Next day we drove over to Waterloo to have tea with John and Barbie Fenwicke, and they, too, were anxious. The Waterloo wool cheque for the previous year had been miserably small, like ours, although John was still making a little money with his honey and other enterprises.

'It can hardly get any worse,' he declared. 'The days of Australia riding on the sheep's back are over. Wool prices will come up again, but possibly not in our lifetimes. The Korean War was a boon for wool growers, but we'd hardly want to wish for another war.'

My father was still trying to clear land, but it was very slow going, and he didn't have the funds to pay someone to help, although he had the boys helping with the livestock and pulling out suckers and regrowth. They were eight now, and able to pitch in with many of the paddock tasks, so in the mornings they rode off with Dad and Katrina on the truck and returned in the afternoon.

We all went on with mustering, drenching, crutching, chopping wood, tending the vegetable garden, milking Molly (who seemed glad to see Katrina back), mending, darning, making butter, feeding the animals and generally turning the wheels of existence. Katrina and I were glad to be home, although once again I stayed awake at night worrying about the family's financial situation. Although my parents had never mentioned such a possibility, my biggest dread was that someday we might have to leave.

And in no time at all we were back on the train to Grandma's. The nuns advised that they would have a boarding place for me in third term, after the August holidays, but in the meantime, I was able to spend more Saturday time running around Double Bay with Libby, who did not seem to mind that I only had shabby, hand-me-down clothes, apart from the one good jumper and tartan skirt for Mass on Sundays.

The next holidays coincided almost exactly with the summer Olympics in Rome. Again we crowded around the kitchen radio to listen to delayed broadcasts as Murray Rose and John Konrads and Dawn Fraser swam their way to victory and as runner Herb Elliott annihilated the competition in the 1500 metres. Once again, we set up hurdles in the front yard and tried our hand at athletic pursuits.

Katrina and I were home to help with the shearing, both in the kitchen and in the shed. Katrina was becoming an expert fleece handler, now almost able to throw the fleece on the sorting table in one go, and she began also to take an interest in classing. My father had taken some classing lessons in Armidale, so that he would not need to hire a classer, an extra expense. He started teaching Katrina, and allowed her to tackle the first sort.

The debt caused by the drought still hung over my parents like a sword. By the fire in the kitchen they discussed ways to make some extra income. Dad could make it known that he was willing to paint pictures for people and they decided to sell an antique rug and a couple of pieces of antique furniture in the living room. 'What about my engagement ring?' said Mum, but Dad said no.

I lay awake in my bed wondering what I could do to help. We were too far away from town for me to get a job, so in desperation I began writing what I hoped might become a best-selling children's story, Enid Blyton style. Perhaps I could save the family. But when I read the chapters I had written they seemed banal and clichéd. I threw them on the fire.

After the bales of wool had gone off to market, Mr Brien arrived one Saturday evening with steaks and a bottle or two of whisky. Mrs Brien had gone to the other side of Walcha to visit one of her children for a few days and he needed company. After dinner the adults settled down to listen to a radio play on the ABC. Being now twelve years old, I was allowed to stay up for a while, sitting in a corner with my book.

When the play was over my father, a sheet or two to the wind, exclaimed, 'That was bloody terrible. Hackneyed writing. I could have written a better play than that!'

Mr Brien, several more sheets to the wind, staggered to his feet, making violent stabs at his pocket. He produced a ten-pound note, which he slapped on the table. 'Oh, so you're a playwright now, are you? Next thing you'll be telling me you can ride the Old Grey Mare standing on your head. Here's a tenner to say you couldn't!' he challenged.

I looked up from my book in surprise. I had never seen a ten-pound note. It was a huge amount of money. But Mr Brien snatched his ten-pound note back from the table and staggered out to his car.

It might have been a week, or it might have been several weeks, later, that Mr Brien roared up to the front door and got out of his truck waving a newspaper, possibly the *Northern Daily Leader*, possibly the *Armidale Herald*. The University of New England's Adult Education Department was conducting a writing competition. There were three categories: poetry, drama and short story.

'You don't get away with it that easily,' said Mr Brien, poking his finger at the paper. 'Try your hand at this. See how you go. You win a prize and you've got your ten quid.'

My father and Old Bill, who had also been alerted, got to work, my father with pen and paper at the kitchen table after his day's labour in the sheds and paddocks. A week or so later, he put me and Katrina on the train back to school.

Boarding school life at Rose Bay bore no resemblance whatever to the life described in the English schoolgirl novels I had read. As a boarder, I may as well have entered the convent as a religious novice. The routine was rigorous, the rules many and complicated, and discipline strict. Enforced silence prevailed for a large part of the day. It was a miserable and anxious time for me, since I kept getting into inadvertent trouble of one kind or another.

My mother wrote to say that the blossoms were out in the

orchard and that my father had written a one-act play and was busy on a short story, both of which he planned to submit to the University of New England competition. A lady in Walcha was going to type them up for him.

The Christmas holidays came around soon enough, and, exams over, one warm Friday in early December Katrina and I were back on the platform at Central Station to take the Northern Tablelands Express to Walcha Road. I had in my suitcase a couple of leather-bound volumes handed out at the school prize-giving night, which made both my grandmother and my parents very happy.

Not long after our arrival home, Mr Grieve's truck rattled up over the ramp bringing not one, but two letters from the University of New England. My father ripped them open and read them right there in the front yard, with my mother peering over his shoulder. We heard her sharp intake of breath and joyful exclamation. It seemed that Mr Robert Wales, of 'Arran', Walcha, had won second place in the Drama category of their recent writing competition for his play *White Bird Passing* and third place for his story *The Searchers* in the Short Story category. He had won two guineas for the play and a guinea for the short story. Enclosed with the cheques were the comments from the judges.

The judges for the Drama category were complimentary and encouraging about the play. The judges for the short story category noted that Mr Wales had a talent for dialogue, and that he should think about writing plays.

We could hardly believe it, but that was not even the best part. The best part was that Mr Brien was probably going to have to pay out on his bet – ten whole pounds.

Poor Old Bill, however, did not even get a mention in the poetry section, which was a bitter disappointment to him, since he had submitted several entries.

Just a few days later Mr Brien drove up, delivering the crisp new note along with a bottle of whisky, which he waved happily as he marched into our kitchen. He opened it right away.

Christmas was a happier one than it might have been, given the way things were. It wasn't just the hangovers from the various disasters. Since we started on Arran, the price of wool had sunk lower and lower, partly due to competition from new-fangled synthetic fabrics, partly due to other forces. How long could we keep going on a declining income?

Chapter 27

Plan B

My father began to see a way out of our difficulties: he was going to try to supplement his income from sheep and cattle with some playwriting on the side. He used his prize money from the competition to purchase a small Olivetti portable typewriter, which he set at the end of the kitchen table, only to be put aside for meals. He was going to start with a full-length play. The Infant of Prague sat imperturbable in his place of honour on the mantelpiece. If he smiled, we did not notice it.

It is clear to me now that my father was something of a dreamer. He might as well have been standing at the edge of the verandah trying to fly, but he was going to throw his whole heart and soul into this new dream. He was going to give it his all. Since Katrina was home to milk the cow, that summer my father wrote for an hour or so before breakfast, and then again after dinner at night, *tap-tap-tapping* away with only two or three fingers. My mother read everything and made comments and suggestions. He had joined the Fellowship of Australian Writers, and its newsletter brought news of more writing competitions. There was one being run by the Far West Queensland Theatrical Association, with quite good prize money. He put the full-length play aside for now and embarked on a new one-act play, which he planned to enter in the Queensland competition.

'If you win, can I have a watch?' I asked. I didn't have one, let alone a fancy one like the girls at school. He said yes.

Soon afterwards he learned that the city of Coffs Harbour, up the coast to the north of Port Macquarie, was planning a centenary to mark the city's founding. As part of the celebrations, the local arts council was running a playwriting competition. They wanted a full-length play.

By the time we went back to school in late January my father was well along with the play for the Queensland competition, and as soon as he finished that he was going to complete the one for the Coffs Harbour competition. He wrote only a couple of hours a day – there were still sheep to be tended, fences to fix – but I noticed that he was no longer clearing land.

Katrina and I arrived back at Rosemont to find a new piece of furniture in the corner of Grandma's living room: a large walnut cabinet containing a state-of-the-art black and white television set. This was an unexpected thrill, but alas, the only thing that Grandma and Aunt Phil authorised as suitable watching were religious services on Sundays and classical music concerts. Otherwise the television sat sadly in the corner with its walnut doors firmly closed.

~

The May holidays were notable for several things. First, I came down with a high fever, and my worried mother drove me into town to see Dr Dodd.

'Straight to Tamworth Hospital with you, my girl,' said Dr Dodd, and so down the ranges we went, winding past Woolbrook and Bendemeer and Kootingal with its chicken farms. It was another bout of pneumonia. It was most disappointing to have to miss several days of my precious holidays in this way, but it did lead to the next notable thing: my first bra.

When I told my mother I wanted a bra like the other girls at school she took me to Treloar's without argument. We tried on some white cotton bras and came away with two. I could barely wait to take them home and sew my school number into each of them.

As we approached Winterbourne, me proudly wearing one of my new bras, we found bulldozers and graders and trucks busy moving earth and rocks to make a new road. The road down by the Old Stone House to the Winterbourne Creek was being diverted, and Walcha Council was about to build a bridge over the creek, a little further upstream from the ford. All the years of lobbying had finally paid off. Since they had already extended the bitumen road from town by several miles, almost a third of the way to our place, getting to and from town was going to be much easier.

Almost as exciting, however, was that Grandma's Christmas present to the family had been the funds to put in a septic tank and flushing toilet and my father had begun to install it. The toilet would go in the storeroom and the water for flushing would come from the spring.

As we stood watching my father dig the pit for the tank out beyond the dog kennels, he said, 'Don't let anyone ever tell you that intellectual labour is harder than physical labour. It isn't, not anywhere near.'

As he dug, he found something, an old Ardath cigarette tin. It was covered in rust and dirt, but it rattled. There were things inside. I begged my father to let me have it. I took it to the tank and cleaned it up under the tap there, and then we managed to get it open. Inside were some military medals and, folded inside a thick piece of paper, some old photographs of men in military uniform.

At lunch time, my father and I had a closer look.

'These things belonged to an Anzac soldier from the First World War,' he said. 'See, there's an AIF badge and these medals probably represent various campaigns. They probably belonged to the original owner of the house. I wonder if he is still alive?"

We agreed that next time we went to Sydney we would look up the medals and see what they were, and what campaigns they might have represented. I put the tin under my bed, wondering about who had buried it. Who *were* the original owners of the house? Why had someone buried the tin? Where was the soldier now? What was the story behind these things?

Then Mr Grieve brought a letter with the news that my father had come second in the Far West Queensland Theatrical Association competition, with his play *Wings on the Morning*. It had been a close call, the judges said, but he had lost to established Sydney dramatist Marian Dreyer, which gave him great heart. If he had to lose, it was reassuring to lose to someone well known in the field. He hadn't won but the cheque seemed to me like a generous amount, so I was still hopeful of receiving my longed-for watch. Where was my watch? Everyone at school had a watch.

But my parents couldn't spare the money for a watch, although as a consolation my mother gave us two shillings each the following Saturday to go to the pictures to see *The Big Country*. Going to the pictures had become a rare treat, because there was a widespread depression on the land now. Money was tighter than ever, and at our place every economy that could possibly be made was being made. Relatives in Sydney were sending more boxes of cast-off clothes and shoes. There seemed to be no light at the end of the tunnel. Again, I lay in bed at night, fretting about our future. If only we could win the lottery.

Philomena and the boys went back to school a week before Katrina and I did, and we helped scrape the ice off the windshield of the car in the mornings, so that Mum could drive them to the turnoff to get the bus. The younger children had mixed feelings about their new regime; St Patrick's was tolerable enough, but the boys were not happy about some of the older boys who rode the school bus with them, who appeared to enjoy tormenting the younger children. Pas Fenwicke did her best to control things, but she needed to keep her eyes on the road, and it was not always enough.

By the time we went back to school, the new septic tank was fully installed and the winter frosts were deepening and the ground hardening. A few more weeks and the ground would have been too hard to dig. It was a novel sensation, having a toilet practically in the house, and a flushing one at that, although to conserve water, flushing was kept to a minimum. Better still, we had to use proper toilet paper instead of newspaper, because the septic tank would not tolerate pieces of *The Walcha News* or pages of the *Reader's Digest*. Philomena was very pleased.

In Sydney we received momentous news from home: our father had won – not come second or third but won – the Coffs Harbour Centenary Playwriting Competition with *The Hobby Horse*. A telephone call had come with the news at 1pm, as our parents were in the kitchen having lunch. There was to be a prize-giving ceremony at a ball in Coffs Harbor that very evening. My father was excited and wanted to go. But given the very short notice, and not wanting to impose on the kindness of our neighbours yet again, they agreed between them that my father would go while my mother stayed behind with the children.

But as Dad was preparing to leave, Mrs Bloo dropped by on

her way back from town to deliver some items she had picked up for them at the co-op. When she heard of their plan, she wouldn't hear of it.

'Nonsense, Joan! You can't not go. You must be with Bob for this. Anyway, even Blind Freddie can see that you need a break. You can wear your blue dress. I'll pick up the kids from the bus and take them home with me. Off you go, go and put something in a bag.'

It was all arranged. The prize was to be presented along with a song-writing prize at the gala Centenary Arts Ball. It was going to be one of the most glamorous events of the decade for Coffs Harbour. Mum and Dad drove northeast all afternoon and arrived just as the ball was starting. It was raining heavily, but they were welcomed with enthusiasm, were even feted and celebrated. Next day they were shown the sights, including the Big Banana, and the souvenir they brought home was an extra-large bunch of bananas.

Later the news of the ball and the competition and my father's acceptance speech made the front page of the Coffs Harbour paper.

In August Katrina and I came home for the holidays to find our father again at the kitchen table, *tap-tap-tapping* away with two fingers at his little Olivetti. This time he was writing another full-length stage play, but with no competition to enter it in. One of the Coffs Harbour competition judges had been Leslie Rees, head of ABC Radio Drama, who had been very impressed with *The Hobby Horse* and had written encouraging my father to write more.

It was still very much winter and one day I had gone out the kitchen door to the verandah and failed to latch it properly. There was a gale blowing outside and the door flew open, with a huge gust blowing my father's papers off the table and all over the floor. He jumped up and flew at me in a fury, starting to unbuckle his belt.

'Oh no, you don't!' I yelled at him, ducking out of the way. 'I'm too old for that now. I'll pick them all up, I promise, but you're not belting me.'

Where I found the sudden courage for this defiance, I'll never know. But I did. And I had to spend the next hour picking up all the pages of his new play and trying to piece the whole thing back together. Since he had not numbered the pages, this was tricky, but eventually it was done – although Dad was still fuming. The play was called *The Grotto*, and it was a Romeo and Juliet-style drama set among the immigrant Italian community in his old haunt of Woolloomooloo, where his small factory had been.

But there was more news. Leslie Rees wrote again, to say that the ABC would like to broadcast both *Wings on the Morning* and *The Hobby Horse* as radio plays. Plays produced by the ABC were relayed all over Australia. This was a very great honour. Furthermore, they also wanted the television rights to *The Hobby Horse*. Although he had long ago paid up, this was absolute proof, if anybody needed it now, that Mr Brien had well and truly lost his bet. And it was income, and quite helpful income, too.

'Are we going to be rich, Daddy?' asked Philomena, who continued to live in hope.

~

Shearing came and went and our clip was sent off to market. The bridge was finished, and the road diverted. No more worries about the creek at least, although our boys had picked up some regrettable language from the children of the construction crew, which had to be scolded out of them.

One Monday Mr Grieve churned up the track with mail that

included an envelope our mother knew was the wool cheque for last year's clip. She waited for my father to come home so that they could open it together.

'Thirty-six pounds?' I heard Mum gasp, as she looked over Dad's shoulder. 'Is that all? Are you sure there isn't some more to come?'

But no, there wasn't. The Holy Infant of Prague had not been able to prevent our wool cheque from being the smallest it had ever been. Everyone's was. People in the district were lobbying against cheap, synthetic fabrics and demanding action from the government. Menzies had put a squeeze on credit, severely restricting the amounts people could borrow, and it was sending many people to the wall. The biggest problem for us was servicing the accumulated debts. Other people were feeling the pinch, too. John Fenwicke was investigating selling insurance; Pas Fenwicke was looking into nursing positions in Tamworth or Armidale.

There was an election soon after we got home from school, and we all drove into town so that our parents could vote. My mother would never discuss her voting preferences, which she insisted were private, but my father loudly declared his intention to vote Communist. Since the New England electorate was probably not running a Communist candidate, this was empty rhetoric, but it was a signal of his frustration. In the end, however, Menzies won by the narrowest of margins, and my father was disappointed. He thought Arthur Caldwell would have done better.

Leslie Rees wrote again to my father, asking for more radio plays.

Chapter 28

To Seek A Newer World

Christmas had come and gone, and we were looking forward to the Yalgoo fete, to be held in mid-January. But the day before the fete, Barbie Fenwicke rang from Waterloo to say that it was being cancelled. It had been raining heavily, and the deluge had caught the town by surprise. The Apsley River had broken its banks, and within the space of an hour, the entire town of Walcha had been flooded and the two main streets were ten feet under water. Businesses and homes were full of silt and mud, cars and furniture floated in the river, and the Bowling Club building had drifted away and settled in the middle of the oval.

The entire town came out to help with the clean-up, working tirelessly for days, piling up and collecting debris, sweeping out homes and shops and offering beds and meals to those left homeless. Later the council built high levies along the river banks to head off another such disaster, so this flood remains the worst natural disaster the town of Walcha has ever suffered.

A week or so later I came in from picking spinach in the vegetable garden to find my mother sitting at the kitchen table with a pen and paper. 'I weeded the beans,' I said, expecting a gratified response. But there wasn't one, and she didn't look up. 'What are you doing?' I asked.

'I might as well tell you,' she said. 'I'm composing a For Sale advertisement. Your father and I are thinking of selling the place.

We think it might be time to move back to Sydney.'

Sell? Sell Arran, our beloved piece of earth? Leave our home, the broad skies, the hills and gullies, which we loved so much? The news hit me like a punch to the gut. Although it shouldn't have come as a surprise, since this was my worst fear realised. I was stricken.

Katrina, too, fought back tears when I told her. 'What are we going to do?' she sobbed. 'This is our place! It's *our place!*'

Despite our straitened circumstances, this was surely a difficult decision for our parents to make. Our six thousand acres had finally defeated them. Their grand experiment had been a failure, their dreams turned to ashes. Although for our mother there would have been some relief mixed with her grief, they had both toiled so doggedly and invested so much of themselves into making their farming venture work that to watch ten years of their lives wither away to nothing must have been deeply painful. But there was no help for it.

On the other hand, with my father's writing, there was a way forward, some big hopes for the future. Indeed, he was now fully determined that this was where his new life lay – as a writer.

We children were inconsolable. Before I went back to school I went from verandah post to verandah post to take my farewell – of the hills, the broad sky, the pine trees, the willie wagtails, the wild rose bushes in the gully, even the eagles and crows.

A few weeks after that a huge transport truck arrived to take away all our cattle, Dad and the boys herding them up the ramp at the yards, the big door shutting behind them with a bang. And then went the sheep. That took two or three more large trucks, and finally they were all gone. Our faithful work dogs, Annie, Bluey and the young Puck, who had replaced Baxter, were farmed out to new homes. Mick Brien took the Old Grey Mare.

Then my father went to Sydney on the train, taking Philomena with him. They were both to stay with our friends the Whites while my father looked for a job and for somewhere to live.

Aunt Phil went up on the train to help our mother pack boxes, cases and what was left of the good furniture. It was a sad business, but for our mother, not without a feeling of release. These had been hard years for her, and part of her was looking forward to the relative ease of city life.

During this time the Russians put a man into space and the Cuban Missile Crisis distracted everyone's attention for a while. Then one Sunday morning my mother arrived in the pale-blue Holden utility truck to pick us up from school and drove us to a cramped two-bedroom flat in a red-brick building near the waterfront in Double Bay. My father was working as a labourer on the roads, and my mother had agreed to take a job on the switchboard at St Margaret's Hospital. Philomena was to start at Barat Burn and the boys were at Double Bay Public School. 'Love Me Do', was just about to hit the airwaves.

Our great farming experiment was over. A new life was beginning.

Lost in the move was the cigarette tin with the photographs and medals from the First World War. We will never know, now, the full story behind them. But I suspect that we were not the first family to have our hearts broken on that rocky piece of bushland.

~

Within a few months of his return to Sydney, my father had been offered a job shifting scenery at the ABC's Gore Hill television studios. He continued to write at night. His play *The Grotto* was produced by Doris Fitton's Independent Theatre to some acclaim the same year we moved to Sydney, and was also adapted for radio.

Not long after that both our parents were promoted – my father to a job in Presentation (where he made trailers for upcoming shows and programs) and my mother from the switchboard to the hospital office. We moved to a larger flat, a ground-floor duplex with a garden out the back.

So, life got better. And although our accommodation was still somewhat cramped, there were pay packets and flushing toilets and meat and vegetables bought from a new-fangled supermarket. Now reinvented as Robert Wales, playwright, my father threw himself into the life of a Sydney bohemian, and a throng of actors, poets, writers and ABC types drifted in and out of our Double Bay flat, drinking wine from flagons and eating spaghetti Bolognese around our dining table into the small hours. His newfound celebrity status threw him into the path of a flock of eager actresses and patrons of the arts, and the temptations became overwhelming. Plus, it was the swinging sixties now. Without the family realising it, my father became something of a ladies' man.

His play *The Cell* was performed by the Independent Theatre in 1966 and was adapted for ABC television, and later, retitled *The Swallow's Nest,* for BBC television. There would be some money coming from the sale of the Walcha property, not much after paying the debts, and Dad began to chafe about the lack of writing opportunities in Australia. We could hear our parents arguing in their bedroom into the night.

'How can we possibly move to London?' Mum would say. 'Philomena and the boys are still at school, and we don't know a soul there. Besides, the children have had enough upheaval for now.'

My father argued that he could get plenty of introductions, and that he was being stifled in the cultural desert that he now perceived Sydney to be.

When the money from Arran did finally come through, we

ganged up on him and insisted on putting a deposit on a house. Katrina, still only eighteen, had spotted a ramshackle but spacious terrace house around the corner from us in Cross Street, and arranged a family inspection. We all fell in love with its wire-pulled doorbell, its ancient plumbing and its winding staircases. And she knew, we all knew, what hung in the balance.

But there was more upheaval to come. Because, after the move to Cross Street, it turned out there was something else, something we had not seen coming. At the ABC my father had met an attractive young Englishwoman, Clare Richardson, and they had fallen in love. She provided a perfect escape hatch.

So, to our shock and sadness, our parents separated in 1968 and divorced the following year. It was hard for us to understand this. How could he leave us, leave our mother? Theirs had always seemed such a love story – they had been through so much together. After all that my mother had sacrificed for him, how could he cast her aside? How could such a rift possibly happen? We had not noticed their growing apart. But there it was.

The lovers left for London and the upheaval was complete. Our father had, to all intents and purposes, deserted us. He had disappeared from our lives forever.

Aidan and Robert, then sixteen, never saw him again.

When she heard the news of the divorce, our Scottish grandmother sent my father a letter from Greenock saying, 'Kindly never communicate with me again.' This was the same message she had sent him when our parents married, twenty years before.

Epilogue

In Which I Finally Fly

In the spring of 1970, Libby Hughes, the girl I had met on my first day in the Rose Bay Convent senior school (and still my best friend) and I, clutching our books and hand luggage, boarded an Air New Zealand DC-8 at Mascot Airport. Flying at last. As the plane rose above the New South Wales countryside heading north, I looked down, trying to make out the hills, the paddocks, the shearing sheds, the bush roads, but then as we gained altitude they turned into a blur of wide brown land, and then we were beyond the clouds, soaring way over the earth.

Libby and I planned to spend some time travelling in Greece first, and then find work in London. For me, it was more than just the fulfillment of my dreams; I was chasing after my father. I refused to allow him to abandon me.

In Greece I lucked into a job on an archaeological dig on Evia and spent two subsequent summers on another dig in Crete. At the end of the first summer, Libby flew from London to meet me in Rome and we hitchhiked our way back to London through Italy, Switzerland, Germany and France.

In London, I mended fences with my father and met my new little brother, Duncan, before the romantic in us took Libby and me to Cambridge, where Libby landed a job in Heffer's Bookshop and I one in King's College Library. Back in London a year later, a job in a travel agency gave me a chance for more European travel, but eventually, with my third English winter approaching, the longing for some Australian sunshine became overwhelming, and I returned to Australia just in time for a scorching Christmas. Libby followed a few months later.

If you had asked me about my ideal job, I would have said working with a writers' organisation. And after a few years working for the Australian Elizabethan Trust and the Australian National Playwrights Conference, the Australian Writers' Guild came calling, and I spent ten happy and event-filled years there, during which time my partner, Mil Perrin, and I had a son, Alec.

That relationship didn't last much beyond Alec's birth, and in the end, I married George Kirgo, an American screenwriter, and the funniest man I had ever met. Alec and I moved with George to Los Angeles, where I manoevered myself into a dream job with The Writers Guild Foundation, dedicated to the preservation and promotion of the work of screen and television writers in the US. I was just where I wanted to be, surrounded by some of the world's great storytellers. Better still, because a part of our work was screenwriting archive and history, during this time I met and got to know many of the people who had written the films that had come flickering across the screen of the Civic Theatre in Walcha, all those many years ago.

In 1977, Katrina married Rob Blomfield, as she had sworn she would as a child, and went to live on Karori, which they still own. Together they run a successful sheep property and merino stud in Walcha, producing some of the softest fine wool in the world. Not so long ago they built themselves an award-winning eco-house at their second Walcha property, Hole Creek. It sits on a hill above a peaceful and picturesque valley, overlooking Arran's still-uncleared back boundary, where hawks and eagles circle in the wind. Our links to Walcha and our history have never been broken.

When long-distance phone calls became cheaper, I was able to call Australia more often, and sometimes after a conversation with Katrina in Walcha about rainfall and ram sales and wool prices, the dreamspace in my mind would take me back to another time, another place, another life. I might not notice as my car left the 10 freeway and began the curve round the La Cienega exit to enter the gridlock heading north, past the used furniture displays on the sidewalk, past the vast parking lot of Toys 'R' Us, past the jammed-in makeshift taco and burrito signs, past the slightly grimy gas stations. My head would be back in those days so long ago, in that place so far away, with the grey haze of the gum trees, the wide blue skies, the distant call of the crows, the barking of the dogs, the bleating of a hundred sheep.

For our parents, our life as sheep farmers was a continuous round of grinding toil accompanied by setback after setback, disappointment after disappointment. They were inexperienced, undercapitalised and under-resourced, and yet they had done their very best. But they were not wasted years. It had toughened and strengthened each of them and given them both inner resources and an appreciation of life that neither of them ever lost.

Ironically, my father's move to London was just before the Australian Government began to lend more support to the arts, and the market for Australian writing began to expand. Television drama was taking off, and small theatres were springing up everywhere. Had he stayed, he might have had a perfectly good career in Australia after all. But I suspect nothing would have kept him in Australia; he was after a new adventure.

My mother became a successful career woman, working her way up through the ranks at St Margaret's, eventually becoming the CEO of St Margaret's Private Hospital. She had several suitors but never remarried. On a 2017 visit to Katrina, she fell and broke her femur, and at the time of writing she remains in the nursing home in Walcha, her memory fragmenting in a muddled fog which sometimes clears enough for her to ask, puzzled, 'I'm in Walcha? Really? So are Mick and Budge still on Winterbourne? Is Mick still drinking?' Or, 'Do you know how Pat and Buddy are?'

She does not remember that they all died years ago.

For us children, our life at Walcha was a joy, a charmed time, a time full of wonders. The delight we took in its trees, rocks, paddocks, animals and birds is embedded deep in our very bones. Even its seasons – the hot summer days with the crickets shrilling in the gully, the first frosts of autumn, the bitter chill of dark winter mornings, the hum of the bees around the spring blossoms in the orchard and the plum tree – wound around with a reassuring certainty. The shape of the sky for us will forever be defined in some sense by the blue and smoky-grey hills that surrounded our little homestead. We can all truly say that our childhoods were happy ones. But over and above that, our experiences gave all of us a sense of responsibility, a willingness to turn our hand to any challenge, and a resourcefulness and self-sufficiency that few childhoods today can match. Most of all it gave us a resilience, an ability to overcome misfortune and setbacks, that has stood us in good stead over the years.

The small excitements that punctuated the rhythm of our days – visits to Cheyenne, Mr Grieve and his teeth, Oskar Kokoschka, lambing, Cassius, shearing, a winter snowfall, Lucky the pig, new kittens, the Christmas presents down the creek – are etched forever in our collective memories. And it is in these reminiscences that Philomena and the boys in particular recall our father, lost to them before they were ready. He died of lung cancer in London in 1994, with Clare, Duncan and me by his side. Katrina and Philomena had visited only a few months previously. According to the doctors, the cancer may in fact have had its roots in the lung disease that had taken us to Walcha in the first place, so many years before.

Whenever we five get together, when visiting our mother or Katrina, the conversation always comes around to those days. 'Someone should write all this down,' one of us invariably says, and then all heads turn to me. And so I have.

Acknowledgments

This book might never have seen the light of day without my friend Linda Aronson, who urged me to keep writing this story in the first place, and who patiently read three drafts and gave invaluable notes and suggestions. Grateful thanks to both Linda and Mark for their input and for much more.

I am also indebted to those who read various drafts and helped with comments, recollections, corrections or even just enthusiasm: Katrina and Rob Blomfield, Richard Glover, Margaret Pomeranz, Anne Gorman, Meg Howrey, Barry and Carmel Oakley, Clare Wales, and Janet Withers. Yet others supplied information, memories, anecdotes, and sometimes photographs: Mark Austin, Virginia Austin, Vaun Blomfield, Burgh Blomfield, Carolyn (Bunky) Blomfield, Pas Fenwicke, Jane Lieb and Anne Fenwicke Murray. By some serendipitous miracle Catherine Crowe discovered old colour photographs of her 1961 visit in a bottom drawer and passed them on via Anne Gorman just as the book was finished. One of them now graces the front cover. Thanks to you all.

The staff at the State Library of NSW patiently brought out box after box of microfilm holding ancient copies of *The Walcha News*. Let's not take libraries for granted, nor let them die out.

Speaking of libraries, this is my chance to pay tribute to all the authors of all those books borrowed from the Walcha Library that I read as a child. It was their books that helped make a remote bush childhood so rich and interesting, from Enid Blyton to Mary Grant Bruce to Geoffrey Trease.

Finally, thank you to Lyn Tranter, who shepherded me through another edit before she agreed to represent me, and to Martin Hughes, who liked the book enough to publish it, and whose helpful and sensible comments were invaluable in getting to the final version. Thanks also to the entire team at Affirm Press, including editors Kylie Mason and Cosima McGrath, who could not have been more supportive or professional if they tried.

www.ingramcontent.com/pod-product-compliance
Lightning Source LLC
Chambersburg PA
CBHW031423150426
43191CB00006B/374